# RIPPLE

Michael J. Seminetta, III

ISBN 979-8-89112-852-1 (Paperback)
ISBN 979-8-89112-853-8 (Digital)

Covenant Books
11661 Hwy 707
Murrells Inlet, SC 29576
www.covenantbooks.com

# FOREWORD

If I were told in 1984 that I'd be asked to contribute to a book about addiction in the future, I wouldn't have believed it—especially if the book I'd be asked to contribute to would be written by my own son. Nonetheless, the following is a story of addiction, written from the trials and tribulations of my son, Michael III—my namesake, named after myself and his grandfather, Michael Senior.

This is the story about the boy whom I loved unconditionally before he was ever born—the boy who would become a baseball star in the neighborhood, a good-hearted person, a leader of men who will maybe change the world someday.

My boy became addicted to drugs and has literally battled addiction for over twenty years. You'll read about his baseball career full of accolades, championships, pizza, and, most of all, memories that will last a lifetime. You'll read about family vacations and funny moments that all families could relate to. He'll also talk about stealing, lying, being manipulative, being incarcerated, as well as his feelings of despair, self-loathing, and depression.

He'll tell you of the love of a father and son and the bond we have forged through it all that will last until the end of our days here and the love he has for his mother, his sisters Cara and Jessica, his stepmom Dona, and his stepbrothers Patrick and Daniel.

I think it's very obvious these days that addiction has no boundaries. It can affect anybody at any time, right under our noses, no matter your religion, background, ethnicity, or financial status. It can reach out and touch the most insulated.

My son is very brave to be putting himself out there like this. I imagine it's not easy to put all the ugly moments of your life in a book for all to read. I'm not sure I'd be brave enough to do what my son has done. I'm very proud of him for doing this. He realizes that there is a cause out there that is greater than his own self-comfort. A calling for him to use what he has learned from his personal pain, misfortune, hard times, as well as happy times to not only help himself as he goes through the healing process but also help others battling addiction, along with their families who sit by tormented, having to helplessly watch the destruction of a loved one.

If you're an addict or if you have a family member or a friend who is an addict, I'm here to tell you that you're not alone. There is hope for better days ahead, and that is the most important message that my son will try to convey to everybody who reads the following pages.

Michael, I'm so proud of you for writing this book. For putting yourself out there for the world to see and hopefully learn from. I know it wasn't easy. What foresight on my part, huh, kid? As I said at the beginning of this foreword, I knew you were going to change the world before you were born.

Sincerely proud father,
Michael J. Seminetta Jr.

In the remaining years of his life, while in the process of writing this book, my late grandfather, Grandpa McCann, would joke with me, saying, "Michael, have you finished your book yet?" I'd say, "Not yet, Gramps, I'm working on it." "Okay, when you make your first million, I'm going to need to borrow some money." "No problem, Gramps." My Grandpa McCann was one of the very few people in my life who always kept it real with me. When he knew I was screwing up, he'd let me know it. When I'd see him, there were never any fake smiles or any "Hi, Mikey, how are you?" Grandpa McCann knew damn well how I was, and it was always, "Michael, sit down, buddy, let me talk to you. You're screwing up again, and what are you going to do about it?"

I'm very grateful I had the chance to sit with my grandfather on his backyard deck, clean and clearheaded, and tell him how much I respected him for that. On that sunny Sunday after Mass, after an hour of heart-to-heart discussion with him, he gave me a big bear hug in perfect Grandpa McCann fashion, complete with a few powerful back pats, and told me that as far as he was concerned, all the dumb things I've done was "water under the bridge." Then he said something that had a profound effect on me, something I've kept close to my heart and have never shared with another living soul…I'm still at it, Gramps.

Unfortunately, my grandfather passed away before this book was complete. I'm indescribably grateful for his powerful presence in my life. My grandpa just always did everything right. He was a good man, my grandfather, the type of man that I aspire to be like, as I'm sure all my male cousins do. He died surrounded by his family and all of us grandchildren. Undoubtedly, he died and soared straight into God's hands. And I'd be willing to bet that God attached him to Michael's detail—the Archangel—to make sure nobody steps out of line up there. I love you, Gramps. See you on the other side.

Also, for my late grandfather, Grandpa Seminetta. What to write? The truth, I suppose. First off, my grandpa Seminetta never missed any of my baseball games. It's funny, I still remember that feeling I'd get as a kid seeing his truck pull up to the ball field. I can still picture him in my mind, sitting in the bleachers in his work boots, faded blue jeans, flannel, and his fishing hat, twenty feet tall, and fuming! Ready to give the umpire a piece of his mind over a bad call—at my minor league games! He always kept his cool, though. Well, at least until Little League.

Regrettably, I never had the privilege to know my grandfather as a grown man. When I was getting mixed up and involved with hard-core narcotics at sixteen to seventeen years old, getting into trouble, and lying about it all, it put a bad taste in my grandfather's mouth. And more so in my grandmother's mouth, which most likely made it even more bitter for my grandfather. I haven't spoken to my grandpa Seminetta since my late teens, early twenties, nor with the rest of that side of my family. I've made a few futile attempts to reconcile with my grandmother over the years, but I believe that side of my family has formulated a pretty negative view of myself and my sister, Cara. I concluded the best thing would be to just let it be.

One of the biggest regrets in my life is that I didn't get my act together before my grandpa Seminetta died and that I never had a chance to sit down with him face-to-face, as a man, and apologize for my conduct and explain myself and tell him how sorry I am for shaming his name, and that I'm dedicating my life to honoring that name, and that I love him and I miss him. There's no doubt in my mind that after a well-deserved swift kick in my behind for my behavior over the years and maybe a minute or two of ball-breaking, my grandfather would say to me, "It's okay, kiddo, forget about it," and he'd embrace me.

I know he's now looking down on me, and he now knows what's in my heart, and that gives me some peace. I still think about my grandpa momentarily quite often. I can feel his Sicilian blood running through me... Anyway, I miss you, Grandpa.

And last but not the least, for my godmother—my *favorite* aunt Terry. During my criminal years throughout my twenties, while I was ripping and running the streets, completely disregarding the law, my godmother was on the beat, serving the city of Chicago as a police officer and ultimately retiring with lieutenant bars upon her shoulders.

During those years, when in her presence, I could literally feel the disappointment radiating from her, and rightfully so. For the most part, I was a disappointment and a real jerk. I imagine my aunt thought of me as a criminal, a liar, and a junkie. And although I was all those things those days, to a more serious and dangerous degree than I like to admit or that my family could probably fathom, I believe God put me through that life and didn't allow me to perish from it because he knew I was a strong-minded, tough SOB who would take my licks like a man, eventually learn from my mistakes, and ultimately play a role in helping addicts and their families dealing with a substance abuse problem and possibly this entire drug situation running rampant throughout this country. God was teaching and molding me so he could use me. One cannot teach and help others on a subject they've never lived through and experienced firsthand. That connection and understanding wouldn't be there. It was imperative that I went through what I've put myself through over the years. I know that now. And I'd like my godmother to realize that also.

It's important to me that my godmother knows that, in a way, I was also on "the beat." And like she has done, I'm now trying my best to accomplish my form of public service in the only way I know how to.

So for you, my lovely, awesome, and *favorite* godmother, I'll try my best to never disappoint you again. Just keep in mind—baby steps! I love you from the bottom of my heart.

This book is for the three of you.

*****

The following is an account of personal experiences from my life—my life pertaining to my struggle with substance abuse. I do not claim to have addiction all figured out. There is still so much I don't understand. One thing I do understand, though, is that it is becoming more and more of an increasing heartbreaking problem—not only for addicts themselves but also for every life they touch. Their mothers and fathers, brothers and sisters, family and friends, and ultimately, society as a whole. Drug addiction affects all of society and humanity in many different ways, even if they aren't very apparent, because essentially we are all part of the same picture.

This book is the result of experiences from situations and personal journeys throughout my lifetime—some good, some bad. It would be an overwhelming challenge to acknowledge everybody who has inspired me to write it, but for the sake of my existence, I'd like to thank the two people who brought me into this world and who have both taught me priceless lessons—my mom and dad. I love you both very much.

I'd like to dedicate this book to the individuals who have perished to their poison. I know most of you didn't give up; you just ran out of time. Your lives and deaths were not in vain. Someone somewhere learned something from each and every one of you, somehow. I'm sure of that.

I dedicate this book to all of humanity—young and old, male and female, white, black, brown, and yellow, rich or poor, addicted or sober—but especially, I dedicate this book to the men and women who have courageously attempted to step outside their own minds, dominated by the destructive nature of substances and drink, and have ventured into the unknown to recreate their lives. The lives they deserve and the lives that they were put on this earth to lead.

Salute to you all.

# PROLOGUE

*Boom! Boom! Boom!* "It's eleven o'clock, checkout time." *Boom! Boom! Boom!* "Please, sir, checkout time."

Those were the first sounds I heard upon awakening on that cold and wet November morning that now seems so long ago, and, man, were they ear-piercing. I jumped out of bed and hurried across the dingy motel carpet to the door because, for the love of God, I didn't want to hear any more banging. Too late. *Boom! Boom! Boom!*

"It's eleven o'clock, checkout time. Please, sir, I have to clean the…"

Before the nice Indian woman could finish her plea, I swung open the door. "I heard you, okay? Just calm down, I'm coming. Please just give me a few minutes." I shut the door, turned and sighed, and went and sat on the edge of the bed for a minute, lit a cigarette, and blankly stared at the floor.

One minute into my day, and I was already consumed with thoughts of worry and helplessness. See, I only had about three or $4 and some change left over and, worse, no morning "fix" that would allow me to function and try to imitate a normal existence. Showering, eating breakfast—both out of the question. Showering would require energy I did not have, and I had no time, anyway. This little Indian lady seemed nice, but I could tell she had a mean streak. Eating breakfast—forget about it. My stomach usually remained in knots until I used for the first time of the day.

I guess you could say that taking care of my basic human needs was not on my list of top priorities. Having no permanent continuous shelter didn't bother me much at the time, and as far as food was concerned, my diet usually consisted of ninety-nine-cent double cheeseburgers from McDonald's every day. Maybe a couple of candy bars and a fountain drink from a gas station. That would be sufficient enough for me. My food consumption probably cost, on average, about seven to $8 per day. The rest of all the money that quickly passed through my hands daily, often hundreds of dollars, went toward my self-destruction. And that was the one thing I seemed quite content on.

I got up and gathered my belongings, which were no more than some clothes and some travel-pack cosmetics in a plastic shopping bag and a rolled-up dress sock filled with pipes, spoons, and syringes. I went over to the sink, brushed my teeth, splashed some water on my face, and took a very, very quick look in the mirror. I usually slept in cheap motel rooms when I wasn't sleeping on someone's couch or in my mother's car. Three or four nights a week, I'd shell out $40 for a cheap room so I could enjoy some solitude and clean myself up a little bit. I'd stop at a nearby drugstore and pick up some razors and travel cosmetics. So the night before, in between blasts of cocaine, I showered and shaved. But the clean shave didn't hide the truth. What I saw in the mirror I didn't like, and so I never spent much time looking. I turned away, lit another cigarette, and headed for the door.

When I opened the door and stepped outside, the sunlight hurt my eyes. Having spent the entire night in a dark motel room with the shades drawn, geeking out on coke, it took me a moment to focus. I used to love the sunshine upon my face, but during that time in my life, it just bothered me. Most drug addicts become very nocturnal, and I was no exception. Up all night, sleep all day. Unless, of course, the cleaning lady kicks you out at 11:00 a.m. "checkout time."

I had spent the previous night smoking cocaine until about 4:00 a.m., which I then shot my last few bags of heroin and fell asleep. When I left the motel room at 11:15 a.m., I wasn't yet fully withdrawing from the heroin, but I soon would be. So I figured, for no other reason than habit, that my go-to crime of retail theft would do. Not because I believed retail theft was no big deal, by no means. It may sound like committing a felony theft was an easy decision for me to make. It wasn't. I hated it and knew it was wrong. Yet I couldn't control myself. It was the quickest and easiest way to make fast money and, as long as I was fast, had the lowest probability of me getting caught. So off to one of the many major hardware/appliance stores I went.

It was about noon when I walked through the doors. Without making eye contact with anybody, I walked straight to the tool section, the Craftsman Combo Kit. It was about the size of a small suitcase and contained a drill, a circular saw, a reciprocating saw, a flashlight, and two 19.2-volt battery packs and a charger. The kit sold for around $220. But if you drank at any of the bars I'd sell them in, you could get one for $100 even—if you ran into me first, that is. They usually went pretty fast. I once sold four of them in about thirty seconds. I can't tell you how many of these combo kits I've stolen in the past. A thousand maybe? And that's not including brand-new socket sets, individual saws and drills, generators, snowblowers, etc. There was a two-year period when I'd go to multiple stores daily or go into the same store multiple times, and I'd have ten to twenty different items in my trunk within an hour. But here again, my heart beating fast, I picked one up, tore off the security tag, and nonchalantly walked out of the store while staring at a discarded receipt I'd keep on me to make it seem like I just legitimately purchased this thing. The young girl at the front checkout counter actually said, "Thank you, have a good day." I shit you not.

The entire theft—from enter to exit—took sixty seconds. Literally. And when I was safely away, about a block from the store and I knew I'd gotten away with the first felony of the day, the worry and helplessness I felt after waking up in that motel room on Cicero Avenue that morning completely vanished. It vanished because I now knew I could get what I wanted and needed.

I pulled into a bar parking lot on 111th Street right off Pulaski Avenue and didn't even make it inside. I sold the stolen tool kit right in the parking lot to some gentleman in a white pickup truck going to the bar for his "lunch." With $100 now in my hand, it was quite possible I was the most content person in the world. Knowing I was on my way to buy drugs was all that my mind cared about at the moment. Only an addict knows that feeling of relief, knowing at least for the next eight hours or so they didn't have to do anything illegal or morally wrong and could eat and at least try to act like everything was normal.

I jumped back in the car, fired up a cigarette, popped in my favorite CD, and took off. I turned up the volume, rolled all the windows down, and made my way to the hood. Sixty-Ninth and Hoyne was a hop, skip, and jump away, and within ten minutes, I was in familiar territory. I hooked up with my heroin dealer and then stopped at a drug spot and bought a bag of cocaine.

I drove around inside Marquette Park for a couple of laps and smoked the cocaine. When it was gone, I pulled over. On the passenger seat next to me lay a bottle of water, a tablespoon, a lighter, a syringe, and four ten-dollar bags of heroin wrapped in tiny tinfoil packages—the contents of my dress sock. This pile of paraphernalia, when put through the motions, would become the ultimate high. Well…at least that's what I believed at the time.

I unfolded the tinfoil packages until the powder from all four bags lay in the spoon. Next, I took the syringe and stuck the tip into the bottle of water and pulled the plunger back until the chamber filled. Then I picked up the spoon and squirted the water from the syringe into it. I flicked my lighter and held it under the spoon until the wet clumps of powder disappeared and all that remained was a clear brown liquid. I picked up a cigarette and with my teeth tore off a tiny piece of cotton from the filter. I then dropped the cotton ball into the spoon, stuck the tip of the syringe into the cotton, and once again pulled the plunger back. The brown liquid slowly filled the chamber, and the spoon went dry.

Then, just like in the movies, I held the syringe upright, tapped the bubbles to the top, and squeezed out any air. Next, I grabbed my dress sock, tied it around my left arm above my elbow, and waited a few seconds until the veins on my forearm became thick and visible. Then I stuck the needle into the usual vein and pulled the plunger back a little bit until a stream of blood shot into the chamber. When it did, I slowly pushed the plunger until the warm brown liquid was completely emptied into my bloodstream. When the syringe was drained, I pulled the needle out of my arm, untied the dress sock on my arm, and sat back in my seat.

About six seconds later, the heroin hit my heart, which became warm and slightly cramped and slowed as it pumped the drug throughout my body and straight into my brain. The whole process took seconds, literally, and every bit of physical and mental pain completely melted away—well, for a while at least. Shooting heroin always delivers the desired effect, assuming that what you purchased was indeed heroin. The four bags I just shot were indeed heroin, and as I sat there staring out the window into the park, looking at nothing in particular, my desired effect took hold and the body high settled in.

I lit a cigarette, grabbed my coffee, got out, and went and sat in the grass. I lay back and fell asleep without a thought in my head. When I woke up a short while later, my mind was instantly flooded with thoughts, and I couldn't turn it off. Find money...how? My next fix...when? Where would I go? What would I do? I promised my dad I'd call him and stop by and see him. I'd be sick later that night...I hate this...

To make a long story short, my next little scheme didn't go as planned. And a short while after waking up on that cold grass in Marquette Park, I was in handcuffs. I'm sure it's very hard for somebody to imagine how a person could actually feel a strong sense of relief while being transported in the back of a police car to lockup, but that's exactly what I felt—relief.

I had been released from prison eight months earlier. For seven and a half of those eight months, I spent my days like the one I just described. And now it was over—again. I survived a seven-and-a-half-month binge, essentially, and I was relieved. The utter madness was over. I was on my way back to prison—again. No bonding out, no probation, no supervision. No slap on the wrist. I'd already exhausted all those alternatives. People who have been to the county jail numerous times, have numerous convictions on their background, and are on parole from the joint don't get slapped on the wrist. They get thrown into the mix of the American prison system. In my case, the Illinois Department of Corrections, and that's where I was headed—again.

That didn't bother me, though. In fact, everything that should've bothered me in the back of that police car did not. What really bothered me was that I was shooting about $200 worth of heroin a day, and I had about six hours before that indescribable and crippling pain hit me from withdrawal. That's all I could think about. How uncomfortable, and restless, and depressing the next few weeks were going to be for me.

The day ended with a nice police officer handing me a much-needed cigarette through the bars of my cell after the booking process. After he lit the cigarette for me, he said, "Good luck, kid. Snap out of it, man. You seem to be a bright person. You don't belong here. You're young and have your whole life ahead of you." *How cliché*, I thought. I heard that from just about every officer who ever booked me. And I wondered why they would always say something to that note to me. Maybe they saw something in me that I was incapable of seeing myself? I said, "I know, thanks." But deep down, I didn't see what many people seemed to see, and in my head, I was saying, *Thanks for the smoke. Now please shut up and leave me alone.*

But they were all right. I did have my whole life ahead of me. And that day was the first day of a transformation that would last, well, forever. Over the next decade, I'd slowly evolve into the man I was destined to become. The sunshine would never again bother me.

# INTRODUCTION

First and foremost, I'd like to apologize to any of my family members who were shocked by the graphic nature of what they just read. If that was too much for the ones who had no idea, you probably shouldn't read this book. I have to be thorough, put it all out there, and be brutally honest. There are many things I've held close to my chest most of my life that you're about to read. Just a warning.

The following is an inside story of just one of the ways addiction starts and progresses, told by somebody who lived it firsthand—me. My name is Michael. This is the first literary work I've ever done and the first time I've attempted to tell a story. I never went to school for writing. In fact, I never did that well in English class, so forgive me if this book isn't written with perfection. The only thing I can promise is that I'll try my absolute best to accomplish an autobiography that will make my readers think. And while I'm at it, I hope to make you laugh a handful of times, shed a tear at least once, but, most importantly, gain some understanding and hope. Addicts are not bad people trying to get good. We're sick people trying to get well. And although it may sometimes seem like we have given up all hope, we're still trying to get right. The human spirit doesn't give up. I don't believe God created it that way.

This book contains two parts. Part 1 is my personal autobiography. Part 2 is a type of self-help/guidance book. Both parts will be centered around addiction and substance abuse. I won't be getting into every intricate detail of my life. This book is about the subject of addiction.

It is my wish that all who read my book and story understand that I didn't write it for sympathy. People of my breed don't want sympathy. All we seek is peace and true genuine happiness, which we can only find within ourselves. There are some sad stories in this book. I'm all good, though. I'm solid. My past has enabled me to write this book and has given me the opportunity to help young adults and teenagers who are struggling with chemical dependency and also help their heartbroken and confused families who have no idea what has become of their loved one. So I'm grateful.

I'm currently thirty-eight years old. Growing up in Chicagoland, I come from a hardworking middle-class family made up of some pretty awesome folks—union workers, police officers, a fireman, overall down-to-earth, decent Americans. I grew up in a wholesome neighborhood, played sports, and attended private high school.

At nine years old, my parents divorced. With my mother struggling with addiction herself, I began using drugs at a very young preteen age and living a double life—one of school and sports and structure with my father and another of unrestrained fun with my mother on the weekends throughout my teenage years. By the age of sixteen, I was a cocaine user and an intravenous heroin user. A junkie. Needless to say, I became a liar, manipulator, thief, and a downright strain on my family, friends, and society. I wasn't inherently bad. I wasn't a natural liar and thief. My conduct over the years was by no means a reflection of the type of family I grew up in. I engaged in this behavior for the sole reasons of deception, desperation, and addiction.

Over the course of about ten years, I completely destroyed all semblance of normalcy in my life. I was far from the type of individual I was raised to be. Friendships, opportunities, family life, and happiness are just a few of the things I allowed to pass me by through my own neglect. Eventually, my "criminal career" of theft, burglary, and other various acts such as drug dealing fed my addiction that was up to an average of around $300 per day toward the end. I racked up a dozen felony convictions and an overall seven years of incarceration between the revolving doors of the Cook County Jail and four separate state prison sentences.

Sometime around the age of twenty-five, I began to realize the weight and reality of my condition and situation. I had plans, goals, and aspirations once upon a time, and although they were badly distorted, I wanted my life back. I became disgusted with myself. I finally began to realize that drugs don't work and that I'd never be happy and live up to my full potential if I didn't commit to changing. And although I still had a lot to learn and endure as a twenty-five-year-old young man, I made the decision to try and find a solution. Thus began my journey to happiness.

It proved to be long, hard, depressing, and quite confusing to change my thinking and lifestyle, but I couldn't give up. Eventually, with the accumulation of years of hard work, self-realization, reading, searching, rehab (twice), more jail time, relapse after relapse, and refusing to give up, I began to learn how to stay clean and also that I actually enjoyed being clean. I also learned not only what I wanted out of life but, more importantly, what I wanted to contribute and, most importantly, who I was.

I believe the greatest outcome from this crazy situation I've been involved in and have put myself through over the last twenty years is not only my current outlook on life and mental state but also the book that you're holding in your hands. Again, part 1 is my personal autobiography. Part 2 is a kind of self-help informational section for addicts and their families. My only motivation for writing it was to help. And I know in my heart that this literature has the potential to help many people. It's very detailed, very graphic, simple, and I hope very informative (in regard to the clinical aspects of addiction). It was written with love. I know from personal experience that many affected families will absolutely relate to my story and struggle with substance abuse and all the chaos it can bestow upon a family and hopefully will also learn a lot from reading this book.

I didn't write this book for self-recognition or for profit. My motivation again was to help—a contribution. I've read hundreds of books, articles, and papers on addiction and studied addiction in-depth, which has greatly assisted me with the knowledge to put this book together. But the main component I utilized when writing this was actual experience.

I wrote this book with great hopes that anybody concerned with a substance abuse problem, or knows somebody who is, will find hope, strength, and guidance in the following pages. That they, too, will realize that no matter how far down one has gone into the trenches of addiction, they can still break free of that lifestyle and learn how to live life fully. Really live it—consciously.

My past has been long, and many would consider it hard-core. It could have gotten worse, though, if I didn't wake up when I did. I've seen worse. Addiction always continuously gets worse. I don't believe in the "rock bottom" concept for the simple fact that it always gets worse. There is no point in an addict's life where things have gotten as bad as they'll get if they continue to use. The only "rock bottom" I can think of that can rightfully be the ultimate bottom is death, and if that happens, well, nothing else really matters.

My past experiences are what makes it possible for me to discuss this particular subject. And if men and women could be inspired to turn their lives around and tap into their full potential after reading these pages, then all the confusion, pain, and downright mental stress and anguish I went through in my past were well worth it. I write this book with love in my heart, with a full heart, and I hope it is passed on to you reading it. I love you for simply being a human being and, like me, for traveling through this life.

I hope you enjoy what you're about to read. I hope you see the big picture. This story is not about getting loaded and telling "war stories." This story is about getting knocked down again and again and still being able to get back on our feet with our heads held high. It's about taking responsibility for our actions and not crying or complaining about how "horrible" our lives may have become. It's about coming to the realization that life is a continuous growing process that will last until our final breaths. It's about going to sleep at night with a smile on our faces despite the "problems" in our lives, having no regrets and knowing that we're living our life to the best of our ability despite all external conditions. It's a beautiful thing when one realizes that in life there are no "problems." There are only situations, most of which we cannot control, and more often than not, which we ourselves are responsible for putting ourselves in. Every situation we encounter contains priceless lessons. Missing these lessons is a shame. True sin.

To sum it up, this book is about learning how to pump the brakes, slow down, take a deep breath, chill out for a moment, and ask ourselves who we are. And like that popular song by the Commodores: be "easy like Sunday morning." Enjoy.

# PART 1

The longer I live, the more I realize the impact of attitude on life. Attitude to me is more important than facts. It is more important than the past, than education, than money, than circumstances, than failures, than success, than what other people think or say or do. It is more important than appearance, gift, or skill. It will make or break a company...a church...a home. The remarkable thing is we have a choice everyday regarding the attitude we will embrace for that day. We cannot change our past... We cannot change the fact that people will act in a certain way. We cannot change the inevitable. The only thing we can do is play on the one string we have, and that is our attitude. I am convinced that life is 10 percent what happens to me, and 90 percent how I react to it. And so it is with you... We are in charge of our attitudes.

—Charles Swindoll

# CHAPTER 1

I'm a Leo, born on August 21, 1984, the same year Michael Jordan was drafted to the Chicago Bulls, Bruce Springsteen dropped his *Born in the USA* album, and Ronald Reagan was president. I was given the name Michael Joseph Seminetta III. My father, Michael Junior, is Italian—Sicilian, actually. And my mother, Colleen, is Irish, which made me a witty, incredibly good-looking, stubborn, potato and pasta-loving Dago. I'm not famous or rich, just a simple American guy. There are probably only one hundred people who know me outside my immediate family, give or take.

I grew up in Evergreen Park, Illinois. It's the first suburb directly southwest of Chicago. From my front porch, a two-minute walk north would land you in the city, yet Evergreen Park is a small-town kind of place. It's a middle-class, all-American neighborhood in every sense of the phrase. Great for raising children, I suppose, lots of nice parks, groomed lawns, great schools, parades and firework displays on the Fourth of July, an annual carnival, a couple of beautiful churches, shopping malls, and a movie theater, high school sports on Friday nights. We actually have a golf course in Evergreen, which is next to impossible to find that close to the city. And although I've never went golfing at that course in Evergreen Park Country Club, my father took my sister and me there to go sledding as a young boy. We once slid down the hill so fast we damn near crashed into the fence that lines California Avenue. I believe my father and I were the best sled team to ever grace the frozen tundra of Evergreen Park Country Club.

I grew up in an area of the city that referred to neighborhoods not by the name of the town but by the name of the parish within: St. Thomas More, St. Bernadette, St. Bede, Holy Redeemer, Queen of Martyrs. Just a bundle of close-knit friendly communities where the sound of the ice cream truck was always prevalent during the summer.

In the first decade of my life, it was just my mother and father, my older sister Cara, and myself until the chain of events that caused my parents to divorce unfolded. They had their personal reasons. She did this, he did that, so on and so forth. If you ask me, they were both young and not yet mentally, emotionally, or spiritually mature enough to be in a marriage at that time. My father was eighteen years old when he got my mother pregnant. He joined the Painters Union right out of high school and went to work every day to put food on the table. He was young and stressed out.

My mother was pregnant with my sister Cara at sixteen years old. So they got married. At eighteen years old, she was pregnant with me. I imagine my mother felt that she missed out on a lot in her teenage years. She dropped out of high school sophomore year and was stuck taking care of babies before she even had a chance to grow up. I guess sometime around twenty-five years old, she was determined to have a little fun. She'd go out late at night with her friends, and my sister Cara and I would be awakened in the middle of the night to the sound of my mom and dad screaming and yelling, fighting, throwing stuff at each other. Or my dad would smell marijuana in the basement when my mom would smoke a little weed, and again they'd fight. Most of the time, my sister Cara and I would hide behind the couch in the front room and listen to them fighting, not really understanding why they were.

Really, they never should've gotten married. It was one of those Catholic situations where pregnancy equaled marriage. Anyway, I don't blame either one of them for the family dysfunction we all went through. It was what it was. No hard feelings, no resentments. I love them both very much. My point is, they eventually got divorced when I was about nine years old. My mother went her way, and my father went his way.

Usually, in a situation like this, the father moves out and the mother stays in the home with custodial responsibilities. With us, my father ended up staying in the house and my mother moved out.

During the week, Cara and I stayed with our father, went to school, played sports, and lived relatively normal lives. We'd spend the weekends with our mother. During this time, my mom and dad were on two totally different paths in their lives. My mother was on a bad path, and my father ended up getting remarried a few years after my parents split up. And that's where my stepmom, Dona, and my two stepbrothers, Patrick and Daniel, come in.

Also, my mother had another baby later down the line, and when I was fifteen years old, my baby sister Jessica Lynn was born. So there's my father and his wife, Dona. Then there are my two brothers, Pat and Danny, my mother, and my two sisters, Cara and Jessy. And for the sake of digressing, I'll stop explaining my family tree.

Before my parents' fighting really escalated and they divorced, life was good. I was raised a "God-fearing Catholic," so my mother was always dragging my sister and me to church with her and that side of my family. And that continued throughout my teenage years.

I remember goofing around with my cousin Jake a lot during Sunday Mass when we were both young boys, talking, making faces at each other. And as hard as we tried to contain our laughter, once in a while, it would come out in loud abrupt bursts. That usually led to a tight squeeze on the arm by our mothers. Sometimes we'd get "the look" from Grandpa McCann. "The look" from Grandpa was pretty serious. Any further outbursts of laughter resulted in the complete separation of Jacob and me, and it often came down to that.

After that, I had nothing left to do but pay attention. That never lasted very long, however. I was always drawn to the wall statues strategically placed throughout the entire church. They depicted the events of Jesus's crucifixion and were known as the Stations of the Cross. And the storyline fascinated my young mind.

I spent every Sunday upset toward the end of Mass because when everybody went up for communion, I couldn't go. I had yet to make that sacrament, and I patiently awaited the day when I could make my first Holy Communion. That meant that I, too, could receive Communion with everybody else when we all walked in a single file line to the front of the church. I'll never forget my first Sunday Mass with the family after I finally made my first Communion. The whole family was in attendance, and I proudly walked up and received my Communion with everybody else.

I'll never forget that day because when I look back on it, I find it hilarious. The priest placed the little wafer in my mouth, and when I walked away, I secretly took it out of my mouth so I could examine the body of Jesus Christ. Finally, I had him in my hands! We all shuffled back into our pews, lowered the kneeler, and knelt down to pray. I knelt next to my mother, put my head down, pretending to pray, and stared in amazement at the bread in my hand.

It was round and very small and thin, about the size of a poker chip. In the center was the imprint of a cross. Right before everybody sat back down, I put it back in my mouth and began to chew. That's when my mother looked at me and said, "Michael Joseph, what are you doing? That's the body of Jesus Christ! You're not supposed to chew on it, you're supposed to suck on it until it dissolves." *Oh my god*, I thought. I felt like I had just committed a mortal sin! Apparently, Catholics believe that Communion, after it is blessed by a priest, is the actual body and blood of Jesus. Honestly, as a little kid, this kind of disturbed me. I felt kind of bad eating Jesus. I understood that he sacrificed himself for our sins, but why the hell did we have to eat him too? It just seemed so wrong to me. This Communion business wasn't going as well as I had hoped, but I made sure I never chewed on Jesus again.

I have too many still-frame memories from my childhood to mention, but there are a few that really stick out. For instance, most people remember their first girlfriend. Mine was Colleen Clark. I was in fifth grade. I can't tell you very much about her because we never actually spoke to each other. All I knew was that during a school talent show, it was apparent that she was an incredible Irish dancer. Our relationship began when she asked my friend Brian Young if he would ask me if I wanted to "go out" with her. I was very happy yet terrified at the same time.

I told Brian yes, and I had my first girlfriend. She broke it off with me after about a week. She told Brian that I never talked to her, which wasn't true. I distinctly remember saying hello to her one day by the water fountain. I was crushed.

I remember the look on Mrs. Orth's face, the principal at Northwest Elementary School, when Mrs. Norton, my art teacher, held up the bottle of fake blood. It was around Halloween time. I got my hands on some fake blood somehow, and what happened was that I thought it would be funny to squirt an entire bottle of fake blood into my nostril during art class. I don't know why; I just did. When Mrs. Norton saw the blood all over my face and literally pouring all over my shirt, she screamed, totally freaked out, picked me up, and ran me to the nurse's office, completely oblivious to the fact that it was fake blood.

In my defense, she picked me up so quickly and ran so fast with me in her arms I never had a chance to explain. Then the principal, Mrs. Orth, ran in. I figured I'd just play it out and hope nobody realized it was fake. At this point, I was in too deep. About five minutes later, while Mrs. Orth was holding a giant towel up to my face, Mrs. Norton returned. She just walked up to Mrs. Orth and held up the bottle of fake blood. It took Mrs. Orth about five seconds to process what was happening. Her head slowly turned toward me, and her hand slowly lowered the towel away from my face, and I smiled sheepishly. The look Mrs. Orth gave me is a still-frame memory that will always remain engraved in my mind's eye. Needless to say, she didn't find it funny. Bless her heart. I was just glad that it was the early '90s, and teachers were no longer allowed to physically abuse students with rulers and paddles.

Then there was Erica, my first childhood babysitter. She once made me lunch. She took about a pound of ground beef, cooked it in a frying pan, dumped it all onto a plate, and set it in front of me with a spoon. She made me eat it, and while I sat there shoveling loose hamburger meat into my mouth, she sat there staring at me and kept yelling at me to "chew with your mouth closed." When my mother came home, I was so relieved. As soon as Erica left, I cried my eyes out. Mom fired her.

And of course, there was the time I learned that the Santa Claus I believed in was a total hoax. I was about seven or eight years old when I found out. I was already in bed and realized we had forgotten to leave milk and cookies out for Santa, and lying in bed, it dawned on me that he might get upset and I'd get nothing! So I leaped out of my bed so fast I almost tore the cape off my Superman pajamas. I ran downstairs, and what to my wondering eyes should appear? My mom and dad walking through the back door coming from the garage with bags of presents in their hands.

They actually played it off pretty well. Dad said, "What are you doing out of bed?" as if this was North Korea and getting out of bed was against the law. I told him we forgot to leave out the milk and cookies. He redundantly kept explaining that the presents were for the family Christmas party the following day. But they slipped up when I caught a glimpse of a big pink Barbie convertible car. At the time, it didn't mean much to me. Mom helped me get the milk and cookies and tucked me back into bed. The next morning, what does my sister Cara unwrap from under the tree? A big pink Barbie convertible car! I'd been lied to for years! This Santa Claus didn't even exist!

My dad was my hero. He used to work all day in the Painters Union, and when he'd get home, I'd be waiting at the door for him. He'd get out of his old gray Ford F-150, and I'd run up to him. He'd bend down, open his arms, and say, "Buddiecee." I'd say the same and jump into his arms. Then I'd be glued to his side the rest of the night until bedtime. My mother would cook dinner, and while my dad watched TV, he would simultaneously play catch with me. I'd sit on the floor, he in his chair, and we'd toss the Nerf football back and forth to each other while we watched Cubs games or Bulls games, or *All in the Family, Sanford and Son, WKRP in Cincinnati*, or *Cheers*.

I was no angel when I was a boy. I threw rocks at trains and snowballs at cars. When I was a teen, I smoked cigarettes and stayed out fifteen minutes past my curfew. My furthest memory of really getting into trouble, though, was with my best childhood friend, Joe Cucio. Joe and I had a pretty exciting adventurous friendship. We were hunters also.

My father would come outside on the front porch, and Joe and I would be hiding in the bushes holding a string. That string would run from the bushes, through my front yard, across the street, and into an empty lot which was all grass. The other end of the string would be tied to a stick, which would be holding up our animal cage (a.k.a. milk crate). Under the milk crate, usually some lettuce or a piece of fruit. My dad would walk out onto the porch, see us, and say, "What are you two knuckleheads doing?"

"Ssshhh, we're trying to catch a rabbit, Dad."

"How long have you two been sitting in those bushes?"

"Not long, about three hours."

"Oh, alright then, good luck."

One day, though, our eccentric imaginations went too far. We had the bright idea to paint Joe's neighbor's tree house—without permission, of course. And with my father being a painter and having a workshop full of tools and paint, we had everything we needed to do the job. So while my dad was at work, we raided his workshop, loaded up my wagon, and hauled everything down the street for three blocks until we got to Joe's neighbor's backyard.

What we didn't realize was that the beautiful red paint we chose wasn't paint. It was paint colorant. Paint colorant doesn't dry unless you mix it with regular paint. We painted the tree house without any particular pattern or sequence. We just kind of rubbed the brushes around until there were red blotches of colorant all over. I remember asking Joe, "Do you think your neighbor is going to get mad at us?" Joe said, "Dude, it looks good. Why would they be mad at us? We're doing them a favor. Maybe we'll get some money." "Yeah, you're right, I guess," I said.

Long story short—when Joe's neighbors came home and saw what we were in the process of doing, they called Joe's parents. Joe's dad called my dad, and my dad, after working all week, had to spend the weekend repainting the tree house. I think I got grounded for a few days. What really bothered me, though, was that my dad banished me from his workshop. "Michael, you better never go in my workshop again unless I'm with you. It's dangerous."

That really bothered me. It was fun to go into the workshop. It was dirty, smelled like paint, was full of tools and sharp objects, and there were these fascinating magazines hidden in the ceiling... Play something or another, I don't really remember. Anyway, it didn't bother me for very long that I was banned from the workshop.

Shortly after that incident, I watched the movie *Predator* for the first time, and I was too afraid to go down in the basement alone, anyway, for the next couple of years.

I played a lot of baseball when I was a kid. A lot. From T-ball through sophomore year of high school, my dad was my coach. I think the fondest memories from my childhood are my "glory days" of baseball. I played in the Evergreen Park Athletic Association on 91st and California Avenue, Norris Field! I played T-ball, minor league, Little League, and Pony League there. Out of those ten seasons, we were in the championship seven times and won six of them. I also played Fall Ball, and there was always all-stars.

All-star season was fun. We'd travel around and play different townships from the Chicagoland area. Traveling was great, but they never compared to home games at night on Norris Field. Norris Field was my hometown field of dreams. It resembles a small major league field. Beautiful grass, pitcher's hill, dugouts, fencing for home runs, bleachers for the fans, announcer's box above home plate, concession stand for food and snacks. But best of all—the field is equipped with lights. It's a great place, and for years my father and I spent many summer nights there. There were many nights when my dinner consisted of Tombstone pizza slices, nachos, and blue Slurpees. Baseball and junk food!

When you're fourteen or fifteen or sixteen years old, in regard to baseball, at fourteen years old, you enter Pony League for three years. Either that or you play high school ball at fifteen. My freshman year, I went to Marist High School. I tried out for the baseball team and made the roster. Yet this meant that I couldn't play for my father, who was coaching the Braves at Norris Field for his final year. I was glad to have made the team at Marist; however, my heart and my loyalty were with the Braves at Norris Field. Although this was the beginning of my high school baseball career, this was also my last year I could play ball at the athletic association on Norris Field.

So my father doesn't know this (he will now), but I walked out of practice one day at Marist, went home, grabbed my gear, and literally ran up to Norris Field where my dad was holding practice with the Braves. I remember walking up to my dad, who had a look of confusion on his face because he knew I had practice with the Redhawks at Marist that day. I lied to him.

I told him this BS story about overhearing the head coach at Marist talking to the assistant coach about how so-and-so was a better player and that I'd be on the bench all season. The fact was, I didn't particularly like playing for Marist or this coach, who was a twenty-two-year-old teacher whom I wasn't very fond of. Actually, I wasn't very fond of the entire school. Well, I shouldn't say the school. The school in and of itself was great, but the school population—it seemed to be completely populated by stuck-up rich white kids from Orland and Tinley Park, which is why I transferred after freshman year. Anyway, as for baseball, like I said, my heart and loyalty were with my father and all my brothers on the Braves. So my dad just said, "Okay, get out there and stretch." I spent that year playing for the Braves.

My father seemed to be the type of coach that kids were drawn to. He was a tough coach with knowledge and love of baseball that I've never seen in any other coach, with the exception of Mr. Dupree. Mr. Dupree was the father of my dad's best friend growing up, Joe. Sadly, Joe was killed in a work-related accident when I was about seven years old. However, Mr. Dupree helped my father coach his teams every year. I can't talk about baseball without mentioning this man. He was just as much my coach as my father was. Anyway, kids loved being on my father's baseball teams and having him as a mentor and coach. Plus, we won a lot and not because his teams were stacked with talent. I mean, we always had talented kids on our team—there was me, Sammy Rizzo, Timmy Braun, Kevin Deering, Tyler Klein, Greg Moss, Joey Shield, Billy Smith, Jimmy Lagoni— we were all talented ball players. But that wasn't why we always won. We had fun. We had barbecue and pool parties. Kids had a blast playing for my dad. We all learned a lot, and my dad pushed us hard. That's why we won.

My father is the type of guy who watches professional sports and calls the play before it happens. Or he'll make a comment, and seconds later, the announcer on TV would say the exact same thing. My father's saying was, "I forgot more about baseball than this guy ever knew." Anyway, his formula worked, and we won quite a lot of baseball games throughout the years.

Still to this day, we have a section in my father's basement shelved and filled with relics of all the fun we had back then. We have countless trophies, some quite large from winning championships and all-star tournaments. I have no-hitter plaques (I was a pitcher), home-run balls and game balls galore, banners, and flags. I have dirt from shortstop from old Comiskey Park, and I have a couple of cool pictures of me playing on that field. I think I still have old uniforms in my drawers. I was always number 17—like Mark Grace.

Oh, since I'm on the subject, I should mention that I'm a Cubs fan. For the first thirty years of my life, it was ridiculous! Until about the 2014–2015 season when the Cubs hired Coach Maddon and the organization put together the team who would win the 2016 World Series for the first time in 108 years. I have fond memories of driving with my dad in his truck as a little boy, trying to imitate him chew on sunflower seeds and spitting the shells out the window while listening to WGN radio cover Cubs games in the summer.

Most people I know personally are White Sox fans, being I grew up on the South Side of Chicago. My entire family on my mother's side are all White Sox fans. Every girlfriend I ever had (with the exception of one bright and beautiful young lady named Trish) has been a White Sox fan. You can't blame them, though, as they just don't get it. The fact is, you won't find very many White Sox fans outside the South Side of Chicago. The Cubs, however? You can go anywhere in the world, and you'll come across Cubs fans. Harry Caray and the seventh inning stretch. Ron Santo, Mark Grace, Sammy Sosa... Bill Murray! I mean, come on. "Go, Cubs, go! Go, Cubs, go! Hey, Chicago, what do ya say, the Cubs are gonna win today!" I love being a Cubs fan.

We have better uniforms, a better home field, a way stronger fan base. A man could hardly pay attention to the ball game during short shorts season at Wrigley Field. Everywhere you look, it's distraction after distraction! Well, now that I think of it, it's pretty much the same situation at US Cellular Field. The White Sox have some pretty good-looking fans too... Anyway, even here on the South Side of

Chicago, White Sox territory, when the Cubs won the World Series in 2016, even here it sounded like the Fourth of July around ten thirty on that night. There may be just as many Cubs fans on the South Side as there are White Sox fans?

I only played one year of high school baseball as a sophomore at Brother Rice, where I transferred to after my freshman year at Marist. But unfortunately, I was kicked off the team. I was pulled over by the Evergreen Park Police with my friend Ray Marzano. They found a glass weed pipe, and I was charged with a "crime" for the first time in my life at age sixteen (great work, Evergreen Park Police). The charge: possession of drug paraphernalia.

The fact that the courts ended up sentencing me to supervision for six months was not good. But what really hurt me was that I was wearing my Brother Rice baseball jacket at the time I was arrested. The police ended up informing the school, who informed the athletic director, and I was forced to quit. And to make matters worse, my father, who was a Brother Rice alumnus himself, was offered an assistant coaching position, which he took. He had to finish the season coaching without me being on the team. And that was the end of my baseball career. I haven't played since.

I went to Brother Rice High School, which is located on Ninety-Ninth and Pulaski Road. It was a great school, Catholic—which was good not because I was a devoted practicing Catholic but because if there had been girls there, my grades would've been worse than they were. Fortunately, though, I graduated on time in 2002. I guess I may have gone on to college, but my addiction began well before then, and my thoughts and associations were centered on and revolving around getting and staying stoned.

Above the doorway at Brother Rice is a sign that reads, "Act manfully in Christ Jesus." Passing that sign every day for three years, the essence of the phrase never had a meaningful effect on me. Instead of acting manfully and responsibly, I spent my time in school screwing off. I'd go to the library with my buddies Joey Govea and Tim Burns, and we'd do one-hitters in the back. Second period, my buddy Tony De Gasso and I would go play hacky sack on the football field and smoke joints. I actually have photographs of smoking pot in the cafeteria at Brother Rice.

Although I did a lot of stupid stuff in high school, which my father paid about $5,000 a year for me to attend, Brother Rice did have a positive effect on me. I honestly cannot pinpoint exactly what it was, but I had a sense of being part of something that was bigger than myself. That may sound lame, and as much as I hated school, attending Brother Rice balanced that out. It was a fantastic school. I did learn a lot there. I'd be lying if I said I didn't. You cannot go to a school like Brother Rice and not learn anything, no matter how big of a screwball you are.

The mayor of Tinley Park, Mr. Zabrocki—well, before he became a mayor, he was a counselor at Brother Rice—called me into his office one day and was genuinely concerned about my grades, which had slipped badly my senior year. I went from being a B-honor roll student my freshman year to failing almost every class my senior year. I did end up graduating on time, though. And although they may not know this, men like Mr. Zabrocki and "Doc" Mathius, the dean, made me feel comfortable talking about what was going on in my life at the time—which were not ordinary teenage problems. The men who make up the Brother Rice family, both past alumni and current students, most likely became or will become good men.

Anyway, I'm getting ahead of myself a little bit, so allow me to back up to the time when my mother and father got divorced. I was still very young. I believe I was about nine years old. The last time I remember my mother living at home was an ugly scene.

For a couple of months, my mom and dad were separated. My mom stayed at our home with my sister Cara and me, and my dad was living with my grandma and grandpa Seminetta. While they were separated, my mom met a guy named Steve through her cousin Ket (Karen). Although I was very young at the time, I remember my mom had a party at our house one night. Steve and his friends came over and were drinking and shooting pool on my dad's pool table. I now know how bad of an influence this guy and his friends were on my sister and me, but at the time, we thought they were cool. My sister and I spent the night running around the house, sneaking cigarettes and wine coolers. My mom let us stay up late that night. Eventually, the party died down, and Cara and I went upstairs to bed. My mom and Steve also went to bed…in my parents' bedroom.

As I said, my father was in the painters' union, and as I explained, he had a workshop with all his tools and painting equipment in the basement. Well, this particular morning, he had to get some tools and brushes for work that day. So before he went to work, he stopped by the house early in the morning. I'll always stand by my father and my opinion that his anger was justified that morning. He walked into his house only to find his wife sleeping in his bed with another man. I didn't witness his initial reaction. But what my mom told me later in life, his initial reaction was to grab a solid glass lamp and literally smash it over Steve's face.

I remember waking up to the sound of banging and screaming. I remember it still, vividly. When I ran downstairs and into the kitchen, my mother was standing there, completely naked, hysterical. Steve was laying on the floor in the middle of the kitchen, and my father was standing over him, beating him with a wooden pole. There was blood all over the floor. I was nine years old, and I was scared. I had never seen my dad like that before. Sicilians are known to have bad tempers, but this was intense. My dad was beating this guy to death. I felt bad for Steve.

I started crying, and I can still remember the look on my dad's face when he noticed me standing there. If my dad hadn't noticed me standing there crying, he wouldn't have stopped. There's a high probability he would've killed him. When my dad saw me, he stopped, and Steve got up and stumbled out the back door. When he was gone, my parents were to have their last fight ever. It was to be the last time I'd ever see my parents fight or yell at each other.

The fight ended up in the backyard. They were screaming and yelling at each other. My mother slapped my father, he hit her back, and my sister and I grabbed his legs. My mom ran out the backyard, and my dad ran after her. Cara and I just stood in the backyard, crying, hugging each other. A few minutes later, they both came back. While my father was hugging us and telling us he was sorry and that he loved us, my mother was calling a cab. I guess my dad figured he should just let it be and let my sister and me leave with our mom. He probably thought we would go to Grandma and Grandpa McCann's. But that's not where my mom would take us.

The cab showed up in front of our house about ten minutes later. My mother and sister climbed into the cab, and before I did, too, I ran up to my father and hugged him. He told me he loved me and that he was sorry. I told him it was okay and that I loved him too. Then he said, "Go with your mother, it'll be okay." I climbed into the yellow car, and we drove away. We drove around for a few minutes, spotted Steve walking, and he got into the car. The cab driver said, "Where to?" Steve said, "Sixty-Third and Central," and off we went. My father moved back into our house, and for the next few weeks or so, my mother, my sister, and I lived at Steve's house on Sixty-Third and Central.

If my father had known that we were going there and what was to go on, he never would have let Cara and me go. Well, that was the beginning of...I guess you could call it a fork in the road that suddenly came into existence and completely changed the trajectory of where my life was headed. For everything going on during that time of my life, I think I could pinpoint that that was the beginning of my troubles when I look back now. I had to grow up way too fast during the most impressionable time of a young boy's development.

# CHAPTER 2

Sixty-Third and Central was where Helen, Steve's mom, lived. We arrived there at about 8:00 a.m. My mother put my sister and me in this huge waterbed in Steve's bedroom and told us to try to get some sleep. She gave us each a kiss and walked out of the room. Here I was—I just witnessed my dad beat a man half to death, watched my mom and dad fight, took a cab ride for the first time in my life, and to a whole different section of the city. I was lying in this giant waterbed, in a strange room, surrounded by all these posters on the walls: Grateful Dead posters, black light posters of giant marijuana leaves, a half-naked blonde chick with a "Kiss Me I'm Irish" tattoo on her ass. Then all of a sudden, the walls began to rumble and the windows began to shake. I later realized we were about a half block away from Midway Airport, and every eight minutes or so, a giant airplane would fly by literally a hundred feet over the house. And here was my mother telling me to try and go back to bed! *Yeah, right away, Mom.*

I was nine years old at the time, and I was about to be introduced to a particular lifestyle that was totally different than the lifestyle I had been living. I didn't realize how bad of an influence this would be on me because, frankly, I would have a blast for the next eight years or so. There were parties in Steve's backyard almost every night. Everybody was in their late teens, early twenties. Steve was young, his friends were young, and they partied. The thing I immediately noticed about these people was that they didn't conduct themselves like the traditional grown-ups I've always known. They kind of treated me like I was part of the crowd.

Steve always had these two giant house speakers in the backyard cranking out Led Zeppelin or Pink Floyd—music of that sort. I fell in love with it. And nobody seemed to mind if I had a beer. I'll never forget the first time I met Rallo (Ronnie). Rallo was Steve's best friend, and he was always at these backyard parties. One particular time, this guy said, "Hey, come here, kid." I walked up to Rallo for the first time, and he said, "You wanna make ten bucks?" I said, "Sure." He said, "You see that girl over there." The girl he was referring to was his girlfriend, Kim, and she was a hottie. He said, "Go over to her and go like this." Rallo took his hand, put it up to his mouth, made a V shape with his middle and index finger, stuck his tongue between the V, and started flicking his tongue… Yeah, I did it, not knowing any better. When I did, Kim started yelling at Rallo, and the whole backyard broke out in laughter. I think that was the first $10 I ever earned.

A few minutes later, Rallo said, "Mikey, go grab me a beer and grab one for yourself." I was so excited. I went and grabbed two cans of Budweiser from the cooler. I remember some young girl said, "Hey, kid, what are you doing with that beer?" Before I could respond, I hear Rallo say, "Leave him the hell alone. What do you think he's doing with it? Mikey's cool, he could have a beer."

Rallo was about nineteen years old at the time, and I thought he was the coolest guy I ever met. He was loud-spoken and always at the center of attention, arguing and fussing. Always made sure nobody was messing with me. You could say he took me under his wing. I now realize how absolutely corrupt that sounds, but it was true at the time. If somebody said, "Why is this little kid out here? It's midnight," Rallo would say, "Mind your freakin' business. Mikey's hanging out with uncle Rallo." (In the future, Ronnie and I would place ourselves in some dangerous situations and have a lot of fun. He would also become the father of my baby sister, Jessica Lynn. But we'll get into all that later on in the book.)

You may be reading this and wondering where my mother was during all this. She was around. She was paying attention to Cara and me, and she was there if we needed her. She was also having her own fun—in and out of the bathroom every ten minutes. At the time, I just thought she had to pee a lot. Later, I'd find out that her boyfriend Steve was the man with all the blow.

My sister Cara and I were usually side by side, and we didn't really care that much that our mother wasn't paying too close attention to us. We were too busy having our own fun, which usually consisted of stealing cigarettes or sneaking pot roaches out of the ashtrays. The first time I smoked pot was with my cousin Jake. I was nine years old. Seriously. We used to take cigarettes from my mother's purse. One day, in her pack of Newport Lights, we found a joint. We took it and we...well, we smoked it. There's really no story behind it. And I don't remember if I got high or not, but I do remember the excitement I felt doing it.

There was a lot of marijuana smoking at these parties in Steve's backyard. I'd take the "roaches" out of the ashtrays and sneak away and get stoned. I'd walk halfway down the alley, duck down behind a garbage can, light the little joint, take a few hits, then get nervous and throw it down. Then I'd smoke a cigarette and walk back into the backyard, completely unnoticed.

My mom would periodically call me over and ask, "Are you okay, buddy? Are you having fun? Are you hungry? Do you want to go to sleep?" My mom never told me it was bedtime. She would ask me if I was tired, but she never made me go to bed, which I thought was cool. And although she was drinking or getting high and letting my sister and me run wild, she always made sure we were okay. I'll admit that she went to the extreme, but she always made sure we were having fun. And we were, always.

In the few weeks we actually lived at Steve's, I discovered or became aware of at least many things. One of them being hard liquor—Schnapps, to be more precise. There was a party going on as usual. My mother's two cousins, Ket and Emma, stopped by Steve's. I remember Ket telling my mother she had to run to her apartment and would be right back. I asked Emma, who was driving, if I could come with. She said yes, and the three of us got into her car. Ket lived in an apartment about a half mile away. I had been there a few times with my mother. Her apartment was on the second-floor roof of some building, and you'd have to walk up this huge, steep set of wooden stairs in the alley to get onto the roof and into the apartment.

When we walked into her apartment, they decided to have a couple of shots of peach schnapps. They were both already drunk, and I asked them if I could try some. And just that easy, I had a goddamn shot glass in front of me. I did a shot, and as hard as it may be to believe, I liked it. Ket went to the bathroom, and Emma poured us another shot. Then a third. I remember on the fourth shot I had, all within about five minutes' time, mind you, before I drank it, I lifted the shot glass up and said, "To Ket," and knocked it back. Emma started laughing and yelled into the bathroom, "Ket, Mikey made a toast to you! You're so cute." I shit you not, I remember all of this like it was last night.

Ket came out of the bathroom and said, "Ah, thanks, dude." We all did another round together and then Emma said, "Come on, I'll take you back to Steve's." The last thing I remember was walking across the roof and feeling dizzy. When Emma and I reached the giant staircase, she said, "We better go down on our butts." We sat down on the stairs and, while scooching down each step, we were laughing hysterically. Then it's a blank. A total blackout. My first, at age nine.

The next thing I remember was opening my eyes, and I was in Steve's bed, hanging over the side. Steve was kneeling down next to me, and I was vomiting into his shirt. He was catching my throw-up in his shirt and saying, "It's okay, dude, you'll be okay, get it up." I could hear my mother in the other room screaming at Emma. I guess when Emma pulled up to Steve's, I was completely unresponsive, and Steve had to carry me into the house, and my mother flipped out. Then it was a blackout again. I remember waking up in the process of throwing up, and then it was like somebody turned off a light switch. When I woke up the next morning, Steve was sitting right next to me on the bed playing Nintendo. If my memory serves me correctly (and it usually does), he was playing Moto-bike. I woke up and he said, "You okay, little man?" He handed me the controller and said, "Here, it's your turn. I'll go make you something to eat." My mother was lying next to me, still asleep. I didn't wake her up. I just grabbed the controller and started playing Moto-bike like nothing had happened.

When I think back about this now, twenty-six years later as I'm writing, all I could really say is that it was unfortunate, and I still don't understand how that could happen. Maybe because I couldn't imagine myself allowing a child to drink alcohol, let alone hard liquor. I've done a lot of bad things in my life, which you're going to read about in this book. But I have never harmed a child. It does make me mad that this was allowed to happen to me. In fact, writing this book has been hard, and a lot of emotions have surfaced, especially after telling that story.

However, I want to be clear here. I didn't tell that story to out Ket or Emma or my mother—who is more responsible than anybody for letting that happen. I love Ket and Emma. They're my family. They were young and dumb when that happened. In no way, shape, or form did they give me alcohol to intentionally cause harm to me, I know that. It was just young ignorance on everybody's part. I told that story because it's a part of my life. Obviously, it affected me. I wouldn't remember it so well if it hadn't. Again, I love Ket and Emma and my mother. I don't harbor any resentments. However, it always amazed me when people like Ket and Emma, who are still alive and well in our family, have made comments in the past (when my sister Cara and I were in our twenties and totally screwed up) to the tone of "What is wrong with those kids? They're drug addicts and thieves and always in trouble. I can't believe it." Really? You just don't understand what happened to us kids, huh? Part of the reason I wrote this book is so I could sort all this out in my head. As far as any of my family members reading this book, I'd like you all to understand that there are many things my sister Cara and I went through at such young ages that made us more susceptible to becoming drug addicts. I'm not a bad person, and neither is my sister.

My mother was not making the greatest decisions, and I realize that her lifestyle was causing my sister and me to be exposed to things we should've never been exposed to at that age, or any age for that matter. Now, as a grown man, all I could say is that it's just the hand I was dealt. I'm not mad. I'm not sad or angry about my childhood. I'm all good, and so is my sister. In fact, not only do I love and embrace every aspect of my past, but I wouldn't change any of it if I could. My childhood wasn't horrible. It was pretty crazy, but for the most part, I was a happy kid. I had a lot of fun. A lot of fun… I probably had an excessive amount of fun. Some of the funnest times were camping trips. My mother and Steve were always taking us camping.

My mom was always an outdoors kind of person. Throughout my teenage years, we were always going camping. I could still picture us now: my mom driving, Steve in the passenger seat, my sister and I and our two cousins, Jake and Kelly (who were with us a lot when we'd go camping) in the back seat sitting on pillows and blankets, and the hatchback stuffed with tents and all kinds of camping gear as we fly down the I-294 expressway. For the record, this car my mom had at the time was a little white Geo Metro. Or as Steve called it, the smoke box, and not because the car smoked but because it was always filled with reefer smoke; other motorists, I imagine, probably thought we were all nuts. We'd pop in a CD (the *Fly by Night* album by RUSH sticks out in my memory), and by the time it was over, we'd be there—Jellystone Park in Demotte, Indiana. It was a Yogi Bear-themed campground—such a cool place.

There was a small lake with a big waterslide, canoe rentals, game room, swimming pool, mini-golf course. There were small gravel roads throughout the campgrounds, and there were golf carts you could rent to cruise around. It was awesome. At night, we'd all sit around the bonfire and listen to James Taylor or Cat Stevens or the Grateful Dead, smoke pot and drink beer, barbecue, and roast marshmallows. When I was between ten and fourteen years old, camping was a very regular escapade for us, and I loved every trip. Essentially, we'd go into the woods for two to three days and live off hotdogs and chicken, cans of cold beer, and good music.

When my mother first left home, we only stayed at Steve's for a little less than a month. Then my father, along with my grandma and grandpa McCann, were worried, I guess, and tried to talk some sense into my mother. So after our brief stay at Steve's, my mom told my dad she didn't want the house. Ultimately, my parents agreed that they'd divorce. My mom got an apartment on Ninety-Second and Pulaski Road, which was only about a half mile from our home on Ninety-Second and St. Louis. Anyhow, the parties that used to take place in Steve's backyard were now being held at my mom's new apartment.

When my parents' divorce was finalized, my dad stayed in the house, my mom had her apartment not far away, and they "shared" my sister Cara and me—joint custody, I believe it's called. Cara and I slept at the house with our father during the week. We had our own rooms; that's where all our things were and because it was our home. My dad had to go to work early in the morning, so he would wake Cara and me up around 5:30 a.m., and because my mom's apartment was only five blocks away, he'd drop us off there on his way to work, and it was my mother's job to get us off to Northwest Elementary School, which was only a couple of blocks away.

Quite often when my father dropped us off for the early morning parental exchange, he didn't realize that my mom was up and waiting for us not because she had set her alarm but because she hadn't been to sleep yet. Not every time but many times, my sister and I would walk into an all-night party—alcohol all over the place, strange faces, all of them sitting in the front room geeked out on blow.

My mother would put us in her bed and shut the door, then wake us up an hour later to go to school, although I never could go back to sleep. How could I? I'd get upset sometimes because I'd have to use the bathroom, but I'd be too shy to come out of the bedroom. I never told my mother that. Many times, I'd have to peek out the door and wait for my mom to get up so I could get her attention, just so I could pee.

During the week, I lived with my father at home. I remember for the first six months or so we had no furniture in the front room. My dad and I had a Nerf basketball net taped to the wall. That... was awesome in my eyes as a nine-year-old boy! We'd play horse or Around the World. The front room was our own personal basketball court. It was fun for me, but in retrospect, I can only imagine the stress and loneliness my father was dealing with. But he never showed it.

He, my sister Cara, and I would all sleep in his bed together. And slowly but surely, within about a year, my father got caught up on all the bills and turned our house into a nice home once again. He worked his ass off doing it, and now that I'm a grown man myself, I respect him for that more than he knows for providing us with a stable home to live in.

My dad always made sure Cara and I went to school every day. He attended our parent-teacher conferences. He had dinner on the table every night and food in the fridge for our lunches. We did our homework and were involved in sports. Cara played softball, volleyball, and I think she was a cheerleader too. I pretty much just played baseball ten months out of the year.

He also disciplined us when we got out of line. Once in a while, we'd get a hard swat on the behind. When we were small children, he'd make us sit in the corner for time-outs. That sucked! He would make my sister and me sit in the corner for a half hour! My sister and I would be fighting or whatever, and he'd say, "Get your little asses in the corner and don't move until I tell you to." It was like a prison sentence. I remember I'd always be thinking to myself, *God, please don't let him forget we're in the corner.* He never forgot, though. In fact, most of the time, he'd send us to the corner, then spy on us the entire time to make sure we didn't move. My father was very adamant about making sure we learned our lesson. Cara and I would spend our half-hour corner sentence making faces at each other from across the room. Then out of nowhere, we'd hear him say, "Oh, you just added five minutes." Often, he'd join in on the face-making, and the three of us would all just end up goofing around again.

My father was never abusive. Not to criticize my sister Cara, but when she was fourteen to fifteen years old, she and my father would butt heads a lot. She was out of control, and so was I. However, when we were with our dad, I hid that side of my personality. She didn't as much. Plus, she was two years older than I was. She had a confusing, rough childhood like I did. I understand my sister. She's my best friend still to this day, and I'll always be on her side and have her back whether she's right or wrong. But she had a tendency to exaggerate things sometimes. I'm not saying my father was perfect in the way he handled everything, but they bumped heads a lot—my sister and father. I was the type of kid who would sit there quietly when I was getting yelled at for something I did. She'd argue. There were times he and she would be fighting and arguing about smoking, curfew, or getting a detention in school, and she'd run away. When she came home, she'd get in more trouble. My father has lost his temper and would spank us once in a blue moon, and she would equate that to "beating." My father never beat either of us. He was strict, that's all. And thank God because our mother didn't discipline us at all.

The only serious butt-whooping I remember my dad giving me was when I was in seventh grade. I went to public school up until the eighth grade. Because there were no religion classes in public schools, the thing to do was to enroll your children into what was called CCD. CCD stands for Confraternity of Christian Doctrine, or more commonly, "Catechism." It provided religious education for Catholic kids attending secular schools.

Anyway, I went every Monday night from 6:00 p.m. until 8:00 p.m. at Most Holy Redeemer on Ninety-Fifth and Central Park. My friend Steve Follaird and I would walk to CCD together and smoke weed walking through the alleys on the way there and then spend the entire two hours goofing around. This particular night, I was playing with my teacher's keys. Mrs. Kinsella had a collection of key chains, and she'd always let us play with them. I was playing around with her keys—Steve and I were getting on her nerves, which was hard to do. She was a very cool teacher. Anyway, we were being disruptive, and she told us to leave the classroom. The thing is, when we walked out of the classroom, I still had her keys.

We went out into the parking lot and located the Volvo, as indicated on one of the key chains. We spotted it, and I hopped into the driver's seat, while Steve climbed into the passenger seat. We drove around the parking lot a few times. Right when I was parking it back in its spot, who walked outside? The head lady of the CCD program. She used to stand at the front door and say goodbye to all the students as they left, and class was about to get out. She saw us, and we knew it. But then she walked back inside. So we weren't sure if we'd been made. This lady was probably in shock.

I managed to sneak back into the building because I had to get Mrs. Kinsella's keys back to her. So I kind of just ran by the classroom and tossed the keys through the door on the fly. Then I walked home. Long story short, the head lady did see us, told Mrs. Kinsella, and in turn, she called my father (who, by the way, was very good friends with her husband, George, which I had no idea at the time). That walk home was very nerve-racking. I wasn't quite sure if I'd been busted or not. When I turned the corner, I could see my dad sitting on the front porch, just waiting for me. As I approached, he said, "When the hell did you get your driver's license?" Busted! Let me tell you this. I wish I was wearing a few extra pairs of pants—for padding. The belt strap lashes would've been a lot less painful. He cracked my little ass about four or five times!

But on the weekends, it was party time with Mom. That was the other half of me, a young party animal. The lifestyle I lived on the weekends with my mother matured me well beyond my years. What it also did was make it extremely hard for me to relate to kids my own age. Whether in school or playing baseball, I felt different. I was different. There's no doubt about that. I'm pretty damn sure I was the only kid in my grammar school who drank and smoked pot every weekend with people fifteen to twenty years my senior.

As much as this would upset my father to hear, Steve was a fun guy to be around. My weekends were almost always spent at my mother's throughout my preteen and teenage years. My mom dated Steve until I was about fourteen years old, and he was always there. My mom bounced around from one apartment to the next like it was going out of style. It seemed like every six months or so she'd tell us, "Michael, Steve, I'm moving. You guys need to get a truck and help me move this weekend." It was insane! But fun.

Steve always had pot. Always. And when I was about twelve years old, my mother allowed me to smoke it. My mom and Steve were always taking us places. We'd go to the woods and walk the trails, smoke a few joints, and toss the Frisbee around. We'd go hiking at Starved Rock or Waterfall Glen. At night, we'd go downtown to Lake Michigan but not before stopping to get some Al's Beef and an Italian ice from Taylor Street. We would go to Al's Beef and eat, then go across the street and each get a large Italian ice (any of my readers who are from Chicago know how good this is). We'd all pour out a few inches of our Italian ice, and Steve would pull out a bottle of rum and fill all our cups back up to the brim. After finishing one of those, you were pretty tipsy. Then we'd go down to the lakefront on Ohio Street beach and lay a blanket in the sand and hang out all night. Play Frisbee, go swimming, get stoned.

One time, Steve and I climbed and scaled the side of the Shedd Aquarium. The Shedd Aquarium is a museum/zoo for sea animals in downtown Chicago. On the lakefront side of the Shedd Aquarium, the building is rounded and made of glass, and there are these cat-walk-type blue planks going around it. It was about midnight, and Steve and I climbed to the third catwalk, smoked a joint, and watched the dolphins and whales swimming around. This type of stuff was awesome to a young boy.

I was absolutely intrigued by how my mother and Steve just partied and did fun things all the time. And at such an impressionable age, I just followed. In the future, my father would ask me, "Why didn't you tell me about all this that was going on?" What the hell was I supposed to say? "Dad, Mom lets us smoke pot and drink alcohol. Oh, and that guy you beat up, I get high and drink with him every weekend."

By the time I was fourteen years old, I'd seen more things and done more things than the average twenty-five-year-old living a party lifestyle. When I was with my mom every weekend, I was always involved in adult situations and around adults, many of whom were going through addictions of their own. I was an extremely precocious boy.

By the time I was in sixth grade, my father had established a nice home for us on Ninety-Second and St. Louis, and Cara and I were old enough where we no longer had to be dropped off at our mom's in the morning. My dad would leave for work at about 6:00 a.m. and then call the house around 7:00 a.m. to wake Cara and me up for school. There were many times when, after spending the weekend with my mother, I'd manage to come up on some weed. Usually by taking some from Steve or sneaking some from my mom's purse. I'd pinch a little bit and bring it home to my dad's when Cara and I would go home on Sunday night for the school week. My dad would be at work when Cara and I got up for school. I'd eat a bowl of cereal and watch cartoons for a half hour, then make a pipe out of tinfoil and take a few hits before heading out to elementary school.

Sixth graders are, what, twelve years old? My first time taking LSD, I was in sixth grade. I split a tab with my cousin Jake. It was a little white blotter—a very small square piece of paper. We got it from a guy my cousin bought weed from in the neighborhood. I remember it was a school night, and my dad let me go over to hang out with my cousin Jake for a couple of hours. By the time Jake and I got it, took it, and let it kick in, my dad was already back to pick me up! He was unaware I had just dropped acid a half hour before, but I remember by the time it was kicking in my dad and I were driving home down Kedzie Avenue. The lampposts and streetlights? As we would approach each one, they were slowly falling onto the hood of the car! I don't know how I survived that ride home without freaking out.

I went straight to my room when we got home, and I spent the next eight hours sitting on the roof outside my bedroom window listening to my Pink Floyd's *The Wall* album on repeat, smoking cigarettes and starring at the trees. The hallucinations were intense. I don't know if it was because the LSD was good or because I was so young, but I sat there on the roof tripping and freaking out on the dancing tree leaves blowing in the wavey wind until about 5:00 a.m. The next day, my sixth-grade English teacher, Mrs. Sula, yelled at me for falling asleep in class. The nerve of that woman.

Before I move on to the next chapter, I need to mention something that I promised myself I would weave into my story. Not because I necessarily want to, but sadly, most addicts can relate, and the main reason I wrote this book was to help. And now's a good a time as any to get it into my autobiography.

When I was around eleven years old, my mother had already moved out, and it was just my father, my sister, and I at the house during the week. My father worked overtime a lot to catch up on everything, so once in a while, he'd have my cousin John Michael babysit. Johnny was a little older than I was—he was probably about sixteen or seventeen at the time—and he was the best babysitter I ever had. Much better than Erica, the ground beef girl. Because he was my cousin, it really wasn't like having a babysitter at all. It was like, well, hanging out with my cousin. We'd smoke cigarettes, climb out onto the roof of the house and hang out, walk around the neighborhood or whatever. He had his friends over a few times while babysitting, and one of them was a little bit older than Johnny was. He molested me, this guy. A couple of times, actually. There were a couple of times when I was alone with this guy for a few minutes for whatever reason. It wasn't very graphic—meaning I wasn't penetrated or anything like that. But it did happen.

For years, I told nobody about this. Nobody. When I was about twenty-three years old, I told my father. He was more upset than I was about it. He wanted to know the guy's name and where he lived. It wasn't important, though. What was important was that I got it off my chest. Up until now, my father was the only person I ever told. But now that the entire world knows, let me say this: I'm cool, really. It was a long time ago. I'm not the only person in the world this has happened to. I just hope that by me revealing this, it will inspire others to get it off their chest as well if they've experienced it. Something that I thought didn't bother me much felt great to get off my chest.

I read somewhere that one in every four chronic drug addicts has had something like this happen to them when they were very young. Like I said, I'm not unique. Honestly, it doesn't bother me anymore. It didn't mess my head up. I don't need therapy. I love having sex, with girls. I'm not a sexual deviant. And most of all, I don't want to talk about it. So please, if you happen to know me and you're reading this, like I said in the beginning, no sympathy. And after reading this book and you see me, don't bring it up. Thanks.

But if you're reading this and something like this has happened to you, don't sweat it. Some people are just scumbags. Talk to somebody you love and trust. You may have buried the memory deep inside and think it doesn't affect you. It does. It can be like a secret stress lying dormant in your mind, and you never think about it. Or if it does bother you and you do think about it, more often than not, you'll adopt unhealthy means to dull or mask it, like utilizing drugs as a coping tool.

Sit down with somebody you confide in and tell him or her how much it pissed you off or how confused you were at the time. You'll feel better, I promise you. It wasn't your fault. Fault implies intent, and nobody intends for something like that to happen to them at such a young age. If it did, it could still be affecting you, even if you're not aware of it. Get it out, shake it off, and move on. Speaking of moving on…

# CHAPTER 3

To me, losing your innocence means knowing right from wrong and choosing to do things that you fully understand are wrong. When my drug use began, I didn't fully recognize that it was wrong. I was drinking and smoking pot before Officer Nowicki, the neighborhood DARE officer, walked into my fifth-grade elementary class with all his little posters and flash cards to teach us that drugs and alcohol were bad. It was a rush, and it was fun to do these things. How could that be wrong?

I can remember those school assemblies with Officer Nowicki. He'd show us pictures on the overhead projector of various paraphernalia and cartoonlike images of drug addicts. They had on dirty clothes, ripped jeans, basically bums made to look like they just spent a year living in an alley. He didn't show any pictures of regular people like me. So since I couldn't relate to the dirty bum, I figured I was all good. I didn't look like that. I honestly thought that people who didn't live like my mother and her boyfriend never had any fun. At least not the fun we had.

Almost every time I did something, whether it be going to the movies, playing sports—basically anything—I'd want to smoke some weed beforehand. In seventh grade CCD, I went joyriding in Mrs. Kinsella's car after getting kicked out of class. In eighth-grade CCD, I won a contest in class, and myself and another student got to go on a trip to the United Center to see the Chicago Bulls play in a playoff game. This was when Michael Jordan was on the team. Scottie Pippen, Dennis Rodman, Mr. Jackson was the coach. This was the greatest basketball team to ever exist. The Bulls were on their way to a second three-peat. It was very exciting. My teacher owned a Skybox Section, and that's where my classmate and I would be watching the game.

We were supposed to meet our teacher at Bleeker's Bowling alley, which was only a few blocks from my house, and from there we'd drive to the game with our teacher. I insisted to my father that I wanted to walk up to Bleeker's. Naturally, he was suspicious towards my decision to keep declining his offers to drive me up there. But I kept telling him, "I'm fine, Dad, I just feel like walking." I was about fourteen years old at the time. It's not like I was a little boy, so he said to me, "Alright then, have fun."

I was walking down an alley, totally oblivious to the fact that my dad was following me. He was probably expecting me to be smoking, which I was. Weed. My dad caught me smoking pot!

He couldn't understand why I felt the need to smoke pot before such an exciting event. He couldn't understand why going to a Bulls game with Skybox seats was not enough excitement for me. To be honest, I didn't understand either at the time. But what really bothered him was the fact that I was getting high in the first place. And his confusion was centered on where the hell I got weed from. I had no answers for him. I just clammed up. It disturbed him a lot. I think he was more worried than mad. I was just relieved that it was just the pot smoking he knew about. It would've killed him if he knew of all the other things I had done.

When I got home from the game that night, which my dad reluctantly let me go to, he had a long sit-down with me. He kept asking me why I wanted to get high before something as exciting as going to a Bulls playoff game to see Air Jordan play from the Skybox. I didn't know why. I think that was the very first time I realized that I was doing something wrong. Because you have to admit, my dad had a pretty good point.

About a year before that playoff game, I got involved with huffing. Whippets, nitrous tanks, Glade Air Freshener, "hippie crack." Anybody who has been to a Grateful Dead concert or understands what I mean by "Wa Wa Wa Wa" knows what I'm talking about. Huffing produced a very short, yet very intense high. And while I was at my father's all week—with no access to the freedom and fun I had with my mom on the weekend—huffing did the trick.

The high lasts about forty-five seconds, then you'd huff or inhale more chemicals. The high was strong. Back then, I didn't understand why, but I understand now it was because millions of brain cells were being killed with every hit. The brain "freezes up." It's actually very, very dangerous. The brain seizes up and all motor skills completely vanish, yet you're still semiconscious. What that means is, for example, after taking a hit and the brain freezes up, one can fall over. You know you're falling. You know it's going to hurt. But you can't do anything about it.

Now why anybody would want to feel that helpless is beyond my conceptual knowledge. But back then, I liked it, and I did it all the time. I'd huff if my dad was at work, or if he ran to the store. The high wore off fast other than the inevitable pounding headache afterward, so he never knew. There was a short period when I'd huff pretty much every time I was alone. Pardon me for saying this, but normally, when a teenage boy is alone or has the house to himself for an hour or so, most likely, masturbation is his personal pastime. Mine was getting high.

That may sound like I was using drugs because I was lonely or sad or trying to escape some feeling I wasn't comfortable with, but that wasn't the case. I was getting high all the time, any way I could, simply because I liked getting high. Period. In fact, I don't think I ever used drugs to "escape" until the last few years of my heroin addiction, which I'll be discussing soon. But with huffing, there's one story that sticks out in my memory.

I would go into the shopping center and suck the nitrous oxide out of all the cans of mousse. I don't recall who I was with (well, actually, I do remember who I was with, but I'm not going to set him out there on this). Anyway, we went into the grocery store this particular day with the intention to get high. I was pushing a shopping cart around the store filled with random items, stuff I just threw into the cart to make it look like I was shopping. Clever, right? In the baby seat part of the cart, I had about ten cans of Finesse Mousse. I was probably on my third or fourth bottle when I inhaled the nitrous, blacked out, and fell back hard. I cracked my head on the floor and woke up with the manager and two other employees standing over me, cans of mousse everywhere!

The store manager either had this problem before, or he was a huffer himself because he seemed to know exactly what I was doing. Consequently, I was asked to leave and never return. And this was a problem because this is where my dad went grocery shopping, and sometimes he'd make me come with him to help.

My father eventually became wise to my little huffing habit. About two weeks after he caught me smoking pot before that Bulls game, he found some plastic bags with spray paint in them. He took me to Christ Hospital to see a drug counselor. She told me and my father that I may be developing a drug problem. She was sharp, this one. She also said something about having a long road ahead of me if I didn't stop. I wasn't really paying attention, and my mind was just completely closed off to the notion that I had a problem. A problem in the sense that I couldn't control myself or that I had all sorts of trouble in my life because of getting high.

Being so young, my father didn't want to believe it either. I swore to him that I was just experimenting and that I'd never do it again. So that was the only visit to the drug counselor. Actually, my huffing stage was about to be over anyway. I probably huffed less than a dozen times after that. Not because it was wrong but because I'd progress to something else.

Right around this time, my mother had a new place—again. It was a small two-bedroom house with a huge backyard. She also had a new boyfriend named Dean. I warmed up to him pretty fast. Probably because he let me smoke pot with him. Dean was a truck driver and also a drug dealer. Not a nickel-and-dimer either. From my understanding, he sold a lot of cocaine and marijuana. Obviously, I didn't know all his business because I was a fourteen-year-old kid. But bits and pieces of hearing things and snooping around led me to believe he was getting a lot of drugs from out of state. His brother was also a truck driver, and about once a month he'd drive to Florida and every time he'd return, he'd come over, and they'd lock themselves in the bedroom for a few hours.

I'd be at my mother's for the weekend, and Dean would say to me, "Mikey, go cut the lawn for your mother and I'll give you some weed." I'd cut the grass, and afterward, he'd take me into his room, pull out his big lockbox safe from under his bed, and tear off a chunk of weed from this huge compressed brick. It would be so compact that when I'd break it up, the little bud he'd give me would turn out to be a half ounce. I liked this guy.

Dean was cool to a young boy like me. I know now that he wasn't cool. Dean was a great cook and would make breakfast for my sister Cara and me on the weekends with our mom. Dean set up horseshoe pits in the backyard, and we'd barbecue, drink beer, and pitch horseshoes all weekend. Among other things, Dean was a heroin addict. And naturally, my mother became one also. That's when I was exposed to a whole different type of lifestyle—one I'd be living in the near future.

This period in my life also marked the time when I first went to the West Side of Chicago to buy drugs. I didn't know that my mom was in trouble because I didn't know all that much about heroin. One day, Dean woke up and he kept telling my mom to hurry up and get ready. I asked my mom where they were going. I wasn't stupid, and I didn't have a normal traditional relationship with my mother, so she just told me, "Dean wants to go get some shit." I asked if I could go with, and my mom said no. After arguing with her for a few minutes, Dean said, "Just let him come, let's go."

It was a summer afternoon, it was beautiful outside, and I won't lie—I was nervous. Well, not really nervous. More anxious because I had a relative idea of where we were going. We flew down I-55 expressway and got off on Pulaski Road, then headed north. We made a right turn on Roosevelt Road, and the farther we drove, the more the surroundings changed. Dean parked the car on a side street off Kedzie Avenue about a block south of Roosevelt. There was a house in the middle of the block where about ten black dudes were standing. Dean got out, ran up to the house, and came right back. He got back into the car and said, "It's going to be five minutes." We all sat there in silence. There were cars full of people parked all up and down the block, apparently waiting for the same thing.

A few minutes later, the guys by the house waved their hands in a "come on" motion. Dean, along with about twenty other people, jumped out of the car and they all disappeared into a gangway. Within thirty seconds, Dean was back in the car. I remember pulling away and about a block later, Dean said, "Shit, slick boys." There was an unmarked Chicago narc car right behind us.

For whatever reason, the narcs didn't pull us over, and about a mile later, Dean pulled over to the side of the road. My mom told him to please "wait until we get home." Dean said, "Screw that, I'm sick." I didn't know what "sick" meant then. I remember sitting in the back seat and I could see Dean holding a lighter up to a spoon through the reflection in the window. I didn't actually see him stick the needle in his arm because my view from the back seat was limited, but I have seen movies like *Basketball Diaries* and *The Goat*, so I knew what was going on. I couldn't comprehend the nature of what I was seeing. It was strange how on the way there Dean drove like a madman, swerving in and out of traffic and speeding. Then after he shot up, the ride home was slow and smooth. I remember thinking two things: one—this dude is messed up. And two—is my mom doing this too? For the first time in my life, in regard to drugs, I knew this situation was not good.

Both of their habits rapidly progressed, and every time I'd return to my mother's for the weekend, she seemed a little more messed up each time, and things seemed more and more chaotic. Soon they were taking me boosting with them. Dean would steal VHS Walt Disney movies from K-mart or the mall. And occasionally, I'd steal a few also. We would drive to the city and sell them for $4 apiece to this Arabian man who owned a deli. We'd hit two or three different stores and accumulate forty to fifty videos in thirty minutes flat. That's about $150 to $200. On the way to the West Side, we'd stop here, stop there, hit the deli, and by then we'd be in the general area already where we got the drugs from.

I didn't go every time, but when I did, it was exciting. Dean and my mother were sick, withdrawing heroin addicts; I was just a kid having fun, not really knowing any better or being conscious of the fact that this was all completely illegal. It wasn't really a big deal to me at the time. I can't pinpoint the first time I did cocaine, but it was around this time during these trips to the West Side that summer between seventh and eighth grade. There was a dope spot that sold "Tape bags." Those were $20 bags of powder cocaine wrapped and sealed in folded wax paper. At fourteen years old, I was allowed to buy my own bags of cocaine. And I did, and I loved it.

Dean's habit was pretty bad. Again, he started stealing for drug money because his drug-dealing "business" didn't go so well. I was at my father's for the week when the Justice Police Department kicked in my mother's front door. When the police raided the house, Dean had the key to his lockbox in his pocket. The police took the key and opened the safe under the bed. I believe there was a couple of ounces of cocaine and about a half-pound of marijuana. He was arrested and taken to the Cook County Jail. His bond was $10,000, and my mom spent two weeks gathering it up from his family to bond him out.

I remember the following Saturday after Dean was arrested, I was at my mom's, and she woke up crying. We didn't have a phone (this was before everybody had a cell phone). My mom told me to go up to the corner store and call Zorin on the pay phone. Zorin was some friend of Dean's—fine specimen of humanity, this guy was, let me tell you. Anyhow, I was scared because my mom looked like she was dying. I asked her if she was alright, and she just said she was sick, to go call Zorin and tell him to hurry up. She wrote his number down on a piece of paper, and off I went.

Zorin showed up about a half hour later. My mother gave me a hug and a kiss and walked out the door. Those few hours were some of the loneliest I ever had. I was completely depressed. I wanted to call my father so bad and just tell him to come get me. But at the same time, I was worried and wanted to see my mother walk back through the front door. That's what my father never understood when he'd ask me why I never told him what was going on. I was embarrassed, and confused, and scared. I had absolutely no idea how to even start a conversation like that with my father.

Dean was bonded out of jail, and they continued to get high. Within a few months of going to court, he copped a plea deal and was sentenced to ten years in prison. And because my mother was letting him sell it out of her house, she was sentenced to one year in prison. Dean would end up doing four and a half years. My mom would serve sixty-one days.

I was at my dad's again for the school week when she was arrested. She was supposed to pick me up for the weekend and never showed up. I waited on the porch for about an hour. I started calling a few phone numbers of places she may be. I ended up getting a hold of one of their friends, and the guy simply said to me, "She's locked up," and hung up the phone.

My grandma and grandpa McCann took my sister Cara and me to Dwight Correctional Center to visit her. Dwight was a female prison in Central Illinois. It was hard to see her there. But that little time off the street cleaned her up a little bit, and she looked great and seemed to be her happy self again. While she was gone, though, it was like I was missing something in my life. I was upset that she was in prison, and I missed her a lot. But I also missed the freedom I got from going to my mother's every weekend. I looked forward to that, and it was gone for a few months.

I tried to entertain myself. I was staying with my dad full time now. He had remarried, so my stepmom, Dona, and my two stepbrothers were living with us. I had baseball games going on. School was coming up. I actually started going to the park with friends from junior high. I was a little shy because I never hung out with them outside school. While they'd be hanging out at the park and whatnot every weekend, dating each other, going to the mall or movies, what have you—I was at my mom's every weekend partying with people ten to twenty years older than myself. As hard as I tried, I could hardly relate to kids my age. I tried too. For the life of me, I did.

While my mother was in prison, something random happened. I ran into her old boyfriend, Steve, at a White Castle restaurant. He was a coke dealer and a crackhead. It was a brief encounter. "How are you, how's your mom, blah blah blah." I ended up buying a half teener off him, which was a $40 bag of cocaine. That was the first time I brought cocaine into my dad's house.

I didn't do any the night I bought the coke. My dad had remarried, as I said, so not only was he home, but my stepmom, Dona, and my two stepbrothers were home as well, which was great. I enjoyed having brothers in my life. However, I guess I was a little hesitant to get high surrounded by my family.

When I got home, we all had dinner together, my brothers and I played some video games, and I went to bed around 10:00 p.m. like usual for school the next day. I woke up the next morning, and my father was already gone for work. Dona was in her room, getting ready for work herself. I dumped a little pile of coke on a Rod Stewart CD case, did a couple of lines, and got ready for school. I did another line and left the house.

I walked through the alleys, smoking cigarettes until I reached Central Jr. High School. I was completely wired when I got there. The first period I had was gym class. All I remember was sitting in the corner of the gym toward the end of class, feeling horrible. I was coming down or crashing from the coke, and I had left the rest at home. I told Mr. Burke, my gym teacher, that I had a headache, and he told me to just sit down and take it easy. You can't blame the guy for not really knowing what was wrong with me. I'm sure the last thing he'd think was that his fourteen-year-old gym student was jonesing for coke.

My drug use usually went over everybody's head. Not only because I was unbelievably young but also because I hid it well. Between going to my mother's every weekend and running wild and doing whatever I wanted to, and then returning to my father's all week where it was structured and I went to school every day—there was no semblance of continuity in the transition. It was like having a personality light switch. Living this double life taught me how to be a proficient liar, and I became a very manipulative young man. As time passed, I became very good at hiding my drug use from everybody.

I didn't realize I was becoming this type of individual. It kind of happened unconsciously. Deep down, though, I knew the things I engaged in were wrong. So I did my best to hide it from the ones I wanted to keep in the dark. That's what addicts do. And I was good at it. I had to be—I was no longer innocent.

# CHAPTER 4

I had a very eccentric childhood. It may seem that it was pretty rough, and it was at times, but for the most part, I was happy. In fact, I was blessed as a child. As much as I've sometimes led others, and myself, to believe that I had a hard childhood, I now realize I didn't—comparatively. Not only do many people come from dysfunctional, split-up families, but there are also many who've had it far worse than I. In the last few years of chronic addiction, when things were really bad, I've been in project buildings and drug houses, and I've seen things that are too heartbreaking to even write about. Young children and even babies who are totally neglected and abused. Kids who don't have a chance at growing up normal. After seeing some of the things and situations I've seen, my complaints don't hold much merit.

I've always had what I needed. I never went hungry. My father always took me shopping for clothes and shoes when I needed them. I was always in school and involved in sports. I went to and graduated from one of the top high schools in the state. My dad was always taking me fishing or to Cubs games. My stepmom Dona's mother, Grandma Senese, had a lake house in Wisconsin. We've spent many weekends up there, fishing in the boat, playing football in the huge backyard. We'd venture up to Wisconsin Dells every summer to walk the shopping strip or go to Noah's Ark, which is the biggest water park in the world. Great fun! We went on a couple of nice vacations to Myrtle Beach in South Carolina. We'd rent a condo right on the oceanfront. My father and I went golfing on one of the many gorgeous golf courses Myrtle Beach is known for. I lived in a nice home, always surrounded by people who loved and cared about me. My drug use was never a reflection of the type of family I come from, both on my mother's side and my father's side. I come from a good, law-abiding, morally grounded family. My mother, my sister Cara, and I are really the only ones within our family who have battled serious substance abuse disorders.

I'd also like to make something clear: my mother and father were young, had kids, and got married for all the wrong reasons. And they did fight a lot when they were together. It was crazy, let's not get confused here. They did fight a lot, but they were happy a lot of the time also. Before things boiled over and they got divorced, they took my sister Cara and me to Florida, and we made the rounds. Disney, Universal Studios, and I also got to meet Goofy and Mickey Mouse. My sister and my dad rode Space Mountain. I wasn't tall enough. Not that it really mattered. I wouldn't have gone on that ride, anyway, at the time. What I'm trying to say is that it wasn't all bad, and I was very upset when they divorced.

After the divorce, my mother was always taking us places throughout my teenage years—camping, Great America, the movies. She took my sister and me on a ski trip. That was fun. My mother, sister, and I had never been skiing before. I think we each took a tumble down the hill a couple of times. My mother was always a very spontaneous woman. She'd wake us up on a Saturday morning and say, "Let's go horseback riding."

I'd also like to say something on my mother's behalf. I'm sure if you're reading this autobiography, you may have painted your own picture of my mother, and it may not be very good. But let me say that not only is she great, she's also a good person with a bright spirit. She's very nice to everybody she comes across. She has just one major flaw: addiction. My mother has been struggling with substance abuse since she's been a young girl herself. People who've never personally, mentally, or physically experienced a major addiction, such as an addiction to drugs or alcohol, cannot pass judgment. They truly don't understand what a chemically dependent addict goes through on a daily basis, even though they'll swear up and down they do. "There's no excuse," "Just say no," or they say "I understand more than you think." Just because one reads a book about addiction and learns about the effects on the brain, physically, neurologically, etc., or just because one witnesses the lifestyle of an addict does not mean they understand what an addict is dealing with. Like the Big Book of Alcoholics Anonymous says: "Behind their opinions is a world of ignorance and misunderstanding." I can't explain it better myself— however, I'll try to in the second part of this book.

My mom is an awesome person. She could brighten up a room with her energy. She always made sure my sister and I were with her for church on Sundays growing up. Afterward, we'd go out for breakfast with Grandma and Grandpa McCann. She made dinner for us when we were with her for the weekends. I'll admit, discipline was not her forte, and she let us use drugs and alcohol. However misguided her reasons were for that, it was wrong. She knows that now. But my mother loves me just as much as my father does. Here's a perfect portrait of the type of person my mother is:

My little sister, Jessica Lynn, was about eight years old. I was about twenty-three. I walked into the kitchen and my mom has twenty pancakes stacked onto this huge plate and she's pouring syrup all over them. It was the biggest plate of pancakes I'd ever seen in my life! My baby sister is standing on a chair next to the counter, watching her and laughing hysterically. I said, "What the heck are you guys doing?" Jessica said, "Mommy asked me what I wanted for dinner, and I told her I wanted twenty pancakes." My mom looked at me and smiled, then handed my baby sister this gigantic plate of pancakes. I said, "You're crazy, Mom." She said, "I know. You want some pancakes?" "Sure."

That's the type of person my mother is. There's not one uptight bone in her body. And even though she may have taken it too far, she always made sure we were happy. I'm not saying she did a perfect job raising her kids. She'll tell you that herself. She exposed my sister Cara and me to a lot of things she shouldn't have. I believe she tried to over-compensate for her own shortcomings by letting us do what- ever we wanted to because she didn't know how to deal with her own substance abuse problem and didn't feel she was ever in a position to punish us or yell at us. She just left that up to our father. I have got- ten high with my mother. But I know in my heart that if she could change the past and be a better influence on her kids, she would.

And that's enough for me not to hold any resentments. If it wasn't for my mom, I wouldn't be who I am today, and I love who I am.

Also, if it weren't for my mother, my taste in music would probably be of a different quality. My mother introduced me to the greatest music ever made. There aren't too many thirty-eight-year-olds nowadays still listening to bands like Crosby, Stills, Nash, and Young; Eric Clapton; Elton John; Bruce Springsteen. I've seen many live concerts in my life, thanks to my mom. Page and Plant (Led Zeppelin), Roger Waters (Pink Floyd), Aerosmith, Tom Petty, Rod Stewart, Bob Dylan, Elton John, REO Speedwagon, Cheap Trick, Melissa Etheridge. Many of these concerts I went to with my mom. And I wouldn't change that for anything. Great times—great experiences!

Not long ago, I was listening to John Mellencamp. This young kid asked me, "What the hell are you listening to?" Like, indignantly. Like my music sucked! He was about twenty years old, and I legitimately wanted to smack this kid upside his head. I told him, and he said, "Who the hell is John Mellencamp?" Now to me—that's sad. How can a young American man not know who Mellencamp is? Seriously! What's this world coming to! He sure in the hell knew who Lil Wayne was, though… God, that pisses me off. No offense to Lil Wayne… I'm so happy I took after my mom's taste in music.

One thing I have tremendous respect for my mother about is telling me not to change anything about this book. I was concerned about how she would feel, putting all these memories of mine in a book for everybody to see. When I let her read the manuscript, I asked her afterward if it bothered her. She said, of course, it bothered her, but that it was the truth, and "You need to be honest, Michael, if you're going to help anybody." If that's not admirable, I don't know what is.

Anyway, as I was saying, many people have had it a lot worse than I. Despite the fact that I was always stoned on whatever it may be, and as hard as it may be to grasp—taking into account my conduct over the years—I had a good foundation in my life. I come from a family of hardworking, awesome people. There are a lot of police officers in my family. My late grandfather, Grandpa McCann, was a police sergeant. My godmother was a Chicago cop. My mother's twin brother, my Uncle Kenny, is a Chicago fireman. My Uncle Kevin is the V.P. of operations for Metra. All my cousins are in the union. My mother, who is now clean and sober, was a concrete carpenter. Now she works for a restaurant. My father was a union painter for twenty years, then started his own construction company. We still eat dinner as a family almost every night. I come from a very close, tight-knit family.

I don't have to say much on my father's behalf. My mother and father are two polar opposites. But they are both good people. I love them both equally. But I will say this about my dad—he's my rock. He has never let me down a single time in my life. Not once. I can count on him for anything. If it weren't for my dad, I honestly don't know how I would've turned out. I'd probably be a disrespectful punk, or a lost cause. My dad taught me to always respect my elders. In fact, he taught me to be respectful to everybody—as long as they're worthy of it. He taught me to hold doors for people and be courteous. He showed me, by example, what integrity was. He taught me how to work hard and to follow through and pay attention to detail. That the only way to get ahead and build a comfortable life for myself was to work hard at it. He taught me to never let anybody walk over me no matter the circumstance, and to never kiss anybody's ass for any reason. I can go on and on about things I've learned from my father, but one priceless lesson he taught me was this:

One night when I was in my midtwenties, I walked into the family room and sat down on the couch. My dad was sitting in his recliner reading the newspaper and watching *Law and Order*. My stepmom was cleaning and dusting off the pictures and little knick-knacks in the curio. No more than ten seconds after I sat down, my stepmom dropped a glass, and it shattered on the hardwood floor. Now, being a guy, I quickly evaluated the situation within the matter of about two seconds and came to the conclusion that a broom and dustpan would suffice for this particular, and potentially harmful, situation. It made sense to me. It would be quick and easy. Sweep it into the pan, dump it in the can. *Boom*—done.

So while my father just sat there staring at his wife, I ran to the kitchen to retrieve the broom and dustpan from the closet. When I returned to help sweep up the glass, my stepmom said, "What are you doing? I don't want the broom."

I said, "What do you mean you don't want the broom?"

"Because," she said. "Just get out of the way."

I looked at my dad, hoping he'd back me up on my plan of attack here. He smiled at me, shook his head no, and snapped the newspaper back in front of his face. During this whole ordeal, he never moved once or said anything. Here I am trying to be helpful, and I'm being told, essentially, "Your idea sucks, get the hell out of the way." Well, apparently, the proper way to deal with broken glass is to pick up the large pieces and then, with a damp paper towel, wipe up any shards of tiny glass—which, I'll admit, makes a lot of sense... Women! With their better ideas and their finesse.

That night while I was sitting in the backyard smoking a cigarette, still confused, my father walked outside to turn the filter off on the pool. He sat down next to me and said, "Son, you need a lot of practice when it comes to women if you ever want to be in a lasting relationship." Basically, he told me to always show concern, genuinely, and offer to help if it's warranted, or if they need help. But don't always jump up and try to clean up their messes, whatever they may be. Once in a while, but not every time. Girls hate that. And I've found this to be true through the years. They really get tired of the "nice guy."

Anyway, that's when he went on to tell me the laundry story. "Remember when Dona asked me to do the laundry and I 'accidentally' turned all the clothes pink?" he asked me. "Well, from that point on, she knew that if she asked me to do the laundry for her, I would do it. And I knew from that point on that she'd never ask me to again. It's a win-win." My dad and stepmom are hilarious. Living with them is literally like being in a real-life *Everybody Loves Raymond* episode.

There was a period in my life before the real madness began when I was a "normal" teenager. My last few years of high school were great. That time was the calm before the storm, if you will. My mother was clean and doing great; however, she had a little fling with an old friend—Ronnie. Remember, Rallo was the guy who hung out at Steve's all the time when my mom was dating him. Long story short, their fling happened to become a wonderful blessing. And when I was fifteen years old, on October 12, 1999, my baby sister was born—Jessica Lynn.

I was at the hospital when she was born, and for the next five years, I was glued to her side. We were, and still are, best buddies. And school was going well. My grades weren't the best, and I wasn't playing baseball anymore, but at least I was hanging out with people who were actually my own age. And although I never really felt like I was on the same level as my friends from school (not that my level was above them, just different), I still managed to have somewhat of a normal social life.

Junior and Senior year were a lot of fun. Instead of spending all weekend with my mom, I'd still go there after school Friday but only to get a beer run. Then I'd go to the woods with my buddies and throw a Keg party. Or go party at my sister Cara's, who had her own apartment then.

My childhood and teenage years were full of excitement. I admit that I was confused and sometimes nervous when it came to certain things. Things that young men shouldn't be nervous about, like dating girls or simply hanging out with people my own age. That was sometimes hard for me because I never had a social life outside school. I mean, I managed. I lost my virginity at fourteen to a pretty German girl named Allison who was seventeen at the time. We dated for a few months. And I had other girlfriends, and I had a lot of friends in school. But after spending my weekends at my mother' s the previous years and partying with people twice my age, I couldn't relate to people my age. And I'm not quite sure if I ever really fit into any particular group of people.

One thing I wasn't nervous about was trying new drugs. By the age of fifteen, I'd done just about all the drugs that were out there. But I'd soon expel all of them for one particular drug. I'll never forget the day I tried heroin.

It was summertime, July, I believe. I was sixteen years old, and because I was the youngest in my class, I would be going into my senior year at Brother Rice right after I turned seventeen in August. I had about six weeks of summer vacation left, and I was making them all count. This particular day, I remember, it was absolutely beautiful outside—80 to 85 degrees, not a cloud in the sky. I was at my mom's with my buddy Byron, and we had spent the day swimming in the community pool.

About 3:00 p.m. rolled around, and after begging my mom to let me use her car while she went to work, she finally caved. I dropped her off at work, then went back to her place to take a quick shower. Between Byron and I, we had about $80. Our plan was to get some beer and a bag of weed and just hang out and chill at my mom's all night. About five minutes before we left, Rallo shows up at the front door. For the first four or five years of my little sister's life, he wasn't really around much. My mother was clean at the time; he wasn't, so she really didn't want him around. He never really accepted being her father until she was about five years old. But he'd pop in now and then.

Anyway, he showed up and asked what my plans were. I told him. Then he said, "Mikey, please take me to get some dope, I feel like shit." I knew exactly what he meant, and I told him no. He argued with me for ten minutes, but there's no winning an argument with this guy. It's like arguing with a child and ultimately breaking down just to shut them up.

"Mikey, please, dude! Take me to the Westside, let me get a couple of bags of dope, and I'll take you to get some good weed."

What could I say? "Alright, fine, let's go."

"Let me drive."

"No, Rallo, I'm driving."

"Fine, whatever… You never let me drive."

We got into my mother's '86 Grand Marquis and took off. I rolled all the windows down, cranked up the tunes, and after a ten-minute 90 mph drive down I-55, we got off on Pulaski Road. Just like my mother, Dean, and I did a few years before.

We drove deeper and deeper into the hood until we got to Fifth Street and Kostner Avenue. "We're here, turn the music down," Rallo said. I had butterflies in my stomach. Those nerves and fear were not due to the fact that we were in a horrible neighborhood. They were due to the fact that we were a bunch of white dudes in a black neighborhood, where drugs happened to be sold on just about every corner, about to buy something illegal while simultaneously trying to avoid being seen by the dozen narc cars circling the area. When you buy drugs from an open-air drug spot on the Westside of Chicago, it doesn't take much effort to figure out. Especially if you're white. You don't have to explain yourself. When you pull off the main streets, people know why you're there. And as long as you're in the right general area, the dealers promptly direct you to where you want to go. A man pushing a shopping cart up and down the street back and forth made eye contact with us. After a nod between Rallo and him, he waved us into the alley. He pointed down the alley and went about pushing his cart.

In the middle of the alley were a bunch of kids playing basketball on a backboard and rim attached to a garage. As I rolled up the alley to the group of kids, one of them walked up to my window and said, "How many?" I shit you not, this kid was no more than ten years old. Rallo leaned over and told him, "Two," and within seconds, the kid walked to a nearby garbage can, reached behind it, and walked back up to my window. Rallo handed him a $20 bill, and the kid dropped two tiny tinfoil packages into his hand. The kids playing basketball stepped aside, and I drove out of the alley and back onto the main street. The whole deal took about thirty seconds. It was so fast and so smooth I remember thinking, *That was easy.*

Within getting two blocks from the dope spot, Rallo had the two bags dumped out onto a CD case. "Roll a bill up for me," Rallo asked me. "Ronnie, I'm driving. Roll your own bill up." "I don't have any more money, come on Mikey, hurry up." This freaking guy! I pulled a bill out of my pocket and handed it to him. He rolled it up and snorted half the dope on the CD case.

Then, out of nowhere, and completely unplanned, I said, "Let me try a little bit." Rallo looked at me and said, "You sure? Alright, hold on. I'll save you some of this." He did a little more, then handed me the CD case. I told him to hold the wheel for me, and I took the bill from his hand. I stuck it in my nose, held the CD case up, and snorted. The line I did was about the size of a matchstick. It was horrendous! It tasted bitter and felt like I was snorting fire. It took about a minute before the heroin started to drain down the back of my throat. Rallo kept saying, "You feel it yet?"

About three to four minutes after snorting it, I pulled up to a red light on Twenty-Sixth and Pulaski. That's when it hit me. "I feel it… Oh my god."

Rallo said, "Yeah? Yeah, motherfucker! You like it."

I finally understood what Pink Floyd meant by "Comfortably Numb." My body was just that, completely and utterly comfortably numb. It was undeniably the most lethargic, relaxed feeling I ever experienced. Like Vicodin on steroids. My brain completely flooded with dopamine. My face, my arms and legs, even my fingers and toes felt completely relaxed. The high is technically indescribable. It felt like ecstasy was flowing throughout my entire body. And I fell in love with it. Literally.

Byron was in the backseat and kept saying, "Is it good, bro, is it good?" All I could say is, "Good, yeah, it's good." I couldn't even talk. Byron said, "Damn it! We should've bought more. Let's go back."

Needless to say, we decided against spending our $80 on beer and weed. We turned around and went right back to Fifth and Kostner. We bought four more bags of heroin. The rest of the night, Rallo, Byron, and I spent it sitting in my mom's backyard nodding out. I was head over heels for this stuff. Little did I know, heroin would become my solution to everything shortly after that day. Over the next decade, my life would get pretty chaotic and twisted, and I'd end up completely crashing and burning.

# CHAPTER 5

Ask anybody who has been using heroin for a significant amount of time if they enjoy their lives or if there is any type of happiness in them. They will tell you, "No, not at all." In fact, I can pretty much guarantee that any chronic heroin user you happen to run into is not happy at all, and their life is full of all kinds of problems: family problems, financial problems, social problems, legal problems, relationship problems, or health problems—both mentally and physically. However, these problems do not exist in the very beginning.

When I first started using heroin, the high put me on top of the world. I'd never experienced such a stress-free, relaxing, overwhelmingly happy feeling quite like the high heroin gave me. It instantly produced a level of comfortability and pleasure that cannot be gained from anything else. At least that's what I believed at the time. Stress, pain, sadness—heroin completely eradicates all that… in the beginning.

After that first time using it, my friend Byron and I had a new mission every weekend. That mission was to get a car, either my mom's or his, gather together some cash, and take a ride to the west side of Chicago. It was exciting. We knew where to go, it was easy, relatively cheap, and we'd make the trip every Friday night.

The drive alone is a high in and of itself. We'd listen to music, chain smoke, talk, and laugh. Just knowing what we were about to do and the high it would produce is enough to get your stomach in a knot. When we would get in the general drug-infested area, the radio would be turned off, the talking would cease, and the nervous vibrations could be felt throughout the car. We'd make our deal, and once we were in the clear, the radio went up, cigarettes were lit, and the good times rolled on. Only more so.

We'd buy a ten-dollar bag, sometimes two, and we'd split each one. Usually, we'd wait until we got back to our neighborhood, pull over, do a line, and after that, nothing else really mattered. Byron and I would have a blast just driving around aimlessly, listening to Nirvana or Bone Thugs-N-Harmony. Attending social gatherings, weekend keg parties in the woods, movies, girls, hanging out downtown, concert tickets, etc. All those things stopped being important to me. Snorting a few lines of heroin on the weekends proved to be a better time... in the beginning.

For about five months, Byron and I were inseparable on the weekends. Our heroin consumption only consisted of a bag or two on Friday night, more often than not a bag or two on Saturday. That's $20 to $40. We still had money for fast food, gasoline, whatever. We were still at the point where we did heroin because we wanted to—not because we needed to. Heroin wasn't a physical necessity...yet. We still had fun and occasionally went to parties. But we made sure our budget included $30 or $40 every weekend for a few bags.

I remember all that fun we were having started to change about six months after that first time I used heroin. I had spent the weekend at my mom's, as usual. Byron and I spent the weekend hanging out, doing dope, as usual. I went home Sunday night to get ready for another school week. Monday came and went. I had gone to school, ate dinner with the family, and spent Monday night watching *Seinfeld* and *Family Guy* with my brothers. The next morning, I woke up an hour before my alarm clock went off because I had to throw up. I had this horrible pain in my stomach... Maybe it was something I ate? I felt weak and tired. I was cold and shivering, yet I was sweating. I told my stepmom I wanted to stay home from school. She felt my forehead, left some chicken noodle soup on the kitchen counter for me with a little note (she's the best), and she left for work. My brothers left for school, and I went out in the backyard to smoke a cigarette.

I wasn't stupid. I knew that if a heroin habit was bad enough, one could start getting sick from withdrawal. But I had it figured out. That wouldn't happen to me. I didn't have a habit...yet. At least that was my rationalization. I was only doing a bag or two on the weekends, so it never occurred to me (because I was young and dumb and didn't understand these things) that my body had changed over the last six months. More so, my brain, my physical brain had changed how it operates—slowly but surely. And while I was sitting in the backyard smoking, I knew in my heart that I was, in fact, "dope sick." But I didn't want to believe that. "I got this," I thought.

I only felt sick for about two days. I think I stayed home from school on Wednesday as well. Then I finished the school week, and after my last class on Friday, I called Byron. He picked me up in his mother's car, and off we went. I told him about having a cold and feeling a little sick during the week. He told me that he had felt the same way. But after a brief conversation (or shall I say rationalization) between the two of us, we decided it was a coincidence and that it couldn't be the drugs. "Dude, we don't do that much." "Yeah, it's flu season, anyway." "Yeah, plus, you can't get sick from dope unless you do it three days in a row. That's, like, the rule of thumb." Fucking stupid kids we were. Stupid, know-it-all, arrogant little assholes… Anyway, we weren't about to turn around and cancel our rendezvous to the west side we had been looking forward to all week. Plus, we were already almost there before this conversation ended. For the next few weeks, we stuck to our weekends-only agreement…until we didn't.

I believe it was a Wednesday or Thursday when we broke that agreement. I just didn't want to wait until Friday. Why wait until Friday when I had $20 on me and nothing to do after school? It just so happened that I had a "cold" again when I made my first week-day trip to cop dope. And wouldn't you know—after doing a bag, the cold, the stomach cramps, the runny nose, and sweating—they instantly vanished.

Within seven or eight months of doing heroin for the first time, I had a daily habit. And I knew I was in trouble. I tried to abstain myself from doing it. But it was too late. I was addicted; something I promised myself I wouldn't let happen. It did. I know now that it happens to everybody who tries it. I just never thought that every-body included me.

Everything in my life was placed on the back burner. I had to get a couple of bags every day. And after jumping through hoops to get that accomplished without arising any suspicion from my father or anybody else, well, there wasn't much time for anything else. I was lying to my dad on a daily basis. I was always going to so-and-so's house to hang out. Or I was going to the mall and needed $10 or $20. My dad never spoiled us, but I always managed to bum a few dollars from him. Then one day, I just couldn't come up with a good enough excuse as to why I needed more money, and I did something I never imagined I'd ever do.

My father came home from work and decided to jump in the shower. So while he was in the shower, I grabbed his ATM card and jumped on my bike. I flew to the bank, which was only two blocks away, withdrew $100, and flew home as fast as I could, and slipped the card back in his wallet before he got out of the bathroom. I wasn't proud of myself. I felt immense shame for stealing from my own father. At this point, though, I wasn't stealing because I was having a good time, or because I just wanted to do heroin. It was out of complete desperation. I was stealing because if I didn't have dope, I'd become terribly sick. And no matter how hard I tried to get through withdrawal, I couldn't. I'd always fail, breakdown, come up with some money, tell a bullshit story to my dad, and make that trip to the city. Always. I couldn't control it.

None of my friends in school knew I was doing heroin. Byron knew, but he went to a different high school. He went to St. Rita; I was at Brother Rice. One day, I met Tony DeGasso in the cafeteria at school. It just so happened that he did heroin too, once in a while. His buddy Tim Burns had tried it a few times as well. The three of us became instant friends. Once in a while, we'd sneak out of school, sit outside in the parking lot, and smoke cigarettes and pot while we talked about dope. But it was our little secret, and we kept it between the three of us.

Heroin is not like alcohol or marijuana. It's not really accepted in a youthful environment. When people hear that word—heroin—they think of bums, dirty needles, and ugly human beings. Heroin does not discriminate. It isn't only used by inner-city bums and ugly human beings. And 99 percent of beginners snort it at first. One of the most popular growing imports during the 1990s and early 2000s wasn't Eastern fashion or Asian electronics. It was Afghan heroin—and more young people were using it than anybody imagined. Combine that with pharmaceutical companies pushing opiates for pain management and "pill mills" popping up all over the country— heroin use exploded. Now, twenty years later as I'm writing this, one hundred thousand people are overdosing and dying from opiates (mainly from heroin) every year. To put that in perspective, about fifty-eight thousand people died in the entirety of the Vietnam War.

The young man or young lady who looked completely normal at the gas station, and explained to you that their car was out of gas, and could you please help them with two or three dollars for gas just so they could get home? More often than not, they have a drug habit to feed. They've probably asked three or four other people the same thing. With your two dollars, they now have enough to go get a bag so they're not sick. But they hide it well, they seem nice, look normal, and you may have believed their story, saying to yourself, "They look normal, I doubt this young lady is a drug addict. I'll help her out."

The fact is, if you really think about it, people don't ask strangers for money unless they are on drugs. Even if they ran out of gas, a normal person (and by normal, I mean someone who isn't a drug addict) won't walk up to a complete stranger and ask for money. Period. If somebody runs out of gas, they call a family member or a friend to help them. Only drug addicts ask strangers for money. Not my opinion—it's just how it is.

I, for one, was too embarrassed about my drug habit and never did I want my secret to be exposed. Family, cousins, friends, girlfriends, bosses at places I worked, co-workers—I told nobody. But when I was with others who used it, I'd glorify the drug. Everybody else I'd keep in the dark at all costs.

# CHAPTER 6

The summer between my junior and senior year of high school, I met a girl named Clare. She wasn't my first girlfriend, but she was the first girl that I grew to love and genuinely care about. The funny thing was that when we started dating, she invited me to have dinner with her and her family one night, and her parents, after meeting me, informed us that we used to play with each other when we were children. When I was a little boy and lived on Ninety-Second and St. Louis, Clare and her family lived directly across the street. My sister Cara hung out with Clare's sister Eileen, and I guess Clare and I played together on their swing set / sandbox a few times. Small world.

Anyway—I thought she was the cutest, prettiest girl I'd ever seen. She had this little baby face with rosy cheeks, long brown curly hair, bubbly spirit, nice family. She went to St. Ignatius High School, and she had a totally separate group of friends she hung around with. They were all about a year younger than I, and I didn't quite like any of them, but I loved being around her.

I tried to get along with her friends, but I just couldn't stand any of them. I didn't really fit into her social life. I guess I felt comfortable enough to share my secret with this kid named John I was hanging around with one day. He lived right by where Clare lived and was in that same circle. A few days later, my girlfriend knew I did heroin. Shortly after that, she broke up with me. I imagine it was embarrassing for her to be dating a heroin user. I mean, she was fifteen years old. I was sixteen. She made the right decision to get away from me, but I was heartbroken.

She was very upset about the fact I did heroin. But she was even more upset that I lied to her about it, or that I just absolutely wouldn't even talk about it with her. I would rather have her break up with me than expose her to anything that had to do with that crap. She called it lying. I looked at it more along the lines of protecting.

I mention this, not only because I still have love for her and keep in touch but because this period also marked the first time that heroin caused me to lose something. A someone, I should say. My beautiful curly-haired girlfriend.

I got over her by immersing myself in my addiction. And from then on, through my last few months of senior year, it progressed extremely fast. I graduated from Brother Rice in 2002. The summer that followed my graduation, I lived my life like Jimmy Conway in 'Goodfellas.' I was stealing and committing crimes like nobody's business.

I'd go into all the local home improvement stores, literally fill a shopping cart with thousands of dollars' worth of power tools and electronics, walk into the outdoor garden section, and walk right out the gate where my car would be parked. This was before "loss prevention" was a big thing, before cameras were all over the place, and before there were checkout counters in the garden sections at all the home improvement stores. I'd throw everything in the trunk of my car and be gone in twenty seconds. My luck in not getting caught was probably due to the fact there are about two hundred different stores in and around Chicago, so I didn't hit the same one twice for two or three weeks. Eventually, all the stores started putting chains on the gate in the garden sections, thinking that would deter people from walking right out the side gate with a cart full of stolen merchandise. And I'm sure it did deter most people. Not me. I'd load up a cart with power tools, then I'd stop by the hardware section and grab a pair of bolt cutters from the shelf, walk right out into the garden section, cut the chain, and walk out the gate.

Afterward, I'd drive around to all the local bars, or I'd drive by a construction site and pull over. I'd get out of the car, open the trunk, and sell everything for half of what it was worth. A $300 saw I'd sell for $123. An $800 generator I'd sell for $250. Sometimes I'd have $2,000 to $3,000 worth of merchandise in my trunk, and one guy would want everything. I'd say, "Give me a thousand dollars."

They'd counter with $800, and I'd take it. I'd sell it for whatever they had in their wallet. I didn't care. It was all profit, and I'd want it out of my possession as soon as possible. I don't think it ever took me longer than twenty to thirty minutes to sell anything I had stolen. It went fast. There were many times I'd steal a bunch of tools, and before I'd even pulled out of the parking lot, I'd ask a guy in a random pickup truck if he was interested in some brand-new tools, and I'd sell them right there, literally two minutes after I stole them.

I'd walk into a grocery store or a corner drugstore and empty the entire rack of replacement heads for shaving razors into a shopping bag. Then I'd fill another bag up with bottles of Tylenol, Advil, Zantac, Claritin, etc. Then I'd just walk out of the store. As long as nobody saw me loading all this into my personal shopping bags (that I'd bring into the store in my pockets), which only took about ten seconds to fill, and as long as I acted like I wasn't doing anything wrong, nobody even noticed. I'd go in and out of a store in less than ninety seconds. In thirty minutes, I could hit two or three stores and accumulate an entire duffel bag with packs of razors and medicine. Nowadays, shopping centers either don't carry replacement razors on the shelf—you have to get them from customer service—or they are locked up behind glass and you have to ask an employee to open the case for you. A lot of the high-theft over-the-counter medicine items are also behind glass. That's because they are $15 to $30 apiece, and all the local drug addicts were stealing them back then. I'd take all the merchandise to this little grocery store on Lake Street and Cicero Avenue on the west side of Chicago. The owner would take me in the backroom, count everything up with a calculator, and give me $4 to $6 an item. Three or four days a week I'd walk out of there with $300 to $400 in my pocket—all blown on coke and heroin. Mostly heroin.

Rallo and I, when we hung around together? Complete madness. We'd be together for two or three days locked in a motel room, smoking crack and doing heroin. We'd have a pocket full of money and go rob a dope spot on the west side just for fun. That would drive me nuts. I'd say, "Rallo, I have $200, let's just pay for the shit." He'd say, "Fuck that. They aren't getting our money." We've been shot at, involved in high-speed chases. As much danger as we put ourselves in, and all the stupid insane things we did—it was fun.

We never hurt anybody, physically. I'm not by any means condoning anything we did, but I had a lot of exciting times with Ronnie. Nowadays, I wouldn't say he's involved in my sister Jessica's life, but he's around still. So we're still in touch. He comes over and has Thanksgiving dinner with us every year. He'll pop in my mom's house a couple of times a month to say hello. Things like that. So we're still in contact, yes. However, we don't hang out together anymore. He's still a little out there.

Anyway, for that first year of using heroin, all the chaos, crime, and craziness didn't faze me to the point where I was truly aware that my life was headed in a very bad direction. I wasn't considering the consequences. The lifestyle hadn't yet caught up to me, so there was no dire reason to force me to stop getting high. I was using heroin every day, I was never home during the day, and I hid it well from everybody. My father was my main concern. I didn't want him knowing what was going on. Then my secret came to light.

My sister Cara was usually right along with me during my addiction. You'd never know this pretty, petite, little Italian chick was straight-up gangster. In fact, this story is just as much hers as it is mine. We had been stealing from every major retail/outlet/hardware store in the Chicago land area. Chicago Ridge Mall, Ford City Mall, Orland Park Mall—not to mention every grocery and drugstore within a forty-mile radius from where we lived. I remember I had this feeling that we should slow down, or at least go further to somewhere we hadn't ripped off lately. I guess I had that criminal intuition that we were going to get caught. I should've listened to it.

We drove out to North Riverside Mall in my sister's car. The crazy thing was we didn't even need the money. We had about $100 on us and four bags of heroin. Our thinking and logic was that it would be gone that night most likely, so we might as well get some money for the next day. Honestly, who in the hell knows what we were thinking. We stashed the dope in the glove box, parked the car, and walked into the store.

Within two minutes, we were on our way out of the store when we were stopped and escorted to the security room. We were both charged with felony theft because it was over $300 worth of merchandise. And because it was a holiday weekend, we had to spend the entire weekend in the police station lockup until Monday morning Bond Court.

The lockup officers at the police station allowed us to smoke a few cigarettes throughout our forty-eight-hour stay. They explained to my sister and me that instead of towing my sister's car, her purple Saturn that was parked in the parking lot back at the mall, they called our father and let him come and pick it up. I guess when they ran the plates, his information came up because technically it was his car. He had cosigned on the car for Cara. So they called him. And now we were both nervous, my sister and I, because we weren't planning on calling him and telling him what was going on. What we also didn't realize was that when the officer who arrested us asked why we were stealing and if we had drug problems, she would inform our father what our answers to those questions were. The answers being that we were both addicted to heroin. And when our father came to pick up the car, the officer told our dad everything.

Monday morning came, and my sister and I were transported to Maywood Courthouse. Around 10:00 a.m., we were both pulled out of our male and female bullpens we had been sitting in for the last four hours and marched into courtroom 103. Our charges were read aloud, and the judge gave us a second court date and a $20,000 bond each. That meant we each needed $2,000 to get out of jail.

We were in the courtroom for about forty-five seconds then put right back into the bullpen where we remained until about 6:00 p.m. That's when the correctional officers from the Cook County Jail arrived and began calling names and handcuffing everybody that was going to the County Jail. While I sat there, I was trying to prepare myself mentally for my first trip to the County. But it never happened. At least not that day.

My name was called, and I stepped to the front of the bullpen, thinking I was about to be handcuffed. The officer said, "Seminetta, your bond was posted. Step out." Deuces! I felt a sudden rush of relief, instantly followed by a rush of confusion. Who the hell bonded me out? Deep down, I knew. It could only be one person. But my sister nor I called him from the police station.

I stepped out into the hallway, and there was my sister Cara. She said, "Dad bonded us out," with the same look on her face I had on mine. Apparently, he was sitting in the courtroom when we walked out there earlier that day. And while we were sitting and waiting in the bullpens all morning and afternoon, our dad was going to the bank to withdraw $4,000 to bond his children out of jail.

My sister and I signed some paperwork and were released from the courthouse. Our father was waiting on a bench right outside the doors. I had a sneaking suspicion that he bonded me out just so he could kick my ass. As soon as he saw us, he stood up and said, "Let's go. Get your little asses in the car." Then he started walking to the car, Cara and I slowly trailing.

The whole ride home not a word was spoken. When we finally pulled up to our house, my dad pulled into the driveway and said, "We ordered some pizza. And I asked your mother to come over and have dinner with us. We're going to sit down and eat, and we're going to talk. And I better not hear a single lie come out of either of your mouths." Cara and I were still not aware that the police officer we told about using heroin was the same officer who released Cara's car keys to our father. That night, my sister and I, along with our father, stepmom, and our mother all sat there and talked about the fact we were doing heroin. Other than my mother, who had been through this in the past, nobody had a clue. Our dad, Dona, nor Cara and I—none of us had any idea of the seriousness of the situation. Our mother knew. But she also knew that there was nothing she could really do about it.

During that dinner, Cara and I were still sick and withdrawing from heroin. It had been three days since we used. And I hate to say this as I think back, but throughout that whole dinner, the only thing I could think about were the four bags of heroin we had stashed in the glove box before we got out of Cara's car and got pinched. That purple Saturn was now parked in the driveway. I could see it out the kitchen window from where I was sitting.

After dinner, my sister and I went out in the backyard to have a cigarette. I said to her, "Cara, we still have dope in the car." She said, "I know, I've been thinking about it since we left the courthouse." Literally ten minutes after promising our parents that we would quit using drugs, we were doing a line in the basement. And the cycle continued. We had turned into lying and conniving full-blown addicts.

We continued to lie, and steal, and use heroin. About a week before my next court date, I was once again out stealing for drugs. A camera caught my license plate in the parking lot of some store, and a half hour later, about five or six Chicago squad cars were out in front of my father's house. Since I wasn't there, I didn't get arrested that day. They left, but not before leaving my father with a message for me: Turn myself in, soon.

When I finally showed up at home, my dad was in shock. He told me that the detective said that if I turned myself in by the end of the week, the case would remain a misdemeanor instead of a felony. About a week later, after procrastinating and getting daily phone calls from this detective assigned to my case, I broke down and told my dad everything.

I told him that I couldn't stop using heroin, no matter how hard I tried. And I did try. I realize that there are people, like the majority of my family members who eventually became wise to me being a heroin addict, thought that I grew up to be a punk, a liar, and a thief. And although I was lying and stealing all the time, I wasn't a punk. I wasn't blatantly disregarding my morals. I knew what I was doing was wrong. I'm not making an excuse, but before I started doing these things, I had already developed a serious substance abuse disorder. It was too late. My soul knew that stealing from stores and using heroin were wrong, yet my physical body wouldn't allow me to stop. If that makes any sense.

Anyway, I came clean with my father. That's when he realized I had a very serious problem, even if he didn't fully understand it at the time. My dad didn't know how to help me, and he hated that. And I had many hard lessons to learn still at that point. This, in fact, was just the beginning of the storm. The drizzle before the flash flood.

After a long talk and a big hug between my father and me, he drove me to the Detective's Station on Thirty-Ninth and Damen. Because we were told on the phone by the detective that I'd be able to bond out because the charge was a misdemeanor, I wasn't that nervous. They said I wouldn't even be handcuffed, and to bring $100 with to post for bond. They'd fingerprint me and that would be that. So, it never crossed my mind that bringing my cigarettes and having two bags of heroin in my secret pocket would not be a good idea.

The detective was pretty cool. He told my father and me to have a seat and relax while he contacted the State's Attorney. When he returned about ten minutes later, however, the tables had turned. "Well, guys, I have bad news," he said. "Apparently, Michael is out on bond already for another retail theft in Maywood, so the State's Attorney upgraded this incident to a felony." My dad asked what that meant because we were both pretty clueless about how all this worked. "Well, he's going to have to stay in jail overnight and go to court in the morning to get his bond from a judge," the detective said. My dad was asked to leave, and I was transported to the police station on Sixty-Third and St. Louis to spend the night in jail.

I'll never forget that night. I was fingerprinted, my photo was taken, and I was thrown into a small cell with three other people. It was a dungeon! There were benches on each side of the cell, which by the way was the size of a walk-in closet. In the center, against the wall, was a stainless steel toilet covered with urine and vomit. It was a dingy, musty cell with a single dim light bulb flickering on the ceiling. The worst thing, though, were the tiny red cockroaches crawling all over the walls. I stood the entire night.

When I first got into the cell, the other three guys were asleep, two were sitting on one bench slouched over, and the other was lying on the other bench. Not one of them so much as budged when the cop put me in there and slammed the bars shut. For about ten minutes, I just stood there. Then all of a sudden, the man lying on the bench jumped up, went to the toilet, and started throwing up. I knew exactly what was wrong with him. "Dope Sick" was written all over his face.

Because I wasn't planning on spending the night in jail, I had two bags of heroin on me when I turned myself in, and I managed to hold onto them. I was eighteen years old and completely overwhelmed with confusion and anxiety, not knowing what was going to happen to me or how long I'd be locked up. I needed answers. Yet I was very hesitant to say anything to this older gentleman throwing up in the toilet. He looked like a dangerously mean individual. I was wrong, though. After he was done throwing up, he sat on the bench and said, "What do they call you, kid?" I told him my name, and he asked me what I was in for. When I said a felony theft, he said, "Ah, a dope fiend, huh?" When I asked him how he knew that, he looked at me and said, "Kid, I've been around the block a few times. That's what I'm in here for too. A thousand dollars' worth of DVDs."

I asked him if he was dope sick and going through withdrawal, which was an obvious rhetorical question. When he said that he was, I pulled out my two bags of dope I had. His eyes lit up like a kid in a candy store. I dumped both bags onto the bench, made two big lines, and we each did a blast. After his sickness melted away and my high kicked in, we began to talk. I'll never forget that old man.

His name was Freddy. He was an older Black man, probably around sixty years old. He spent the next four or five hours lecturing me like I was a child. I know it seems counterintuitive for a drug addict who's in jail to lecture another drug addict in jail about how they're wrong. But he had lived that life, and I guess he knew things I didn't. It was hard for me to absorb everything he was telling me, but everything that old man told me that night was from his experience with this drug, and everything he told me I'd go through if I didn't stop eventually would come to pass.

He told me about coming in and out of jail his whole life. He told me to try to quit and get some help, and in doing so I'd save myself and my family a lot of heartache and pain. Sadly, though, I've come to realize through the years that the problem with chemically dependent addicts is that they literally don't know how to quit. Knowing that heroin is wrong doesn't change the fact that they're addicted to it. Learning the hard way is often the only way addicts learn. Many addicts don't even consider they have a problem until they have experienced the negative consequences and the grief and all the bullshit using drugs or drinking excessively brings into their lives on the full scale. Not only that, but most addicts don't know how to stop even if they wanted to. And that was me that night.

There's a reason why people who try heroin will want to do it again and again. It's because it's an amazing high. In fact, out of all the harder drugs, heroin is in a class of its own. Nothing really compares to it in regard to the way it makes you feel. But there's also a second reason why somebody would want to use it at all, let alone a second or third time. That reason is because they have no idea of the misery they are inviting into their lives as they try it for the first time. Proof of that lies in the fact that anybody would try it in the first place.

If an individual tries heroin for the first time, obviously they don't understand what they are doing, because if they did, they'd stay as far away from it as possible. When they do try it, it's not very likely they are going to say, "Oh my, what is this incredible amazing feeling? I don't like feeling this good, take it away, I'll never do this again." No—they're going to like it, and like I said, they don't yet understand what it's going to do to them in the near future. So they do it again.

The absolute fact about heroin is this: It will turn your world, your mind, your emotions, and your moral compass upside down. I say absolute fact because that's not my relative opinion. Meaning, relative to me and my situation, it destroyed my life. But maybe for others, it won't. It will. It will absolutely mess up anybody who starts using it. That's an absolute truth; nobody gets a pass. That's the difference between heroin and other drugs.

Throughout my life, I really kept the reality of my drug use hidden from most people. It was unbelievable to most people the amount of drugs I'd ingest. I could never be the type of person who goes out, has a couple of beers, does a couple of lines of coke in the bathroom, and goes home and crashes. One flake of cocaine goes in my nose, I go buy a quarter ounce, a bag of syringes, baking soda, a crack pipe, a big chunk of raw heroin, and I go lock myself in a room for two days by myself. It's embarrassing. I was a sick puppy in my younger years. I wish I wasn't like that when it came to drugs, but I was. Moderation was not a part of my vocabulary.

I've done drugs with people who would almost brag about having a bad drug habit (like it was impressive or cool to have a bad drug habit), and that they knew what I was talking about when I'd tell them they should slow down before it got too out of control. Yes, I've been known to be a "pot calling the kettle black." This is common with hard-core addicts because most of us who have been through the ringer and really understand what happens when you use heavy drugs for long periods of time wouldn't wish that outcome on anybody. Many people I've used with, their drug habit at age twenty-five or thirty mirrored my drug habit at age sixteen. Because I was once in their shoes, I could almost guess how their lives were going to spiral out of control. I could see through them like glass. And I didn't want what happened to me to happen to them. So I'd "preach" to them.

Which would do no good. I know now that no amount of preaching could make someone realize they may have a problem and that they need to change. I mean, who the hell am I? What do I know?—some things people just have to learn on their own. The lessons mean more to us that way. Nobody ever taught me that drugs were bad. Experience showed me that drugs were bad. Until I actually personally experienced what that lifestyle leads to, my brain couldn't understand that there would come a time when I wouldn't be able to control it. I wasn't like those other addicts…until I was.

Anyway, I'm sure that's how Freddy saw me that night in that jail cell. Knowing that everything he was telling me was going in one ear and out the other. And as much as I wanted to believe him, I remember thinking to myself, "This old man is freakin' insane. I'll never end up like that." I'm sure Freddy saw through me like a piece of glass. I kept saying "I know, I know." But the reality was that I didn't know anything.

# CHAPTER 7

I didn't sleep a wink the entire night during my overnight stay at the police station. About 5:30 a.m. rolled around, and the lockup officer began to call off names, and my fellow detainees and I were handcuffed together. Then we were all led outside into the cold January air into the parking lot where a Chicago Police paddy wagon was waiting with the back doors open. We all slowly climbed into the back.

We proceeded to drive around to several other police stations to pick up other detainees. I couldn't tell you where because there were no windows. Soon, though, the paddy wagon was filled beyond capacity, and the mobile jail cell contained twenty to twenty-five men. I felt like a sardine in a little can. And the smell! I can't even begin to describe it. If you could imagine twenty to twenty-five men who haven't showered in two to three days locked in a space the size of an average bathroom with no windows. You have that image in your head? Okay, now imagine four or five of them have thrown up on the floor. And this ride lasted an hour. We finally arrived at the Cook County jail at about 7:30 a.m. We were all shuffled into the basement of the criminal courts building and put into our respective bullpens assorted by which judge we were assigned to.

My charge was a Class 4 felony theft. Finally, my name was called at around eleven o'clock, and an officer let me out of the bullpen, told me to keep my mouth shut and my hands behind my back, and I was led into the courtroom. It was a strange feeling. Complete detachment from society. The courtroom was buzzing with activity. Lawyers walking around, public defenders, courtroom officers, prosecutors. As I walked into the courtroom, I saw my father sitting amongst the general public on the benches. He nodded at me, and before I could even register it and nod back, I was spun around and *boom*! There's the judge in his high chair sitting behind this giant wooden desk staring down at me. He was an old white man with white hair and glasses. Initially, I was quite sure it was God himself.

His name was Judge Porter. The lawyer my dad hired was standing right next to me. And thank God, because everything I had rehearsed and planned on telling the judge completely vanished from my head. All I got out was "Hello." The judge smirked and said, "Proceed." The conversation between my lawyer and the judge might as well have been in Mandarin.

Within a matter of thirty seconds, I was given a 'No bond hold,' and marched away and put back into the bullpen. Other inmates were asking me what happened and if the judge was in a good mood. Right! I had no idea what had happened, and I couldn't care less about the judge's mood. However, because since then I've spent a lot of time in courtrooms, I can now explain that what happened that time in court was this: Because I was already out on bond for another felony case in Maywood, I was now in violation of that bond for catching this new case. I was given a VOBB (Violation of Bail Bond). When my father bonded my sister and me out from Maywood Courthouse, one of the conditions of that bond was that I do not catch another criminal case. And since I did, in fact, catch another case, there was no way that this judge would give me another chance to bond out. So a "Hold" was placed on me. That basically means, in layman's terms, that I'd be sent up shit's creek without a paddle. And so I was. My lawyer, Larry, came back to the bullpen and said, "Mike, they want you to sit in jail for a while. You're going to have to stay in County until we can figure out what Maywood's going to do."

I spent the rest of the day being processed into the jail: being fingerprinted, giving blood, talking to intake counselors. Those counselors' questions were just fantastic. "Um…Mr. Seminetta…Let me ask you, how do you feel right now?" "Oh, I feel great. Wonderful, actually; everything in my life is perfect at the present moment. Now, if you'd excuse me, I'm going to go repeatedly ram my skull into that concrete wall."

Throughout the afternoon and night, I was moved from one bullpen to the next. And by the way, a bullpen is basically a large cage or room used to contain large groups of people. Cook County Jail is the largest on-site jail in the world, and their bullpens are disgusting. Literally, hundreds of criminals from every corner of Chicagoland crammed into cages like a bunch of stinking animals. Hence the word "Bullpen."

About 10:00 p.m. came around, and they started taking approximately sixty to seventy people at a time out to be strip-searched. Complete dehumanization, let me tell you. We were all lined up along this long, dirty concrete wall and instructed to strip. "Listen up! If you weren't born with it, take it off. And for all you geniuses, that means take off all your clothing. Place everything in front of you, then turn back around and put your foreheads and toes on the wall. And for your safety, and the safety of my staff, do not fucking move. The quicker we get this done, the quicker you can get to your beds." And let me tell you, what I just went through in the last twenty-four hours, the only thing I could think about was laying down. I was withdrawing from heroin, I had a migraine headache, my back was in excruciating pain, and all I wanted to do was fall onto something soft.

We all stripped, turned around, and stood face to face with this giant dirty concrete wall while ten to fifteen officers searched all our clothing and shoes. I was standing right next to this older Mexican man. He didn't speak English, so when the officer told us all to keep our foreheads on the wall, I guess he didn't understand. He had his head off the wall and was looking around. An officer came up behind him, took the back of his head in one hand, and literally slammed his face into the wall. Real tough guy, this turnkey was. These Cook County Correctional Officers? Very professional, they were. If you didn't pick up on my sarcasm, what I really mean is that half of them belong locked up themselves. This was before the Federal DOJ (Department of Justice) came in to investigate Cook County Jail back in the early 2000s. Before cameras were placed on every wall, before they took away the Q-tip swab in your penis, or the strip-search lawsuit occurred. The Cook County Jail was a wild place back then. Anyway—needless to say, my head never left that wall until I was told to move.

My name was called again, and I stepped out of the bullpen. I stepped forward, and an officer wrote "MED-DIV6" on my forearm with a big black marker. MED meant medium security. DIV6 meant Division 6. Eventually, a group of about fifty of us were all marched through the underground tunnels to Division 6. And so I went.

It was around midnight when I finally arrived on deck—or to my living unit. Division 6, L1, lower cell 5. When I walked onto the tier, all the other inmates were locked in their cells for the night. The housing unit was a big room—kind of like a racquetball court—with a few tables made of steel and a TV bolted to the wall. The back and side wall were lined with cells. The unit officer told me my cell number—lower deck, cell 5—and as I walked across the dayroom to my cell, all of the inmates who were locked in their cells were hollering out of their chuckholes, which are rectangular openings in the cell doors, saying, "What you is." *What you is?* I had no idea what that meant. *What you is?* I later found out that they were asking me what gang I was in. I didn't say anything. I just walked to my cell.

I was locked in my cell and immediately confused. There were already two people in there, both occupying a bunk. King, who was, you guessed it, a Latin King, rolled over in his bunk and explained to me that the whole jail was overcrowded and that most of the cells had three guys in them. He said, "Just throw your mattress on the floor. I leave to go home in a few days, so you'll have a bunk then." My other cellmate, who was sleeping on the top bunk, woke up and said, "What's up, bro, you smoke." Hell yes, I smoke! His name was…well, I don't really know what his name was, but he told me to call him Moe. He was a Blackstone gang member. Apparently, Blackstones call each other Moe. And that was all well and fine. King and Moe were pretty cool, though, considering. They both told me if I needed anything to just ask. A bar of soap, a ramen noodle, a candy bar, whatever. Moe reached into his little storage box and handed me a pack of kite cigarettes, some rolling papers, and a book of matches. I sat there on the cold floor, smoked a cigarette in the dark, using the toilet for an ashtray, then fell asleep on my one-inch foam mattress.

Before I knew it, I woke up to a loud voice. "On these trays." Our cell door opened, and I walked out of the cell and into the day-room. The echoing sound of about sixty to seventy people filled the room. I was given a plastic tray which contained about a half-cup of cold oatmeal, a quarter-cup of cold powdered eggs, two slices of stale bread with a frozen slice of butter on them, and a half-pint carton of milk. I didn't eat it. I couldn't. My stomach was in knots, my eyes were bloodshot, and I felt like I was dying. I set the tray on the steel table and went back to my cell.

I remained on that wing in the county jail for sixty days. The entire time I was constantly surrounded by violence. Three days into my time there, the deck "went up." The deck going up basi-cally means a gang war erupted. Who the hell knows why. Probably because somebody sat at the wrong table or some stupid shit like that. I was eighteen years old, I wasn't plugged with any gang, and I was nervous. My cellie told me, "Mikey, the deck's going up after dinner. Just stand in the bottom deck, and you'll be cool. You're not plugged, so nobody has any beef with you." Picture eighty young gangbangers brawling, swinging socks filled with bars of soap and crushed-up light bulbs, beating each other half to death. The noise was ear-piercing. A total incomprehensible scene. It's something you have to witness to fully understand the madness. It was like freakin' Braveheart!

The fight went on for about seven or eight minutes. And that's pretty long in fighting time. The whole time this was going on, I stood in the corner of the bottom deck with a few others who wanted no part of it and just stood there, observing this whole insane scene. Thankfully, I was untouched. Then, all of a sudden, like a storm, about twenty correctional officers charged into the room with billy clubs and wearing helmets. They let loose, and for lack of a better description, beat the hell out of anybody standing up. It took them about five minutes to get everything under control and everybody laying on the floor, which by the way was covered in chicken grease and bones. (we were all sitting down having a pleasant county jail dinner when this all broke out).

Then the lieutenant walks in and says, "Strip your clothes off right now and get against the motherfucking wall. I'm tired of you little jagoffs. You're gonna learn a lesson this time." We all lined up on the wall and put our hands up high. This big officer started putting on leather gloves. And when I say big—this guy was six feet and four inches and about three hundred pounds! He started at the end of the line of us, and as he walked up to each inmate, he was slapping them on the side of the head! I was in the middle of the line. I could hear him getting closer. Slap! Slap! Slap! I was thinking to myself, "Is this freakin' guy really going to hit me?" He got to me. Slap! It felt like a polar bear slapped me in the head. My ears were ringing for hours. Anyway, it was a horrible situation. The violence I had just witnessed was completely pointless. Completely pointless. It makes you realize the level of ignorant hatred and unconsciousness that exists out there. All I remember thinking to myself that night while lying on my bunk was, "This sucks. I'm never getting high again." And at the time, I was sincere. More sincere than a person could possibly be. What my problem was, though, was that I didn't understand addiction. I didn't understand the psychology behind it, or the neurology of it. The way my brain processed thoughts and made decisions had changed drastically over the years. I didn't understand that no matter how strong the urge to abstain from using drugs was, I wouldn't be able to. The urge to use them would always win over the intention not to. To be honest, I didn't want to quit using drugs. I just never wanted to come back to this place—this jail on Twenty-Sixth and California Avenue. And on March 20, 2003, the judge in Maywood and the judge at the Criminal Courts building decided to run both of my cases concurrently. And at about 9:00 p.m., one day before the first day of spring, I was discharged from jail on two years' probation.

# CHAPTER 8

At thirty-eight years old as I'm writing this, I believe I now have a basic comprehensive opinion of what it means to be normal. To me, normal people do not do things that cause negative outcomes in their lives, consciously, over again. Maybe to the average normal human being, being incarcerated for their actions would naturally force them to reevaluate their present character, conduct, and temperament, and attempt to correct the problem. But as much as normal people who have never personally experienced a chemical addiction find the phrase "just say no," a discernable solution to chemical dependency—addicts aren't normal.

I can only speak for myself, but I'm pretty damn sure this doesn't just pertain to me when I say that in the very beginning of my heroin addiction, there was something extremely wrong with my attitude, as well as my understanding of the nature of addiction, and my awareness of just the type of character I was becoming over time. I'm not saying I believed that nothing was wrong with my actions or attitude at that time. I'm saying that despite how ashamed I was of my conduct, I couldn't stop.

I have little recollection of what was going on in my young, confused mind at that point in my life as an eighteen-year-old jail releasee with a substance abuse problem. Basically, I believed getting locked up was a fluke and I surely wouldn't let that happen again. If I fully understood my condition and what I was about to put myself through over the next decade, I like to believe that I would've done more to stay clean. One of my biggest regrets is that I didn't complete my probation when I was discharged from jail that first time. I blew the opportunity of a lifetime.

September 11, 2001, at around 8:30 a.m., my friends Tony, Tim, and I had just come in off the football field from smoking a joint and playing hackysack. We all had open school together during second period as seniors at Brother Rice. Our daily routine was to play hackysack and smoke weed on the football field, then sit in the cafeteria and eat nachos and cookies and watch TV for a half hour. Around the entire cafeteria at Brother Rice were TVs hanging on the walls.

We had just sat down when our homeroom teacher ran in and turned all the channels to the news station. The first building had already been hit. I remember thinking to myself, "How could a plane not see that huge building?" Within five minutes of watching, another plane hit the second tower. Before this day, I wasn't even aware of terrorists or Islamic extremists or Osama bin Laden. I knew that what I was witnessing was bad, but I didn't quite comprehend it at the time. How our country was attacked by terrorists. How many families had lost loved ones in those moments. The situation was a lot to process for people my age and younger at the time.

Over the years as I grew up, I started to read a lot of books on history, particularly pertaining to war. I learned a lot about Islamic extremists. History was always the one subject I was actually interested in. And after watching documentaries about 9/11 and the history of Osama bin Laden and Al Qaeda and how it came to be, I couldn't help but to be frustrated. I was angry. They killed 2,984 Americans.

When I graduated from high school, I was already pretty screwed up, but not completely beyond redemption. When I got probation, my father and I briefly discussed me joining the Marine Corps. At the time, it wasn't because I had a burning desire to be a soldier. The main reason for joining the service was because I was headed in a bad direction and thought the military would be good for me. I went to the recruiting office, and the man told me to finish my probation and come back, which at that time I still had about twenty-two months left on that probation.

I was willing to leave home and fight for my country, and I would have. If they would've accepted me, I would have gone to Iraq or Afghanistan in the early 2000s. But they said no, that I had to finish twenty-two months of probation first, all because I was a young kid doing drugs and stole a few tools. I'm not trying to minimize my behavior, but something could've been done. It's a very sore subject for me because I didn't agree with their decision. The trajectory of my life would've been completely averted, and I could've served my country. Unfortunately, because receiving probation doesn't magically cure addiction, I got in more trouble before those twenty-two months were up, and the military was no longer an option.

Although I'm happy with who I am today and there's not much I'd change about my past because it made me who I am today, if there's one thing I could change, I would've joined the military immediately after high school before I committed that petty, stupid crime. Over the years, I've become very interested in history and past events that have affected us all as a species. Again, particularly war. The French and Indian War, and the events leading up to the American Revolution, and then the Revolutionary War are some of the most intriguing things to read about the history of the United States. I became so interested in these things.

I would never say that I would've made it through training. Nobody can be that arrogant, not to mention disrespectful to actual SEALs. But I will say that I would've given 110 percent and I'd like to believe that I wouldn't have quit, if I'd been given the chance. Nobody I know, or who knows me, is aware of this about me because I don't like talking about it, but I regret not getting my shit together faster for the sole reason of being able to join the military. I would've served my country in a heartbeat.

I do know that I blew that opportunity—I don't blame anybody but myself—but not being allowed to join for such a petty reason is one of those things in life that I compulsively try to understand, still to this day. I've yet to understand why. However, I also realize that what I was to go through had to be faced head-on for many reasons. That was the path God chose for me. He chose to mold me in a different way other than the molding I would've received in the United States military. Period. I can't really question it, and I have no choice but to embrace it.

I still daydream about how it would've been had I been allowed to join the military. I watch *Lone Survivor* probably once a month. I search for YouTube videos about SEAL training, and other special operators like Rangers or Green Berets. *American Sniper, Saving Private Ryan*, all the war documentaries by Ken Burns. Ken Burns is the best. His documentary on Vietnam is amazing. I watch these movies every time they're on, and I actually like to be alone because I go into my own world while I watch them. I guess it's just one of those things that will bother me forever that I failed to do. Now, I can only serve my country with my knowledge and wisdom on a subject I happen to be very experienced in. So that's what I'm doing. Maybe that's what I was always supposed to do? Anyhow...

When I was a teenager and throughout my twenties, before I started to grow up and get my ego in check, I took many things for granted. As time passed and my addiction worsened, I spent more time without consideration for the things or people that actually mattered in my life. And by the time I was a young adult—like most young adults—I became extremely wrapped up in the calamity and stress of life. I was living, breathing, and active—but I wasn't consciously enjoying life. My mind was always running, from the moment I woke up until the moment I fell asleep. Running, thinking, doing. I forgot how to just enjoy the present moment. I took everything for granted. When I was in the county jail for the first time, surrounded by strangers, I realized I had taken my loved ones for granted. I took life for granted. The little things that make life beautiful and fulfilling, like eating dinner with my family, taking a car ride to get ice cream, or going for a cruise down Lake Shore Drive. Italian food! Making love! I took all those things for granted, thinking they'd always be there no matter how I behaved. I took my freedom for granted.

I recall being younger and older folks saying to me, "You don't understand," or they'd say, "You'll understand when you're older." That used to aggravate the hell out of me. "I understand, I really do," I'd say. Or "I know." "I know" was my saying. "I know, I know, God, I'm not dumb," I'd say. My father would respond to that with "Don't say 'I know,' just shut your mouth and listen. Capisce?"

"Yeah, Dad."

"What."

"I said yeah… Yes."

"Alright then."—My dad hated the word *yeah*.

Anyway, that always made my ego flare up, being told that I didn't understand. I honestly believed that I knew what I was being told. And I hated that the adult people didn't think that I knew what they were talking about. No particular time or conversation, I just remember hating being told, "You'll understand when you're older." The thing is, though, as I'd get older, and through actual adult experience, I'd gain some type of insight or wisdom into something that, previously, I thought I totally understood. Then I'd say to myself, "Huh, wow, I really didn't understand shit when I was younger."

Well, what I thought I knew about drug addiction and staying clean when I was released from the Cook County Jail at eighteen years old was completely wrong. I underestimated my situation, thinking, "Not me." I believed that willpower and good intentions were sufficient enough for me to stay out of jail. I say "stay out of jail" and not "stay clean" because my intentions were not to never get high again. My intentions were to never go back to jail again.

I had a plan. Basically, my plan consisted of only using once in a great while. But I could still smoke pot every day and get drunk on the weekends. I had everything under control. Like I said, getting locked up was a fluke. I'd handle myself better this time around. Now mind you, I'm still learning and always will be, but I can honestly say that when I was eighteen years old, I didn't understand anything about addiction, life, or about myself. But at the time, as all eighteen-year-olds think, I knew everything! I was Mikey Seminetta. I had been through a lot. Drugs weren't going to take me down.

About thirty hours. That's how long it was after I was released from jail before I had heroin running back through my system. Less than two days. Within a week, I was using every day again. As the first month passed, my habit increased, and I was right where I had been before I got locked up. When I used that first time, a day after I got out, I wasn't disregarding my morals, my resolve, or my common sense. I knew what I was doing was wrong, and I was ashamed

76

of myself. Yet something inside me would not allow me to push the thought of using aside once it entered my mind. It's as if my will-power didn't exist. Or at least, it wasn't functioning properly.

The first four or five months after getting out of jail were actually going pretty well—seemingly. I did start using heroin again right away, but it took about eight months before it caught up to me again. As soon as I got out of jail, my father had a job set up for me. The following Monday, I was to start working for my next-door neighbor's business. Mr. Novick owned a union sheet metal company, Kirby Sheet Metal. Before I started my new job, my dad also took me shopping for a new car. After driving around from one dealership to the next, I finally came across the car I wanted. It was a 2002 silver Dodge Stratus, woodgrain accent, six total miles on it, sitting on the showroom floor. My dad cosigned for me, and I walked out of there with the car for zero down and a car note of $199 per month—thanks to my dad's credit. For once in my life, I was completely happy, and everything seemed to be going great.

I started my job and loved it. My job was to be at the shop on Forty-Second and Western Boulevard at 6:30 a.m., get my work orders, and load this huge International Diesel Truck up with tools, sheet metal, spiral tubing, and various materials and hardware, then I'd spend my entire day delivering everything to all the field-workers that were on construction sites throughout the city of Chicago. My shop foreman told me, "Mike, you'll drive the truck until the next union test comes up in four months. For now, you'll make $15 an hour. But after you take the test, you'll get your Union Card, and you can start your career as a tin man at the shop." That plan never unfolded and came to fruition as it was supposed to. But if it had, I would've been a journeyman at age twenty-two, making about $40 an hour with full medical and dental insurance and a pension plan. But God had other things in mind for me to learn and go through, with a very different test.

At the time, though, I was happy. I was netting about $400 a week, so I had plenty of money in my pocket. I had money for gas and smokes, fast food, and I had money to get a couple of bags of dope every day. My work was located on Forty-Second and Western, and my job was to deliver equipment to field-workers but also to pick up various materials from different factories. Tanks of propane for blowtorches, electropolished sheets of metal, etc. All these different factories were all located on the Westside of Chicago, in some of the biggest drug-infested areas of the city. I'm talking open-air drug markets on every corner. So usually, while making my rounds in the company truck, I'd make my drug runs. It was so convenient. I drove this truck that was huge. The driver's cab was the same as a semitruck, manual transmission with a thirty-foot-long flatbed with gates. So I never was nervous about being seen by the police in an area I didn't belong in. I was "just working."

I'd drive around and pick up supplies, drop off supplies, and get high all day. And because I did all my drug runs at work, I had more time to spend at home. I didn't have to run out the door right after work and be gone all night. I took care of all that crap during the day. Everything in my life was going smoothly, I was happy, and I was getting high. This reassured me that I wouldn't go back to jail, and I wasn't like all those other drug addicts I knew of. I was different. I was in control. Life was good at the time, then it got even better.

I worked on Forty-Second and Western, and I lived on Ninety-Second and Avers. So I'd take Western to Ninety-First Street and Ninety-First Street home, in which I'd drive by my ex-girlfriend's house. Clare was that girl that, no matter how many girls I've been with, she never quite escaped my mind. I was driving home from work one afternoon and I almost ran over Nell. Nell was my ex's family dog, who was running in the street after her backyard breakout. I stopped and called her name, and she actually came right up to me. I picked her up in my arms, pulled into Clare's driveway, and beeped my horn a few times. I was holding Nell by her collar and walking her back to the yard when my ex-girlfriend came outside. She walked up to me with that big smile and beautiful copper-colored curly hair and gave me a hug. I told her I had seen Nell running in the street and just wanted to make sure she got back into the yard. Which, in all actuality, was complete bullshit. I really didn't care about the dog per se; it was just a good excuse to stop by.

She asked how I was doing, and I said, "Great. Everything is going good." Then she asked me if I was "still using that crap." Shit! What was I to say to that question? I told her no. She complimented my new car, and we exchanged cell numbers. I drove away very happy to have seen her, and I just hoped that she'd call. Then she did.

I ended up taking her and a couple of her girlfriends downtown to the lakefront on Ohio Street Beach. We got a bottle of SKYY Vodka and some pineapple juice, laid a blanket in the sand, and had a blast. I remember she got up to go and relieve herself, and while she was gone, her girlfriend said to me, "She misses you, Mike, and she wants to get back together with you." When I look back on this now, it was cute. Clare and I were just young kids who were into each other. When she came back a few minutes later, she came and sat down in front of me between my legs, leaned back, and rested her head against my chest. We spent another hour talking and laughing by the lakefront. Afterward, I drove her two girlfriends home, and Clare and I found a dark secluded area in North Beverly and cuddled up in the back seat of my car.

Our new relationship lasted about four months. Then I lost her again. I was using more and more, which meant I had to sneak around more and more. Money was going fast. My moods were miserable. And eventually, she realized that I was a big fat liar. What I was doing, and more so what I couldn't stop doing no matter how hard I tried, well, it was embarrassing to let it be known. I loved her, but in my eyes, she was this young girl who just wouldn't understand. So I tried to hide it from her as long as I could, hoping that somehow I'd be able to quit and get my life together before she bailed. But again, I failed. She just didn't understand why I used. There were plenty of times when I met drug dealers at fast-food restaurants or gas stations without her even knowing it. There were times we'd go buy weed, but what she didn't realize was that weed wasn't the only thing I was buying.

The last time we were together before we broke up again, I was in bad shape. I had spent the night with Rallo, driving around the city, burning dope spots on the west side. We probably did a couple hundred dollars' worth of crack, and at about 6:00 a.m., when the sun was coming up and the streets started filling up with cars, we headed home. I did a few bags of heroin to mellow myself out and was dropped off on her corner. For one, I wanted to see her, but more so because I didn't want to face my father.

Her parents were gone for work, and I rang the doorbell. Her little brother answered the door and let me in. When I went up to her bedroom, she was still asleep. I lay down next to her, and she woke up kind of surprised. "What's up?" she said. I told her I got up early and just wanted to see her. I remember she went and got a big glass of orange juice, jumped back into bed, crossed her legs Indian style, and said, "You want to hear a cool story I read last night?" I said, "Sure, babe," and she grabbed a book and started to read to me. It was a short story of sorts. I don't remember what the story was about because I wasn't really listening. I was just lying there, staring at her, watching her read, and thinking to myself how pretty and cute she was and how big of an ass I was. While she was reading, I fell asleep on her.

About a week later, she broke up with me again. And that was probably for the best. One thing I can say, though, is that I never exposed her to drugs. She smoked pot, but never had I offered her hard drugs. I didn't even want her to know about it. Her parents liked me at first, until they found out I was a heroin addict. Then not so much. But like I said, I loved her and cared for her too much to get her involved in my life. Any bad decision she made was on her own accord. I was never the type to influence people to do wrong. We'd see each other again, though.

Shortly after my girlfriend and I broke up again, I ran into an old friend of mine that I hadn't seen in about a year. I was pumping gas into my car, and there was Byron standing at the bus stop. About thirty seconds into our reunion, we realized we both had the same destination: the Westside. He hopped in my car, and off we went. We drove to a project building on the Westside, which oddly enough was about fifty yards away from the alley on Fifth and Kostner where we had both done heroin together for the first time about two years earlier. We bought our drugs and jumped back on the highway. I dumped a bag of heroin onto a CD case, snorted it, and when I handed the case to Byron, he said that he wanted to pull over and do his at a gas station or fast-food restaurant bathroom. I said, "Dude, I'm not pulling over, just do it." He insisted that we stop, though. That's when I asked him what he was hesitant to tell me himself. "Are you shooting it?" The smirk he gave me answered my question.

After he did his thing, the conversation began. I told him he was crazy. "Byron, you're crazy, bro! I have never," I said. He told me how much better it was and how I was wasting my dope by snorting it. The ride home was silent for the next thirty minutes. Mainly because I was in deep thought about this whole "wasting my dope" business, and also because Byron was completely nodded out. Then my contemplation ended abruptly. I pulled over in a McDonald's parking lot on Seventy-Ninth and Western, parked the car, and turned to Byron. "I want to try it." Then I proceeded to do the one thing that I swore I'd never do… Stick a needle in my arm.

I'll never forget the irony of the situation. I had a Sublime CD playing at the time, and while I was shooting up for the first time, the song "Johnny Butt" was playing: "Shoot it up, shoot it up, it just doesn't matter, when you resist it anyway. We got a brand-new dance, we got to overcome." I immediately learned how to cook my dope, shoot up, and I fell in love with the drug all over again. This was it! It was like injecting happiness directly into my brain.

Within eight months of being released from the county jail, I landed a great job, was blessed with a new car, gained some trust back from my father, got my girl back—started shooting heroin—lost my job for being late and not doing my job efficiently or professionally, kissed my first union job goodbye, lost my girlfriend again, totally disappointed my father, and once again, guess what? Busted!

I'm not going to keep interrupting my story with trips to the county jail. I've been to the county jail numerous times. Between the ages of eighteen and twenty-two, I spent a lot of time on Twenty-Sixth and California (where the jail is located). The first time was for sixty days. Three months the second time. Six months the third time. A few times the cases I caught were not that serious, like being charged with criminal trespassing for trying to buy drugs from project buildings. Before the previous mayor of Chicago, Mayor Daley, tore down all the project buildings, they were everywhere—up and down State Street: Rockwell Gardens, Robert Taylor Homes, Ida B. Wells, Ogden Courts. I've been in all of them. And if you're white, the narcs will arrest you for just being in the vicinity of one of these buildings. They'd arrest me for trespassing, and I'd be locked up for a day or two. A handful of times, my loving father bailed me out on the more serious charges: $2,000 the first time, $5,000, twice he paid $10,000, $2,500 once or twice.

Every time I got arrested, I'd go through withdrawal in my cell. That meant four or five days of diarrhea, stomach cramps, throwing up every time I'd swallow any type of food or liquid. The body rejects everything for about a week. Sweating and shivering at the same time. Then what follows that is about a week or two of insomnia. You cannot sleep at all. If you do get lucky and nod off for a half hour, you wake up covered in sweat. It takes a good three weeks before the body is seminormal again. Then the promises begin.

You start telling yourself that you won't get high anymore when you get out. And you're being honest and sincere. After an addict's first couple of times getting locked up, they start realizing that they may actually have an issue with drugs. By then, though, it's usually too late to just be able to stop on their own. No matter how many times an addict tells themselves they're done, if they're not fully aware of their condition in relation to being drug-dependent, more likely they're just getting started. What many fail to realize is that drug addicts aren't stupid. There comes a point early on in addiction where we don't relapse because we're having fun, or because we think we can control it. The reality is that we literally don't know how to say no when those inevitable urges floor our thoughts.

For me personally, my promises and good intentions usually lasted two days, maybe three. Then as sure as the sun would set at night, I'd take that ride to the city. And believe me when I say this, it wasn't because I was having a good time. And eventually, it wasn't because I believed I had everything under control. That right there suggests that addicts have a serious chemical imbalance that often entails a very strong mental obsession to use. And that's not an excuse. It's real. The human brain, after using drugs for a significant period of time, literally changes the way it operates. But we'll get into all that in part two of this book.

Anyway, I'd get out of jail, or prison, or rehab, and within a few days, I'd start using again. Within a month, my life would again become complete chaos. And slowly but surely, every bit of happiness I'd rekindle while in jail or rehab would eventually be drained out of me. I'd begin lying, stealing, and using all day, every day. I'd spend my days buying drugs, getting high, and finding ways to get more. There were times that I'd go on two or three day binges without hardly any sleep, and when the money was all gone, and every store in the area was hot, I'd do really stupid, dangerous shit, like actually going and robbing drugs from the actual drug spots. Then within a few months, I'd get locked up again. Honestly, from the ages of eighteen to twenty-five, there's really not much to tell. If I were to write about those years, it wouldn't make for a very interesting story. Well, actually, it would probably be entertaining, but not very positive or helpful to my readers. Plus…plausible deniability.

It was the same old nonsense day in and day out. The only progressive difference was that my habit, my behavior, and my mental health were continuously getting worse. And the worse it got, the worse my personal life became. And the worse my personal life became, the more I'd want to get high. The more I got high, the more I'd want to stop and get clean, but the harder it became. Again, we'll get into the "why" in part two of this book.

My point is that I just couldn't stop! My life was a mess, and I was absolutely heartbroken because of it. By the time I was in my early twenties, my habits and behavior patterns I had established over the years were really starting to turn on me. My life was composed of confusion, sadness, a touch of anger and self-pity, brief intervals of depression, and a whole lot of fake smiles.

# CHAPTER 9

"Only to the extent that we expose ourselves to annihilation, over and over again, can that which is indestructible be found within ourselves."

I came across this quote while reading a book once, and it rang so true that I came to memorize it. I apologize to the man or woman who came up with such finely sequenced words because I've forgotten their name, and I no longer possess the book. I mention this quote because not only is it remarkably true, I believe two things: first, I believe that everything I put myself through, and every hand life has dealt me, in retrospect, has taught me countless lessons that are extremely valuable. Secondly, I also believe that I have found that within myself that is indeed indestructible. The only reason I've found it and have become aware of it is because, like the quote says, I kept exposing myself to annihilation over and over again. For me, it is my desire to pursue happiness and tranquility at all costs. I can deal with all the stress and bullshit as long as I know there will be some joy and balance in the end.

Even though it may seem so sometimes—especially with addicts—the human spirit can never be completely diminished or broken. Never. From my experience, that's impossible. The human spirit is divine. Always has been, always will be. Every human being on earth, despite what situation they're in, generally wants to be happy and at peace. If we all have anything in common, it's that truth.

I previously stated at the beginning of this book that I don't hold much stock in the "Rock Bottom" concept. Like I said, it can always get a little bit worse. Always. I also don't believe in the saying I've often heard people say that "some people are better off dead than living the way they are." Only ignorant people make comments like that. I know because I used to think that way.

From the time we're born until the time we die, we're always learning, and we're always teaching—in one way or another. We cannot suggest death for ourselves or for others because things are gloomy and not the way we'd like them to be or think they should be. God teaches us all in different ways, preparing us for our purpose. I believe our individual destinies and paths are inevitable, and I believe we as individuals will suffer a lot less in life when we begin to embrace that concept instead of always going against the grain or trying to swim against the flow or however you want to phrase it. But suggesting that some addict or somebody who is living a treacherous life would be better off dead, or stating our opinions of how everybody should live their life, especially when we're speaking of someone else's life, it's complete ignorance and unconsciousness.

I believe the first time I recognized my human spirit, or "inner God," or that still voice inside myself that has never been broken just so happened to be one of the hardest days of my life up until that point. We will call it my "rock bottom." I was about twenty-three or twenty-four years old, and I was a stone junkie. I had no life outside being a junkie whatsoever. No social life. All my friends, my cousins whom I love dearly, pretty much everyone I knew, I was too embarrassed to even speak to or go near any of them. My immediate family life was strained because everybody was so disappointed in me and didn't know what to do or say. I'd miss every family party basically out of embarrassment. Weeks would go by when I wouldn't speak to my father other than quick phone calls, once or twice a week I'd show up at home and eat dinner with my family, and it would be nice to eat food on an actual plate with silverware. My father would want answers. Was I okay? Where have I been? When was I going to rehab? I had no answers for him. I was totally lost. Whenever this came up between my father and me, I'd clam up and go silent.

There was no joy, no friendship, no companionship. I had no job, no car, no girlfriend. The only type of sex life I had was occasional one-night stands—usually with girls that were about as screwed up as I was. Thankfully, I was very lucky and never contracted any type of disease or STD because there were many one-night stands, and I rarely practiced safe sex.

I was living on ninety-nine-cent double cheeseburgers from McDonald's and about a $200 to $300 a day heroin and cocaine habit. The heroin alone was suicidal. On average, I was shooting anywhere from two to three grams a day. That's two to three grams of uncut raw heroin. I was buying my own bottles of Dormin pills, which is a sleeping agent used to cut raw heroin. I'd put a half gram of raw heroin on a spoon, dump half of a Dormin pill on it, cook it all, and shoot it up. That's equivalent to doing about eight bags one would buy from a street corner all at one time. Comparatively, I was doing thirty- to sixty-dime bags a day. The unbelievable thing is that my drug use actually got worse than that during my late twenties. I was only twenty-three, twenty-four years old during this particular "Rock Bottom."

Anyway, most nights, I would sleep in cheap motel rooms or on the couches of whomever I happened to be with. I weighed about 160 pounds, which is small for me. Healthy, I'm 210 to 215 pounds. I also had visible track marks all over my arms. If you were to ask me when the last time I smiled or laughed was, I wouldn't have been able to tell you. I was messed up.

This particular day was one of those harder days to get through. Possibly the hardest. The only reason I remember it so vividly is because, well for one, if you haven't noticed, I have a vivid memory, but also because this day happened to be one of the most enlightening days I had up until this point. It was just one of those days you don't forget.

I was the type of addict who would wake up with $1.35 in my pocket, and within an hour or two, I'd have enough money to buy $80.00 worth of heroin, $10.00 for gas, smokes, and enough to run through McDonald's drive-through for a couple of Egg McMuffins. Within an hour, every dollar would be spent, and all the drugs would be gone. Then the process would start all over again: find money, get drugs; find money, get drugs. Some days I'd repeat this insane process three or four times. But for some reason, that day, nothing was going as planned.

I spent the entire day on a mission for money, which was hard because I didn't have access to a car at the time. So I was on foot.

Long story short, I finally managed to gather up enough money for bus fare and a few bags of heroin. Which by then, I was aching and desperate for. My regular dealer had been dry all day and had stopped answering the phone, so I had no choice but to go to the city.

It was around 9:00 p.m. when I finally got on the bus and started making my way to the Westside. Normally by 9:00 p.m., I'd have already gotten high four or five times throughout the day. So I was physically weak and sick. Stepping up onto the bus was a challenge for me. But, with $30 in my hand and heading in the direction of the city, I felt a little bit of relief when I took my seat at the back of the bus. By the time I arrived at the area I wanted to be in and stepped off the bus, it was around 10:00 p.m.

When I walked onto the block where the dope was sold, I was told, "It's going to be about a half hour, they're shaking it up now, come back in about forty-five minutes." Now for anybody who understands, hearing him tell me that was like being told the world was about to end. I was sick too. Throwing up bile sick. Forty-five more minutes!

The dope spot was on Kostner and Van Buren. Highway 290 is about a block away, and Kostner Street has an overpass running above the highway. I was probably the only white person within miles, walking around, which worried me. Not that I was worried about being white in a black neighborhood, but because I stuck out like a sore thumb, and I didn't want to be seen by the police. So I walked to the overpass, jumped the guardrail, and went and waited under the overpass.

While I waited, I threw up twice. It was the longest half hour of my life. On the walk back to the block, I stepped in dog shit and was splashed with water from a passing car hitting a puddle. I shit you not. When I got to the dope spot, there was a line of about fifteen to twenty people. Heroin addicts getting their fix, waiting in a line like they're in a store… Unbelievable.

I bought my few bags and made my way to the gas station right around the corner that had a public washroom on the side of the building. That was my destination. When I walked into the gas station to ask for the bathroom key, the man told me, "Sorry, buddy, it's out of order."

"You're fuckin' kidding me, right?"

"Excuse me, buddy."

"Never mind. Can I get a bottle of water?"

I got a bottle of water and left. I walked into the alley behind the gas station, made a little cubby hole out of a few city garbage cans, crouched down, and took out the works. I dumped the three bags onto my spoon, cooked it up, shot it, and leaned back. Instant relief. Every ache and pain my body had? Gone. The stomach cramps? Gone. Runny nose? Gone. Nausea and headache? Gone and gone. Mental stress? Vanished. I was still a depressed, unhappy person, but the mental stress of withdrawal was gone. All the sickness instantly went away. Literally, within seconds.

By the time my little ritual was over and the realization came to my full attention that I was on Kostner and Van Buren, about fifteen to twenty miles from home, and it was eleven thirty at night and about to rain, I ran back to Cicero to get back on the bus that would take me back to my neighborhood. But it was too late. There were no more buses running.

It was approaching midnight, and here I was on Cicero and Van Buren, stranded. I walked to a nearby pay phone, but when I got to it, I had nobody to call. I stared at the dial pad on the pay phone for five minutes straight, just thinking. Then I realized that out of all the people I knew and all the family members I had, I was too ashamed and embarrassed to call any of them for help. In this case, a ride. I had not one person I was comfortable calling who wouldn't judge me. Not even my father. The five minutes I spent staring at that dial pad may have been the loneliest five minutes of my life.

I walked away from the pay phone, sat on a curb, and put my head down and cried. I didn't cry because I was being a baby or because I couldn't handle it. I had been through days just like this one many times. I cried because something inside me finally let me see my situation for what it was, and at last, I understood just how sick and screwed up my life had truly become. It was one of the most humble experiences I ever had. It was like God opened my eyes up a little bit. Not fully, but just a little bit. I felt like God actually planned this entire day for me, with the roadblocks and trouble I had that day, just so I could have this experience at that exact moment in time.

After a few minutes of feeling sorry for myself, I wiped my eyes and lit a cigarette. What I'm about to write may seem contrived, like I'm trying to fabricate some story. I'm not. This is what happened next: Before I was halfway done with my cigarette, it began to rain again. It was that cold November rain, too! I remember shaking my head, saying, "What next." I looked up at the sky and yelled, "Can you please stop the rain? Please! Jesus Christ, what the hell are you trying to do to me?" Immediately after I was done bitching, lightning cracked through the sky, and a few seconds later, the thunder started rumbling, and it started to downpour. It was surreal. And I started laughing. Not a joyful laugh. More of an aggravated, exaggerated, crazy-person laugh. Then I started walking.

I walked from Cicero and Van Buren to my father's house on Ninety-Second and Avers in Evergreen Park. That's about a sixteen-mile walk, give or take. It took me about six hours. I remember when I walked into my father's backyard, it was about 6:00 a.m., and it was starting to get light outside. I lay down in a lawn chair and started contemplating whether I was going to knock on the door or not. I hadn't seen my father in about a week. About a half hour later, while I was still contemplating and procrastinating in my lawn chair, my father opened the back door to let the dog outside. That's when he saw me lying there. He just looked at me and said, "You okay, son?" which obviously was a rhetorical question.

He took me inside, let me eat something and shower. Afterward, we sat down at the kitchen table and began calling rehab centers. After about an hour on the phone, I finally landed an appointment at the SHARE program in Hoffman Estates, IL. I had been there once before for twenty-eight days. The lady on the phone looked up my file and said, "We're so glad you called. Come in at 4:00 p.m. on Wednesday, and we'll start your detox, okay? And Mr. Seminetta, please show up, we want to help you." That was wonderful, but Wednesday was a few days away. My father was relieved that I had actually scheduled an appointment, but I told him, "Dad, I'm not going to make it." He asked me when the last time I used was, and

I told him, "About ten thirty last night." He asked me when I was going to start getting sick, and I said, "I'm already getting sick." He pleaded with me to just stay at home and try to get through it until Wednesday. And honestly, I tried. I lasted that whole day and slept all night on the couch in the basement.

My father sat there with me the entire night while I slept, and when I woke up the next morning, deathly ill, he was sitting on the other side of the couch, staring at me, eating pistachios, and watching TV. I felt pitiful, and I hated that he was seeing his son like this. When a heroin addict withdraws cold turkey, usually about twelve hours after their last fix, they crash, and their bodies shut down for about sixteen hours due to exhaustion. That's what I did the night before. After that, you wake up, and the real sickness begins. When I had woken up that following morning, it had been about thirty-two hours since I had any dope. I was sweating and shivering on the couch, and the man that I took for granted and disrespected time and time again was sitting on the couch next to me, wiping the sweat from my forehead with a cool rag.

I remember he had cut up a bunch of fresh fruit and put it all in a big bowl. He gave it to me and said, "Mike, you have to eat something; it'll be good for you." I felt horrible already, so I didn't want to say, "Dad, if you mention food again, or even say the word *eat*, I'm going to throw up all over this Italian leather sofa." Instead, I just said, "No thanks."

Now I don't want to paint this picture of my father being a softy. He's a good, kind person. But he's also an old-school, tough Sicilian man. He didn't really say, "Mike, you have to eat something, it'll be good for you." It was really more along the lines of, "Mike, you're going to pass out. Now fucking eat the goddamn fruit! Why do you do this to yourself? You're a real jagoff, you know that. I should put my foot up your ass right now."

Well, I lasted about three hours after I woke up. And when my dad went upstairs for a moment, I threw my shoes on, disconnected the PlayStation, and climbed out of my bedroom window in the back of the basement. Twenty minutes later, I had the game sold to a pawnshop for $60. Within an hour, I had a chunk of raw dope. And instead of making my rehab appointment that was two days away, I lived on the streets for another week until I woke up in a motel room. And I don't have to explain what happened on that day. You already read what happened in the prologue at the very beginning of this book.

*****

I've been through many ups and downs in my life, and I've caused myself many mentally stressful situations. And I'm not talking about everyday stress people experience. I'm not talking about losing a job, or your mortgage is late, or you can't afford your phone bill or utility bills, or your wife or girlfriend left you, or your boss is breathing down your neck, or you have to sit in traffic for a half hour every day. All those things can stress a person out. Believe me, I can relate. I've had cars taken away, phones shut off, lost girlfriends, or have been fired from jobs. All those things suck, and they do cause a lot of stress.

However, the stress I'm talking about is on a whole different level. I'm talking about waking up every morning and believing that your life has no meaning. There is no happiness in your life, only utter depression; you hate yourself, and you can't even cry or express emotion about it because you forgot how to. I'm talking about not knowing who you are anymore. You have no idea why you do the things you do, and you don't have the faintest clue as to how you can change, and you don't really care if you die.

I'm not sharing my story to say, "Look at me, look at what I've been through. Feel sorry for me." I'm sharing my story because there are thousands and thousands of people out there, both young and old, male and female, who are currently living their lives like I had, day in and day out. I've seen them. I'm sharing my story because hopefully, somebody will read it and say, "Hey, this guy has been through all this too, and he made it through. Maybe I can learn something or gain a bit of hope and courage and wisdom if I read on and really pay attention to what he has to say from here on out."

# CHAPTER 10

When I was arrested that November, I don't like to say that it was the best thing that could have happened to me, but it needed to happen to me. God had a plan for me only to reach some sort of high ground; it was going to be a long fight for my hardheaded self. It got to the point, legally, where probation was out of the question. Reinstatement of probation for violating probation was exhausted. My father wouldn't bond me out if my bond was $10 because he knew it was not going to help me. This time I had taken my freedom for granted one too many times. Judges have no problem throwing prison time at you when it takes the state's attorney five minutes to read off your background and inform the judge what you've been up to in the last decade. And I accumulated a very big rap sheet. In fact, my rap sheet had morphed into a rap file. My jacket is five inches thick.

Before I got clean and quit using heroin for good, I was sent to prison five separate times. My first sentence was four years; however, I would get out in four months if I successfully completed Boot Camp. And I did. My second prison sentence after that November arrest was three years. With good time, I ended up doing a year flat. For all you active addicts reading this right now, this is what's in store for you eventually if you do not get your head out of your ass and straighten your life out—prison.

Prison is a whole different world than the county jail. The county jail is just a holding facility while you're going to court. When you're sentenced to prison time, you become not only a convicted felon but you also become state property. And in the eyes of whatever state you happen to go to prison in, you're nothing more than a number. Literally. My number is R46921.

When you're sentenced to prison time, within a day or two the county jail officers load all the convicts onto a bus, and in the case of Cook County, Illinois, you'll be transferred to Stateville Northern Receiving Center in Joliet, Illinois. The Northern Receiving Center (NRC) is a literal warehouse for humans. You'll arrive there around 8:00 a.m., and for hours you're processed into the Department of Corrections (DOC). You're strip-searched, given a medical and dental exam, and you give blood. Actually, "give blood" isn't really the case. They take your blood. It's not optional. If you refuse, they'll strap your ass down. And this blood isn't for the Red Cross. It's for the DNA file that will now be available to every law enforcement agency in the entire country, including the Feds.

Around 5:00 p.m., when processing is over, everybody is walked like cattle to your assigned wing. Each wing is a giant three-story room. About twenty-five feet wide and about fifty yards long. On one side is just a forty-foot concrete wall. The other side is cells. Three stories of them. Each wing has about thirty-four cells, and I believe there are twenty-six wings, Wings A to Z. Like I said, a warehouse for people. You're placed in your cell and basically forgotten about. You remain in your cell until the Administration Placement office classifies you and decides which one of the twenty-five adult male or three or so female prisons you'll be sent to depending on your security/violence level or the amount of time you have to serve. That usually takes two to three weeks.

During that time, you come out of your cell once a week for a ten-minute shower. Period. You're even fed in your cell. There's a locked opening in the wall of your cell, and three times a day, the wing officer will come by and open it, slide a tray in for you, and slam it shut. You're fed about 1,400 calories a day, so you're constantly hungry. That's all.

You have no TV, no music, no books, no pillow. You're lucky if there's a book or a Bible in your cell to read and pass the time. You're also lucky if your cellmate is a halfway decent person. You can be put in a cell with an individual who's in for a DUI or an individual who executed his entire family. You don't pick and choose, and the officers don't care. Let me tell you, after being in that cell for a few weeks, you'd be happy to be transferred to the worst prison in the state. Alcatraz would look like a Holiday Inn—anything just to get out of that box! And most people can't handle it. They will sit there and bang on their metal cell door for hours just to get attention. Myself? Well, I've read the entire Bible in NRC several times. Other than that, I'd lay in my bunk, meditate, and sing songs in my head. I'm surprisingly comfortable in seclusion—probably because I had a lot to think about. And finally, one day, at about 2:00 a.m., an officer will come to your cell and slide a paper bag under the door. That means you will be transferred in the morning, and the number written on your bag coincides with the prison you're going to.

When I was arrested that November and sentenced to three years in prison, I was ultimately sent to K7-Centralia Correctional Center in Centralia, Illinois. It was about five hours south of Chicago. And during that year, something very profound started to take place in my mind, thoughts, and overall attitude towards myself and life itself. One specific day really sticks out in my mind. I went to the yard after dinner one night. For some reason, I didn't feel like working out and lifting weights, so I just went to the far end of the yard, took my shoes and socks off, and sat in the grass by myself. I was just sitting there thinking, smoking cigarettes, and watching all the Latinos playing soccer. The old men were walking around the track, complaining about the living conditions, scheming on how they could sue the state. The younger guys were playing basketball or lifting weights, and the gang members were plotting violent attacks on their opposition. Just kidding.

Anyway—the sun was setting, and the sunsets are beautiful down south. For the first time in my life, I was consciously enjoying the sunset. Not one other thought in my head. Of course, I had seen sunsets before, but this was different. This was pure awareness. I can't describe it. For the first time in my life, I realized how beautiful the sunset was, and I was filled with an indescribable sense of gratitude. I was sitting in the grass in a prison yard, alive, and realizing for the first time in my life how absolutely beautiful life can be, regardless of where you are. And I thanked God that I didn't kill myself during my heroin addiction and the horrible, dangerous existence I had been living. It was an epiphany of clarity, and somehow I knew that I had to get right with myself and my loved ones, and I made peace with my situation.

Despite what any judge thought of me, I knew that God knew my heart was good and pure, and that he had a plan for me. I just felt it—like it was coming from within myself. I finally realized that the only thing standing in my way was myself. More specifically, my ego.

Prison offers many opportunities if you have the mindset and maturity level to see them and utilize them. I graduated from high school, I had a good education, and I knew how to do certain things that many prisoners don't. Like fill out a job application or fix a leaky faucet. So I didn't need to go to school in prison to learn basic life skills. But many people in the joint do need to learn the basics, and if they have the drive to learn them, they can. What prison gave me personally was time away to think. It gave me a ton of time to think and re-evaluate. At night, I'd turn my TV off about 10:00 p.m., climb into bed, put my headphones on, lie back, and think myself to sleep.

I'd think about life in general, how I was going to live and act when I got out, and what I had to do to stay clean. I'd think about my family, food, women. Mainly, though, I'd think of my father. I learned how to really evaluate my thoughts and then decide if they held any value. I learned how to think before I responded or acted, instead of responding and acting impulsively and ignorantly. Prison will change a person's thinking process drastically if they practice and work at it. I've accumulated about seven years of thinking, reading, and meditating over the years when it was all said and done. If one spends their time wisely, their mind can grow extremely strong. Prison itself didn't change me. It's just a building. It can't hurt or kill you. I changed myself through my own efforts. Prison just gave me the time to do so. But ultimately, the individual has got to want to change.

I was removed from the calamity and stress of life, then over the years, I realized that calamity and stress are only created by our actions and our own minds. Objects and situations do not produce stress. The human mind produces stress by its own thoughts and reactions.

Prison is not fun. You're stripped of everything in your life. Everything. And you're completely removed from society. Prison is a violent place. It's filled with chaos and negativity. Just living in an environment like that can be dangerous if you don't have the mental fortitude to deflect it. Most people who don't know any better or don't have a very keen intuition become more screwed up as they naturally blend in with their surroundings. Myself? I was a loner. I always managed to find and befriend three or four semi-normal, decent individuals who were seemingly trying to be better people. Usually older guys. People I could work out with, eat a meal with, or hold a conversation with. It's quite hard to find someone you can have a positive conversation within prison. I didn't want to talk about drugs, or crime, or anything negative. I developed a very reclusive personality in prison. I completely stayed to myself.

You basically have two options in the joint. One—make a bunch of buddies, screw off, play cards, and pass the time easily, and then pretty much leave prison the same exact person you were when you got locked up in the first place. If you go that route, more likely than not, you'll be back. Or two—you can stay away from all that bullshit and get serious about yourself. I spent my time jogging, lifting weights, reading, and writing. I'd go into my cell, roll ten cigarettes, make a strong cup of coffee, and read and write for twelve hours straight.

One day, while doing my time in Centralia, I decided out of utter boredom that I'd write my life story. It took me about three hours. The final draft was about thirteen pages. At the time, I didn't plan on taking it seriously. But when I reread what I had, I wanted to rewrite it and add some things. When I did so, memories and emotions started to flow and surface. Then I wanted to rewrite it again. Within a week, I had notes and ideas written everywhere. On napkins, little scraps of paper, etc. And eventually, I decided that I would write my story. So for the remainder of my sentence, which was about two months at that point, I wrote a little bit every day just to pass the time. What I accomplished in a couple of months was a life story that, in its entirety, contained about fifty-three pages. It was soon put on the back burner, though, and I wouldn't dedicate myself to the project completely until years later.

For the first time ever while serving out my time that year, I thought I gained and possessed the knowledge and willpower to not only stay clean but to succeed in life. And honestly, I did change a lot that year. By that point in my life, I had been through more shit than the average person my age could even begin to fathom. Mental stress, pain, loneliness, guilt, remorse, shame, confusion. Being sick and tired and unhealthy. Literally tired, with not an ounce of energy at all or any type of spirit to face the days that went by. Aimlessly ripping and running through the streets of Chicago with no clear destination for the future.

All my cares and worries in the world couldn't keep me from focusing on anything other than my next fix. Stealing, lying, and conniving my way through life. Manipulating everybody I knew, or at least trying to, including myself. Living in motel rooms. Taking the bus to the inner city to spend all my money on dope, then shooting up in some nasty gas-station bathroom. Hating myself and hating the fact that my life had been depleted to what it was and not being able to stop was a horrible feeling that I cannot even describe.

Knowing how sick I was and wanting more than anything to change and be the man I was raised to be but not being able to is the worst feeling I ever felt. So, after being in these situations, I thought to myself, "I'm in prison, I'm clean, I feel great. When I get out in two weeks, I'm going to do what's right and make my family proud. I got it all figured out. I know how I deal with this now."

I wasn't spiritually sound, though. I didn't understand, still. My ego was still running my life. I was weak and arrogant, thinking I was cured of my addictions because I went to some AA meetings in the joint. Well, how's this for a stressful situation—about twelve days before my release date, God threw me a curveball, high and inside, at 90 mph! Two detectives from Oak Lawn actually came down to the prison and charged me with yet another case—a residential burglary. A crime I committed about fifteen months before. Just when I was ready to come home and start my new life, *boom*! Karma, it'll get you every time.

They released me from Centralia prison on my outdate as planned. However, instead of being happy and ready to start the next chapter of my life, I was in limbo. I now had a $350,000 bond on my head for something I had done almost a year and a half in the past while in the midst of a serious heroin addiction. Something very, very stupid. I won't get into the particulars, but I stole some drugs and some cash from someone's house. And this crime carried four to fifteen years in prison.

> We travel the world over in search of what
> we need and return home to find it.
> —George Moore

I'll never forget that day I came home from my second prison bit. I'll always count that day as a major part of my personal growth and awakening. My father picked me up from the front gate at about 9:00 a.m. We hugged, and he asked me if I was hungry. Boy, was I ever! We went to this little country restaurant down the road from the prison, and I ordered a T-bone steak with three eggs over easy. It came with golden hash browns and toast. I also ordered a side of biscuits and gravy, orange juice, and coffee. My dad just looked at me in awe. I said, "You don't understand, Pop." The waitress said to me, "When was the last time you ate, honey? Geez."

After breakfast, we jumped on the highway and made our way back to Chicago. I tried to enjoy my newfound freedom the best I could, but with this new case hanging over my head, it was hard. I tried to keep a smile on my face for the family. When we got home, walking through the back door was amazing. My stepmom and brothers were there. Enzo, our dog. I had plans to see my little sister Jessy and my mother, and my sister Cara was supposed to stop by. It felt so good to be home, surrounded by familiar faces. People who I loved and who loved me.

For dinner, my dad grilled porterhouse steaks on the grill with rice and asparagus. We all sat at the table as a family and ate a meal together. Talked and laughed. Of course, my dad had to break my balls a little bit about the whole "dropping the soap" thing. And my dog, Enzo, must not have forgotten who I was because like always, he sat under the kitchen table between my legs and rested his head in my lap and stared at me while I ate. Enzo eats well when I'm home. My stepmom always yelled at me when I fed him, but I couldn't help it. I have to share with Enzo.

Around 10:00 p.m., my dad and stepmom were ready for bed. My brothers both went out. It had been a long day. I went down to my bedroom in the basement to relax and unwind. I remember I was just standing in the middle of the family room in silence. Silence! For the first time in a year. It sounded wonderful. It was that calm nighttime silence too. The kind of silence where you could hear the electricity in the walls and the ticking of a clock. I was just standing there, taking it all in. I sat on the couch and a memory arose about how bad of shape I was in the last time I was on that couch. Instead of relaxing and unwinding, I experienced a mental breakdown for the first and only time in my life. A true mental breakdown. It happened so suddenly and came out of nowhere.

I was sitting on our comfy Italian leather sofa in silence, looking around at the home that I'd neglected and took for granted so many times in my life. My father and stepmom have a nice home. It's clean and comfortable. There are always strong family values vibrating throughout the house. Nobody hardly ever argues or fights. We all get along and eat meals together. Somebody's always playing a prank, like putting a rubber band on the kitchen sink hose. It's just a nice place to live. I sat there in complete awareness of all this, and I never wanted to leave again. And I knew that soon, with this old case I was recently charged with, I would have to leave home again and go back to prison.

Out of nowhere, I started to cry. Crying turned to sobbing; while I was crying, I was shivering violently, and this went on for about five minutes straight without recoil. I started to get nervous because I was shaking so bad my spine started to hurt, and I was having an extremely hard time breathing. It got to the point where

I was wheezing and literally gasping for air. And as much as I didn't want to bother anybody, I forced myself upstairs.

My stepmom was standing in the front room, putting some pictures into frames for her photography class, and I think I took her by surprise. I didn't say a word to her. I just really needed to get a hug from somebody. I wrapped my arms around her and squeezed. While I was crying on her shoulder, she kept asking me what was wrong, but I couldn't speak, let alone explain to her what I was feeling inside.

My father must've heard me sobbing, and he walked into the front room. I turned to him and wrapped my arms around him and continued to cry. I hugged him and cried on his shoulder for five minutes straight. In between sobs, all I could manage to say was, "I'm sorry, Dad. I'm so sorry." And he just said, "You don't have to be sorry, son. I love you so much, Michael."

When I finally lifted my head, his shirt was literally soaked in tears. They were not tears of fear. I wasn't afraid of anything at the time. And it wasn't because of the new case. I just needed to let it all out. I'll tell you what it was, and I'm only able to explain what it was because I understand it now. It was pure love. Years and years of emotions and pain that I bottled up over the years just boiled over and poured out of me. And both of them were there, unconditionally, to take it from me. If I had one wish, it would be that every living soul on the face of the planet could experience that feeling of love and compassion once in their lifetime. The vibes in our little house in Evergreen Park that night is what life's all about. Living in the present moment. Peace. Heaven.

After that little episode, I went and lay on top of the picnic table in the backyard, smoked a cigarette, and spent an hour just staring at the stars. Not a care, concern, or thought in my mind. I was completely refreshed. Then I went to bed and slept like a baby. But one thing I've learned in life is this: You can't recover the stone after the throw.

# CHAPTER 11

The following morning, I awoke to the sound of the phone ringing. I walked up the stairs into the kitchen only to see my dad standing there looking at the caller ID. "It says Village of Oak Lawn," he said. After listening to the message the detective left on our answering machine, I decided—well, my dad decided—that we should call him back. Myself? I felt no inclination to extend any type of common courtesy to this cop who waited until twelve days before my release to come charge me with a Class One felony. But I called him back after my father convinced me to do so. This is basically the conversation I had with this detective:

"Oak Lawn Police Station."

"Yes, may I speak to Detective So-and-So?"

"Hold, please."

"Detective So-and-So."

"Hi, it's Michael Seminetta."

"Michael! How's it going?"

"How's it going? Really."

"Yeah. I need you to come turn yourself in."

"Okay, listen. I'm not turning myself in today. You guys could've come down there ten months ago and charged me, and I could've gone on a court writ, and the year I just did could've counted towards this new case. Now that I've been released, I have to turn around and do this shit all over again."

"Well, you still need to…"

"I'm not turning myself in until after the holidays."

"Uh, you can't do that."

"I can do that."

"We're on our way to come get you right now."

"Well, I better hang up and get out of here then."

"You can't leave until your parole officer comes to see you, you'll violate your parole, dummy." – This guy really called me a dummy!

"Sir, fuck parole! You charged me with another case. As soon as I'm in handcuffs, my parole will be violated anyway, dummy."

"Michael, you have to take care of this."

"I'm aware of that. But that's not going to happen until after the New Year."

"That's almost three months away."

"Yeah, well, you waited a year already. You can wait a few more months."

"Michael…"

"Listen, I'm staying free for the holidays. You can run around and try to catch me if that's what you gotta do. I understand you got a job to do. But I'm not running from you. I just need a few months. After the New Year, you can come to my father's, and I'll be there."

"Ah shit! Alright…enjoy the holidays."

"Hey, thanks, you too. I'll see you in January."

I remember that phone call vividly, and that's pretty much how it went. And all BS aside, that detective was not a bad guy. He was just doing his job. Plus, he did me a solid. He never came that day. In fact, it wouldn't be until January 16, 2009, that I was in his custody. That gave me sixty-six days to do nothing but chain-smoke and bite my nails.

My dad, stepmom, and brothers and I went up to Grandma Senese's for Thanksgiving. We had a really nice time. My stepmom's mother had a beautiful house right on Lake Wisconsin. We had a delicious feast together as a family, overlooking the lake outside the kitchen's sliding glass doors. It was snowing. It was beautiful. We were all supposed to stay up there throughout the entire weekend after Thanksgiving and go back to Chicago Monday morning. However, when my little brother Daniel and I were sitting on the pier fishing and talking, we decided we would refuse this calm country weekend and go back to the city Friday afternoon. I told my dad I just wanted to go home and relax and spend the little bit of time I had left at the house in Chicago. So while the family stayed in Wisconsin, Daniel and I jumped in his Jeep and took off back to the Windy City Friday after lunch.

We got home around 5:30 p.m., I made us something to eat, and we sat down and ate together and watched an episode of *Seinfeld*. While we were eating, I asked him what his plans for the night were. Daniel said, "I don't know, we don't have anywhere to chill."

"Oh yeah…that sucks," I said. I knew exactly what he wanted to do. What does every nineteen-year-old want to do when they have the house to themselves all weekend with no parents around? My brother's a good guy. I love him. So I told him, "Dude, you can have a few people over, alright? If your friends break anything or spill beer on the pool table, I'm gonna beat their ass."

A few of his buddies came over shortly after. Then he hit me with the big question. "Mikey, can you get us a run?" And because I had already decided that I was going to relapse hard that night like an asshole, my answer to his question was, "Hell yes. What are we drinking? Round up your money." He came back upstairs a few minutes later and handed me about $100. I just looked at him and said, "Jesus! Alright then, what do you guys want?"

"Um, like, four thirty-packs of Busch, a handle of Captain Morgan…and smokes."

I took a quick ride to the liquor store, and when I came back home, there were thirty teenagers in the basement. "Daniel, get your ass up here," I said. "No more people, bro, seriously. And tell them to smoke in the backyard." I went upstairs to make a couple of phone calls. While I was sitting on the couch in the front room, the doorbell rang. I looked through the drapes to make sure there were no cops standing on my front porch, and what do I see? About eight or nine beautiful females. I answered the door, and one of them said, "Is Daniel here?"

I said, "Yeah, he's here. I just told him no more people could show up…but I guess I could make an exception."

"We'll behave," she said.

"You better."

My buddy Greg (may he rest in peace) came over, and we took a quick ride. I picked up a bag of raw dope and went back home. Greg and I got high in the front room, then went downstairs to party with my brother and his friends.

We had a blast. I had a ton of fun hanging out with my brother and his friends. Especially Toni, who was an incredibly beautiful twenty-year-old Italian fox whom I fell madly in love with over the course of the night. We played pool, got hammered, and listened to about fifty Rolling Stones songs. It was great! My inner teenager came out, and I went to my room and pulled out an old book I had saved from my high school days—*101 Greatest Drinking Games*.

I probably shouldn't have got so drunk, but I did. I wasn't going to crucify myself for it. And as much as I try not to make excuses, I was stressed out. But we had a great time, my little brother and I. I wouldn't take it back to remain clean and sober because I was going back to prison, anyway—another excuse.

Next up? Christmas. My favorite time of year. My dad let me do a few painting jobs for his company, so I had a few dollars in my pocket while I was home. One night after dinner, I jumped on the bus and went to Chicago Ridge Mall. I missed a couple of Christmases in the last few years, so I wanted this one to be good. I bought a few gifts for the family, and a bunch for my baby sister Jessy Lynn, who was about ten years old at the time. I had the most amazing time just walking around the mall, whistling Christmas tunes out loud to myself. Now I like rock and roll...but I freaking love Christmas music!

Then who do I run into? My ex-girlfriend Clare. The one who kept breaking up with me. She was shopping with her little brother, and it was great to see her. I love ice cream like no other person alive, so I asked them if they wanted to get some ice cream together at the food court, my treat. We did, and it was fun. She asked me how I was doing, with that look in her eye that basically meant. "Are you still a junkie?" And for the first time since I've known her, I wasn't high. And other than that crazy Friday night with my brother Thanksgiving weekend, I was clean.

It was a friendly rendezvous, and she offered to give me a ride home. That was the last time I saw her before I went back to prison. I wanted to keep seeing her, but I had something on my plate that

I'd have to face soon, so I was a little quiet and distant that night. Oh well. I didn't want to start something I couldn't follow through on. I wouldn't see her again for four years. Sadly, during that time, she started taking Vicodin for a back problem and ultimately turned into a heroin addict herself. It broke my heart when I found that out. Anyway.

Christmas was great! I made the family Christmas party on my mother's side of the family. And guess what? I got to play Santa Claus! My mom's side of the family is absolutely huge. So in order to get together for Christmas, we have to rent out a banquet hall every year. My cousins Jake and Mikey accompanied me to the backroom to assist me with getting into the family Santa suit. Then I spent the next hour and a half yelling "Ho. Ho. Ho," and letting all the kids climb on my lap while I handed out presents.

You know, it's amazing how much joy can enter your life when you're doing the right thing. That may seem meaningless to those who never really do anything wrong, but for me, it means a lot. For me, doing the right thing meant not using heroin, which I had been addicted to since I've been sixteen years old. That's really the only major malfunction I had in the past. And for the first time in a long time, I attended a family Christmas party with a clean and clear head. And it was beautiful.

Next up? New Year's Eve! Now going to a local pub was probably not the best idea for me, an addict trying to stay clean, even if it was New Year's Eve. My bullshit excuse for doing so was because I was going back to prison, anyway, so why not enjoy myself until then.

My cousin Jake picked me up at home around 7:00 p.m., and we went to a bar on Western Avenue. Twenty-five dollars, all you can drink until 12:30 a.m., and a glass of champagne at midnight. A bunch of people were there I knew, people who were normal. And by that, I mean people who weren't junkies and crackheads. Just good people. I had a great time. I did consume quite a few alcoholic beverages of vast variety, and yet, even though I hadn't shot pool in over a year, I still managed to kick my cousin's ass on the table throughout the night. My cousin's an awesome guy; he just, well, he just can't beat me in pool (you know it's true, Jake).

At midnight, glasses of champagne were passed around, and at the stroke of twelve, we all toasted the New Year. Jacob was standing right next to me, and we gave each other a big hug. I love my cousin Jacob, and it had really bothered me over the years that we weren't as close as we should have been, all because of my personal problems. I knew he hated that I was a heroin addict. I also knew that it was probably something he'd never really understand, that I didn't mean to be that way, but I was ashamed, nonetheless. Anyway, I wished I had a pretty girl to kiss at midnight, but a big hug from my drunken Irish cousin was the next best thing.

The New Year had arrived. I knew that soon I'd have to take that ride back to the joint. I had tried my best to put it out of my mind over the last few months. I didn't ever talk about it, and I think I never even told anybody about my situation. The only ones who knew were my immediate family. Now, it was starting to really bother me.

When January came, I knew that any day now I'd have to face the music. It was a hard pill to swallow, and the stress and depression were unbearable at times. Especially after meeting with my lawyer, Dan, and he informed me that the state would probably ask the judge for a ten-year sentence right off the bat.

About a week after the new year, I had an appointment to turn myself in to the Oak Lawn Police Department. I believe it was a Monday, and the plan was that my father would drive me there later that night after one "last supper" together. Everybody was at work, and I was just sitting at home all morning by myself, trying to prepare myself mentally the best I could. It wasn't going too well.

About an hour before my dad came home from the shop, I was sitting on the couch, blankly staring at the TV, bouncing my knee up and down and biting my nails. I got up, threw some clothes in a bag, grabbed the little bit of money I had, and walked out the back door. I've never claimed to be the best decision-maker, so I wasn't very surprised when I made the impulsive decision to go get loaded one last time. It was stupid, it was wrong, and it didn't make my situation any better. At the time, I thought I did it because I was stressed out. I realize now that stress had nothing to do with it. I did it because I was an addict, and that was the only solution I knew of to deal and cope with the situation. I spent the next week in a motel room called "The Saratoga" on Cicero Avenue, shooting heroin and smoking cocaine. As fate would have it, I was in a gas station buying some drinks and snacks, a police officer noticed me, I was picked up on the warrant, and on January 16, 2009, I was sitting in a jail cell in Oak Lawn, ready (or not) to get this over with.

My first court date, the state's attorney did exactly what my lawyer said they'd do. They put a cop-out offer on the table of ten years. I'd have to do four and a half years if I took the plea bargain. I sat in the county jail for three months. A few court dates later, I told my lawyer I wanted a 402 conference with the judge. A 402 conference means the judge, my lawyer, and the prosecutor all sit down together. The prosecutor for the state argues why I should get ten years, and my lawyer argues why I should not.

For the record here, I've never physically hurt a single person in my life. I never robbed an old lady or stole a purse off somebody's shoulder. I'd never do a crime that scared or hurt somebody. I damn sure didn't deserve a ten-year sentence for a burglary I committed almost two years prior while I was on drugs. I'm not saying I should have been cut loose with no consequences for my crime. But this was a little extreme.

I've never once taken any of my former cases to trial. I always apologized and took my time like a man. I mean, what happened to the punishment fitting the crime? I took some cash and some dope from someone's kitchen table. I didn't break in the door, nobody saw me and was frightened, nobody was hurt, ten years! I realize that many people reading this may not be too keen on how the court system works, but people don't get half that amount of time for discharging a firearm in the middle of a city. There are hundreds of young gang members that I've personally seen get one or two-year sentences for their third or fourth UUW (unlawful use of a weapon). You could rob a bank and get five years. I've been in prison with these sick, perverted scumbags who were doing two- or three-year sentences for child pornography or sexual assault on a minor or rape. They get two years and they're back on the street in no time. The last time I was in prison, there was a guy there for his fourth DUI, and he crashed into another car and killed a seventeen-year-old girl. He got six years. That Chicago cop—Van Dyke—the one who shot that young black kid sixteen times and killed him in the street, he was charged with murder and got six years for that. And he's supposed to be a trusted public servant. ten years! I'll just never understand how these people live with themselves.

I'm not a psychopath. I understand how important it is to have laws and consequences. There would be a breakdown of society if there wasn't. I don't blame anybody but myself for my conduct in the past. I just can't understand how somebody can sentence a young man or woman to ten years in prison for stealing some drugs and cash, and then sleep at night. Especially when it's well known nowadays that there are a lot of good people in this country with drug problems who are motivated to commit crime for the sole reason of getting more drugs, out of pure desperation. If it weren't for a heroin addiction, I probably would've never seen the inside of a jail cell.

Anyway, my lawyer explained to the judge that I just spent a year in prison. He showed the judge a couple of different certificates I was awarded for completing drug classes and for chairing AA meetings while I was in prison for a year. He showed him my diploma from Brother Rice High School. My family was there supporting me. He basically tried to show the judge I should get a break. The case carried four to fifteen years. The judge could've given me four years. I still would've had to do a year and a half. Instead, he decided to give me eight years. Which was better than ten, but still a little extreme.

My lawyer came into the little room I was in, sat down, and said, "Mike, he wants eight years." I just shook my head, looked at him, and said, "Whatever, let's go. Just get the paperwork." And with that, I gave the little pip-squeak—sorry, I mean the State's Attorney—his little conviction he wanted for his career, which I'm sure put a smile on his face, and I signed myself up for a three-and-a-half-year stay in the Illinois Department of Corrections. Yay!

I now smile when I hear people complain about the most minor things, or get all stressed out because, I don't know…they had to sit in traffic for fifteen extra minutes, or the fast-food joint forgot to put ketchup on their burger. It really is funny to me. Talk about a stressful situation; after signing that paperwork, I was immediately thrown back into a tiny bullpen the size of a closet with twelve other guys. Some of them career criminals, some of them young little suburban kids bitching and complaining that the judge gave them five days of community service. I was just sentenced to eight years in prison and I couldn't even be alone for five minutes to cry. And I wanted to cry. But I couldn't.

Next, I had to get shackled and put on a bus back to the county jail where I'd remain for a few days until shipment. When shipment day came, I'd be shipped to NRC in Joliet again and have to spend three weeks in a cell with a complete stranger and wait around until placement decided what prison I'd be sent to. Then I'd be shackled on a bus again and driven down South to some prison where I'd have to stay for three and a half years. I'd have to do this all alone without so much as a hug from my family telling me it'll be okay. That's the stress I felt that day. So you can imagine why I smile when I hear somebody complain about something quite minor.

I ended up being sent to Stateville Farm, which is a work camp right there in Joliet. So, not only did I not have to take a bus ride down South, but I'd be doing my time twenty-five minutes from Chicago. So that was good. I'd spend the next few years working for the state for $43 per month. I did spend ten years getting high and screwing off, but I'm a semi-intelligent individual and I'm a hard worker and very handy. A few officers took notice, and I landed a couple of decent "jobs" on the farm.

I spent the first sixteen months working "behind the wall." The main prison—Stateville—is a maximum-security prison. The entire facility is surrounded by a forty-foot concrete wall. And there's good reason for that. There are people behind that wall that belong there, forever. Stateville is where John Wayne Gacy was executed. The majority of inmates behind that wall have twenty or more years to serve. Many have natural life. NRC is a whole separate facility.

It was built right next to Stateville prison, and the Farm—or minimum-security unit—is behind NRC. Stateville holds approximately 1,500 inmates. NRC is the classification center. It holds about two thousand inmates, but the population flips every few weeks because the majority of the inmates get sent to prisons all over the state once they're classified. The Farm, where I was sent, has about two hundred to three hundred inmates.

I was housed on the Farm but went behind the wall to work in personal property every day for about six hours. My two supervisors were Officer Dunlap and Officer DeYoung. They were both good dudes. They treated me well. By well, I mean they treated me like a human being and not like a criminal. Especially Dunlap. He made those first sixteen months a little more comfortable than it could've been. He was always bringing food to work. Pizza, leftovers his wife made the night before, etc. And for an inmate, it was nice to eat some good food now and then. He was also a smoker like I was. And although cigarettes were no longer allowed in State facilities, I got to smoke a few cigarettes every day I worked. Property was a four- to five-man job, but I did it all by myself because I liked going back there alone and having personal time away from everything. Property was this big old, secluded building in the back of the prison. I had my own desk, radio, bathroom. I'd put on the tunes and zone out all day and do my work. As long as I got all the work done, Dunlap didn't really give a shit. He let me be. He was completely professional, but he was cool about it also. It made the time fly by.

After those sixteen months, I got a job in the administration building working for Officer Barnes. She was a cool lady. We bumped heads a lot because I always liked doing things my way. But she always won out. It was that badge! At first, a group of us just swept floors, mopped floors, waxed floors, buffed floors, things like that. Then I had to open my big mouth, and she found out I was a professional painter. She had me paint just about that whole building over the next few months. Before I knew it, the superintendent was asking me to paint her office. Then the Warden. The Warden actually walked up to me and asked me if I'd mind painting his office. "Yeah, for six months good time, I'll paint it." The guy actually laughed. He was actually pretty smooth, this warden. I said, "Warden, I'm going to paint whatever you tell me to paint." He said, "Mike, if you got time. No hurry." Which was an odd statement, I thought. I must've painted at least fifteen to twenty different offices. Hallways, railings, windows, doors. No exaggeration here, I probably did about $50,000 worth of painting alone. All for $43 a month. Talk about paying your debt to society, huh?

My cellie was an older white guy from Canaryville. His name was Mike too. He was caught with two kilos of cocaine and got six years for it. So he was there the whole time I was. We made sure our time was as easy as can be. I was working in the admin building, he worked at the front gate. We both had outside clearance from Springfield. That meant that we could be trusted outside the gates; we weren't considered escape risks or violent offenders. Now at the time, like I said, smoking was no longer allowed in prison. But Mike and I smoked every day. When Mike's wife and kids came to visit him every weekend, his son would put about eight packs of 'Kite' cigarettes, lighters, and a couple of double cheeseburgers in a McDonald's bag and throw it in the garbage can outside the front gates before he came to visit. It was Mike's job to empty that can. Need I say more?

We'd work all day, then go back to the farm where we showered and slept. We'd cook food, eat, watch TV, and smoke cigarettes all night. The IRT's Tact team (known as Orange Crush in the joint— because they're dressed in all orange, and they'll crush you) tried catching us for two years. Only they didn't know who was smuggling in cigarettes, where it was coming from, or where it was hidden. We stashed all the contraband—tobacco, lighters, etc.—inside the wall where all the plumbing was for the showers. We were in prison, away from our families, so we tried to be as comfortable and have as much fun as can be expected in prison. It helped the time go by. Some may say, "If you're in prison already, you shouldn't continue that behavior of breaking the rules." Whatever. What's that saying? "Don't judge someone until you've walked a mile in their shoes." Spend a significant amount of time on Stateville farm, then they can talk about things like that. Finding some form of enjoyment is a must—rules be damned—if you want to keep your sanity in a place like that.

I didn't spend all my time working, though. After work, I'd work out and lift weights for an hour, shower, then spend my nights reading and writing. Every night, no matter what, I'd read and write for at least two hours. And on the weekends, because I was so close to Chicago, my dad and stepmom usually came for a visit on Saturday or Sunday morning. Sometimes they'd bring my baby sister Jessy Lynn with them. We'd eat munchies, play little games like twenty questions or I spy. We'd be able to hug and kiss and laugh with each other for a few hours. It was nice.

I met a man at Stateville Farm who became a true genuine friend of mine, who I still speak to this day. We actually arrived on the farm on the same day and basically had the same amount of time to do. He taught me a lot of things that made me realize how easy it is to be happy and content, no matter what situation you find yourself in. Because of him, I learned the meaning of living a spiritual life. What he did every day was make me think. He made me realize a lot of flaws I had. Like judging and criticizing people, complaining, or being pessimistic. Every time I did these things, he'd say, "Ohhh, Mikey! Look at that little ego of yours. Relax." I'd say, "Fuck you, Victor. Leave me and my ego alone."

He'd let me read all his books when he was finished with them (as long as I didn't bend the spine), and when I was done, we'd discuss them. These books were no ordinary novels either. They were books on "higher learning," if you will. Books written by great minds and teachers of life. And my eyes were opened to many awesome concepts that I'd otherwise never would have been aware of.

While I was there at Stateville doing my time, I changed more than ever. Change had been taking place within myself since I was in my early twenties and realized I had a bad problem with substance abuse, and more so with myself, but the growing process is so slow sometimes that I never could pinpoint if I was, in fact, changing for the better or not. But those few years, I started noticing the changes that were, in fact, taking place inside myself and in my attitudes, and in my overall outlook on life. And I started coming back down to earth. So if you happen to be reading this, Victor, thank you for helping me along.

I also stumbled upon a certain activity in prison that I've grown to love over the years. The first time I went to prison, I went to boot camp for four months. The only exercise we engaged in was bodyweight training: push-ups, pull-ups, sit-ups, etc. The next couple of times I was locked up, I grew a passion for weight lifting and bodybuilding.

The first time I stepped onto a "weight pile" in prison, well, it's an impressive scene, to say the least. I had no idea where to even begin. Not only that, I was shy, as most men are the first time they walk into a gym and see guys lifting tons of weight. Men's egos come out at these moments in life. Instead of starting out with the little weights as they logically should, they want to lift, or attempt to lift, things they simply cannot, so they don't look weak. When a man can't do what other men are doing, we tend to not even attempt it. Especially at the gym. Unfortunately, that's why most people quit going to the gym a week after they paid for a membership. Laziness, but more so ego.

Anyway, I remember I was sitting on the bleachers watching these guys lift. This six-foot-tall, 250-pound massive black dude walks right up to me and says, "Eh, lil' nigga, you on the weight watchers routine." I said, "What do you mean?" He says, "You ain't gonna get big just sitting on your ass watching the fuckin' weights! Come on, bro, I'll show you some things to get you started," and I did what he told me. Starting out lifting in prison is not like going to the gym in the real world. Most people watch too many movies and have never been to prison, and they have this image that everybody in prison is a bad guy. I was surprised myself how helpful some of these guys were. Straight motivators!

The first couple of weeks are brutal if you're really training the right way. Your physical brain does not like strenuous activity, and it'll tell you to stop. You have to fight through that laziness and soreness. These prison weight piles aren't your average gym scenes. Even gyms where the big guys lift. These weight piles are filled with men who are insanely massive and strong, some of whom have been locked up for ten to twenty years. All they do, literally, is lift weights, eat, and rest. The average guy who goes to a gym and his physique complements all the hours in the gym he spends, guys who you look at and say, "Wow, he must go to the gym a lot." Well, these guys, on average, go to the gym, let's say, three to four times per week for an hour or two. Guys in the joint go to morning yard for two hours, afternoon yard for two hours, and night yard or gym for two hours. They might take one day off to play basketball or rest. I'd say collectively, guys in the joint who are dedicated work out about ten times per week for a total of about twenty hours of training.

It sounds crazy, and a physical therapist would probably say that's overtraining, but it's a favorite pastime in prison. Plus, everybody is kind of frustrated in the first place, everyone's testosterone is through the roof, and nobody has seen a female in quite some time. Not only that, but you're not smoking, drinking, or otherwise toxifying your body. You're eating a balanced diet, even though the food isn't the best. And you're getting tons of rest. It's a perfect recipe for training. I'm absolutely in no way implying that prison is at all a place to be for any reason. But it is a perfect place to get healthy if you happen to find yourself there. And if you, who are reading this, are an addict and haven't stopped using drugs yet, you may very well find yourself there one day in the future if you don't stop.

Anyway—I had no idea about the amount of knowledge and science behind working out and lifting weights: the impact of eating right and consuming the right amounts of protein, healthy fats, and carbohydrates. Yes, carbohydrates! They're important for fueling workouts. Set numbers, repetition count, intensity, rest time between sets in regard to your goals, cardiovascular training—I had the faintest clue as to how many muscle groups, or the individual muscles that make up those groups, there were in my body. I started getting very interested in bodybuilding. I've read countless magazines: *Flex*, *Muscle and Fitness*, *Men's Health*. I've read many training books on progressive resistance training, bodybuilding, powerlifting, nutrition books in regard to correct protein, fat, and carbohydrate consumption that's required relative to your weight, fat percentage, or training routine. Metabolism rate, age—it all plays a role. I've read the Arnold

Schwarzenegger Encyclopedia through and through several times—which, for those who don't know, that's the bible for all things to do with fitness and working out. Needless to say, I really grew to enjoy lifting weights. And the natural high and dopamine and serotonin rush it produces… Wow! Nothing like it. I wanted to consume every bit of knowledge I could so I could do it right.

The first time I lay under a bench press, there were two plates on the bar. The bar weighs forty-five pounds, and each plate weighs forty-five pounds, a combined weight of 135 pounds. I lifted the bar off the rack and let it fall to my chest, I pushed it up, it came back down. I pushed it up again, and let it fall back to my chest. When I attempted my third repetition, I could only push the bar about halfway up, then it pretty much fell on my chest. I couldn't even complete three reps! And I was twenty-one years old at the time. It felt like I was lifting a car. 135 pounds is a lot heavier than it sounds. But I've come to learn that, for a guy working out for the first time ever, three reps with 135 pounds is about right.

Today when I do chest, I warm up with the 135. I'll do a quick burnout set to get blood and oxygen pumping into the area I'm targeting. I unrack the bar and do reps in rapid succession without stopping, and I fail around forty to forty-five reps. What follows that is a two-hour workout that consists of about twenty-five to forty-five sets (depending on how I feel and how much time I have) of a variety of exercises: incline barbell or dumbbell presses, flat bench barbell or dumbbell presses, decline presses, flies, either with dumbbells or a cable machine, dips, etc.

My maximum bench press weight for a one-rep max was 385 pounds at my strongest. It's about 325 to 345 now. But I'm also not in my twenties anymore, and I'd like to still be able to move my arms and walk when I'm forty. Plus, I'm no longer in prison and I don't want to frighten anybody at LA Fitness! (Just kidding.) I had a 529-pound deadlift recorded at my strongest, and I could curl eighty-pound dumbbells with perfect form. I routinely work my upper, middle, and lower back, along with my lats. Arms, legs, abs, shoulders. I can run a 10k without stopping in about an hour.

I'm not writing all of this to brag. I'm sharing this for a reason. After all, this book is not about fitness, it's about drug addiction. You don't just deadlift 529 pounds after going to the gym a couple of times. It took me a long time to achieve that. Hours upon hours of grueling hard work and stress. I've thrown up during workouts because I was pushing myself too hard. I worked my ass off for my gains. Getting off drugs, staying clean, and making a wholehearted attempt at becoming the best version of yourself in all areas and aspects of your life is the same concept. We have to work our asses off at it. If you're drug-dependent, you'll have to work out all those mental abstractions you've created through years of drug abuse. It's hard, strenuous, and annoying, and sometimes depressing work. But if you want the results, you have to put in the work. Buying a pair of step-up shoes, or a freakin' shake weight isn't going to cut it. Hard work, dedication, and your spirit is the way to go. Introspection is the only way to become free from the suffering we cause ourselves through substance abuse. Introspection—It is the *only way*.

If being in prison offers anything positive, it offers a chance to be taken out of the madness we sometimes create for ourselves in life, and it gives one a chance to say to themselves, "Slow down! What seems to be my major malfunction? What do I need to work on? What makes me tick?" And as time goes by, you can't help but to become a more conscious individual—if you work on yourself and your character. For me, an understanding of who I really was, what I wanted out of life, and what I wanted to contribute to humanity occurred within myself.

I was blessed with the ability to be humble and recognize my flaws—the bad ones. The flaws that cause me to self-destruct and stick needles in my arms. And this recognition ultimately began in jails and prisons. Some addicts never recognize these character flaws that cause them to do unhealthy things or that invite drama and chaos into their lives, and they often blame others for the hard life they lead. I know people like this and have dated girls like this. Their situation is always because of so-and-so, or because of such-and-such. It's never because of them, and they never change, and in turn, they're never at peace because they have such a hard time looking in the mirror. And I can understand that.

I believe AA calls this being "constitutionally incapable of being honest with themselves." And as much as I respect AA, that's bullshit. There is no such thing as being "constitutionally incapable" when it comes to substance abuse. That's a cop-out. Unless an addict is literally mentally ill, the human spirit is capable of overcoming anything if you want it bad enough. Some addicts just don't want it bad enough, or they run out of time. I'm not judging them, but that's the hard truth.

Imagine everyday activities that keep your mind going and occupied in this overstimulating world we live in, completely removed from your life. Things that we are all guilty of taking for granted at one time or another: work, family life, driving, eating and cooking good food, playing—no matter what it may be—sports, jogging, TV, going out on the town, parties, sex, etc. Imagine having all of that taken away and having a whole day to do nothing but sit still and calm your mind from its excessive stream of thoughts. A whole day to just sit and shut up and observe your mind and watch how it works and watch your thoughts. Now imagine doing this for a week, a month, or a year. In my case, several years. I'm sure it's hard for some people to understand how somebody could rank going to prison as one of their most grateful blessings, but that's how I feel. If God hadn't picked me up and sat my ass down for a while, there's no doubt in my mind I would be dead right now. It allowed me to evolve and grow and mature more than anything.

I started reading novels for the first time in my life when I was eighteen years old and started getting locked up all the time. Prior to that, I think the only book I ever read was *Of Mice and Men* in eighth grade. But as I kept getting locked up, I started reading a lot. Eventually, as I got older, I read the Bible from cover to cover—a few times, actually. I'd be lying if I said that I learned a great deal from the Bible because I didn't. The only thing I came to be interested in is what Jesus taught and what he actually meant by it. Not what the church said he meant by it, but what he actually meant. All the other stuff, I really didn't concern myself with. Just the teachings and words of Jesus, period.

I came to the realization one day that reading fictional novels like James Patterson books was just a waste of time for me. I'd read these novels and think to myself, *I'm not learning anything from these books.* So I decided if I can't learn anything positive or gain knowledge from it, I wouldn't waste my time.

I've read hundreds of books between the ages of twenty to thirty-five. Many books on the teachings of Jesus and what they really mean. That was a subject I really wanted to understand. I've read books on Hinduism and Gandhi. I really got into books about Buddhism and the teachings of Siddhartha Gautama (the Buddha)—the Four Noble Truths, the Eightfold Path to enlightenment, the dangers of living in a cycle of conditioned existence or Samsara. Buddhism is a very spiritual practice. I love it. Even if you're not a Buddhist and have no desire or intention of becoming one, you can still learn a great deal from it.

Buddhism is not a theology or religion in the normal sense. It's a practice that says meditation and training your mind can show us how to wake up, learn who we truly are, and liberate us from suffering. Jesus called this salvation. Buddha called it enlightenment. What was really interesting to me was that Buddhism predates most religions by hundreds of years. The Buddha lived on this earth five hundred years before Jesus was born. If you learn about Buddhism, and then compare these two spiritual masters, there are a lot of Buddhist undertones in Jesus's words and teachings. It's uncanny.

For a while, I basically got into any books that could possibly help me figure out all the questions I had about myself and why I kept harming myself. I loved reading biographies and autobiographies on musicians. I've read *The Chronicles* by Bob Dylan, *The Doors, Pink Floyd, Room Full of Mirrors*, which is a biography about Jimi Hendrix. One of my favorites was *Pearl*, a biography about Janis Joplin. I enjoyed reading books and stories about how people overcame their demons because that's what I was trying to do. Drugs were my problem, and it just so happens that most of the greatest musicians were drug addicts. Janis Joplin, Jerry Garcia, James Taylor,

Eric Clapton, Kurt Cobain—all heroin addicts or former heroin addicts I should say.

My absolute favorite books, though, are books on inner development, growth, and spirituality. Books by Eckhart Tolle, Jack Kornfield, Deepak Chopra. I mention reading because it's evolved souls like these men and women who wrote these books who made me realize all the unnecessary suffering using drugs was causing me. But more importantly, why I was compulsively utilizing these drugs to cope with myself and life. Reading these types of books over the years ultimately helped me with my own recovery and redemption. And now I know with every fiber of my being that I will never stick a needle in my arm again. Not because I simply read books, but because I learned who I truly am. I'm not going to get into what I do and do not believe in. I'm not very religious. And I'm not yet wise enough to be a spiritual teacher—far from it. Becoming in touch with God, or coming into union with what we believe in, is a path for each his/her own. I believe it's extremely important to learn how to commune with God in our own personal way.

I also spent a lot of time reading and writing because Mr. Stephen King told me to. When I first started writing this autobiography and taking it seriously, my stepmom bought me a book titled *On Writing* by Stephen King. The book was about how to go about writing by the master himself. One thing he said in that book was that in order to become a good writer, you have to do two things: read a lot and write a lot. So I did, for almost ten years now.

# CHAPTER 12

About six months before I was released from prison, my dad and stepmom were ready to move out of Chicago. My father wanted to dissolve his business and move to the house in Wisconsin and start another business, Semos Chicago Style Hot Dogs and Italian Beef, which was a big hit up there in Wisconsin. They had about three years left on their mortgage on the house in Evergreen, so instead of selling the house, the plan was for me to parole there and take care of the house while paying my dad rent for the following three years. And although my dad dissolved most of his business when they moved, he managed to hold onto a few clients who agreed to still use our services when I got home and took over the business.

When I paroled, I moved into the house in Evergreen Park. I was in my late twenties and felt as though I had fallen pretty far behind in relation to where a thirty-year-old man should be in his life. I was ready to move forward and get my life together as fast as possible. I had a beautiful house to live in, a work van to use, a garage full of tools and ladders, and $1,300 in cash to hold me over until money started rolling in.

It was springtime when I came home, so I went to the Home Depot and bought a bunch of flowers, mulch, tiki torches, etc. I spent the entire first weekend fixing up the yard, repainting the deck, and getting the pool ready for the summer. My dad drove in from Wisconsin to spend a few days with me. We got to hang out together and have dinner at Rosangela's Pizza. And I had work coming up the following week. For the first time in my life, I was truly happy and content. Everything was going great, and I was ready to move onward with my life. As hard as it may be to believe, this is exactly what happened to me:

I had only been out for about four months. I was staying clean, working, and staying out of trouble. My dad called me one evening and told me he had been reading the Evergreen Park Community blotter on the internet from Wisconsin, and in the police blotter, it was warning residents to beware of burglaries to garages that were occurring around the area where our house was. My dad called me up and said, "Make sure you're locking the garage up at night," as it was filled with tools my dad had left me to continue on with the business. I told him that I would make sure it was locked.

About a week later, I was working late. One of my customers owned a bunch of apartments and condominiums, and when someone moved out of a unit, I'd go in and get it ready for the next tenant. Painting, minor plumbing and electrical work, tile replacement, general cleaning, things like that. The unit I was working on was going to be occupied the following day, so I had to work all day and night until about ten thirty to get it finished. I believe it was about 11:00 p.m. when I finally pulled up to my house. I noticed a car parked in front of my house, but the car was facing me with the headlights on, so I couldn't tell who it was. Before I could register that it was an Evergreen Park police car, I was surrounded. About three or four squad cars came out of nowhere and boxed in my van. They pulled me out, handcuffed me, took me to the police station, and impounded my work van. They left me in the jail cell until the following morning.

The following morning, I was led into an interrogation room. Two detectives started drilling me about garages and houses being burglarized. I knew exactly what was going on. When an individual paroles from prison, the town they're paroling to is notified by IDOC that an ex-convict would be living at such and such address. So because I was on parole, living in a house that coincidentally burglaries were occurring around, I was considered a suspect. I kept telling the two detectives that I understood their interest in me, but it just wasn't me doing these crimes. I told them I had been working since my release, that I was clean, and that I had no reason to be stealing. But they didn't believe me. They just weren't trying to hear anything I had to say. I told them I was done talking to them, asked for a lawyer, and they put me back in the cell.

About an hour later, one of the detectives walked up to the cell and said, "Mike, I'll make a deal with you. We know what we're looking for. Give me permission to go look in your garage, and if there's nothing in there that we're looking for, I'll get you out of here." I knew there was nothing stolen in my garage, so I consented. He took my keys from my property and went to my house. About an hour later, he returned. He came up to the cell and says, "Okay, there was nothing in there we're looking for. I'll get you out of here. But I'm telling you, if you're doing anything wrong, you better stop. We're watching you." I just couldn't believe this was happening.

I was released from the Evergreen Park Police Station around 6:00 p.m. that day. I walked home, took a shower, and ate some food. I had run out of cigarettes and decided to take a walk to the corner to buy some. When I returned home, my girlfriend and I were planning on watching a movie. We had cut up a bunch of fresh fruit and made popcorn. Right before we started the movie, I told her I was just going to step out on the front porch to have a quick smoke. While I was sitting on the front porch, the Evergreen Park Police pulled back up to my house. They told me I had to come back to the station. I flipped out and tried to walk back into my house, and this cop tried blocking me. I ran—which didn't go well because there were cops everywhere. Anyway, they placed me in handcuffs and brought me back to the station, two hours after they released me! I asked what I was being charged with, and the officer said, "Class 3 theft." I asked, "A theft of what?" And all he said is, "You'll find out when you go to court."

When I finally made it to court a couple of days later, the State's Attorney stood up and said, "The Evergreen Park police were investigating some burglaries that were occurring. They stopped Mr. Seminetta and took him in for questioning. He denied everything and was released. About thirty minutes after he was released, a man named Mr. Rogers came to the police station to report some tools that were stolen from his garage. They took Mr. Rogers to Mr. Seminetta's van that they still had in the police impound, and Mr.

Rogers identified six power tools that belonged to him inside Mr. Seminetta's van."

These cops actually took pictures of the six power tools. There was a small drill, a palm sander, a stud finder, a small shop vacuum, a circular saw, and an impact driver. All old, used tools handed down to me, all belonging to my father. I told my lawyer this, and he asked if we could produce any receipts for the tools. I got a continuance, my lawyer contacted my dad who then drove in from Wisconsin to go through old files from the business. All these tools were old; we had been using them for years, and he couldn't find any receipts for them. So, my lawyer basically told me, "Because you cannot prove they're your tools, it boils down to your word against this Mr. Rogers, and unfortunately, you have a background a mile long." I was in shock. And so was my dad because he knew I was being charged with stealing my own tools! It was unreal.

And what's really messed up is that none of these tools cost more than $80 brand-new. The shop vacuum, palm sander, and stud finder were probably $40 to $50 brand-new. Now a class 4 theft carries one to three years. That's what I would've been charged with if the value of the "stolen" property was under $500. These jagoff Evergreen Park Police put a $100 value on each of the six tools, making the value of these old used tools $600. That makes the case a class 3 theft, which carries two to five years because the value is over $500. And also, in my discovery, I find out this Mr. Rogers lived directly behind the police station. His garage was literally twelve feet from the police station parking lot. Who the hell would burglarize a garage that shares an alley with a police station? They were trying to screw me any way they could.

My lawyer told me the state was offering the minimum, two years for a plea deal. He said I could take the two years and be out in seven months, or I could go to trial, probably sit in the County jail for nine months, and if I'm found guilty, I'd get four or five years instead of two. People would ask why I would take two years for something I didn't do. Well, if those people knew how the court system worked, they'd understand. My background was already horrible. One more case really wouldn't make much of a difference. Plus, it was either sit in the county jail for six months to a year, possibly be found guilty and have to do another year in prison—or take the two years and be home in about seven and a half months. I took the two years. I was only free for four months, and now I was going back to prison for "stealing" my own tools. Life's a trip. It's a real trip.

I was shipped to NRC, again. Sat there for about twenty-one days, again. And was shipped to a prison down south, again. I was sent to Illinois River Correctional Center. When I walked into the prison, I had seven months and one week to do. I'm not going to lie, I was pissed off and full of resentment. I had thoughts going through my head like, "I hate cops. Why would God do this to me," so on and so forth. I sat in my cell for the first few weeks, pissed off at the world. I was finally doing okay, happy, and trying to move on with my life, and *boom*! Completely knocked back down for something I didn't even do.

So after a few weeks of feeling sorry for myself, I bought a TV, a fan, a hot pot, and a radio for my cell. Gym shoes and a couple of sweat outfits. Filled my property box with tuna and protein bars, asked my father to send me the manuscript of what I had written so far, and spent six months lifting weights and polishing up this book you're reading now. The time flew by, and I was again released.

There have been a couple of bumps in the road since September of 2016, and I've had a couple of bad but brief relapses in the beginning, but I've been clean now for about four years, other than a six-month relapse in between that ended in a trip to detox for a couple of weeks. I finished this book, moved to Tennessee, I run the field operations for my father's painting and decorating company he started in Dandridge, Tennessee, and I'm getting ready to take over the reins when he retires soon. I bought a nice truck, a motorcycle, and a little boat. I am working on another book and planning and training for a cross-country bicycle trip from the 9/11 memorial in Manhattan, New York, to Venice Beach, California. All these things I've done in the last few years only. All because I decided enough was enough. All because I don't use heroin anymore. When I was younger, a major problem I had was wanting immediate gratification. I'd get clean or get out of jail and I'd want my life to be put back together instantly.

I'd set these unrealistic goals for myself, and then would get depressed when I couldn't accomplish them immediately. Now I go with the flow, and as long as I'm doing the right thing, I'll be okay. God's gifts come as he decides I've earned them, I guess.

Yet I look around me and I see the country I live in facing a serious substance abuse epidemic. It's all around me. There were times in the last few years when I told myself, "I'm clean, I'm moving on with my life, and I want nothing to do with addiction, recovery, or dealing with other addicts. I just want to forget about it." However, I'd also think to myself, "I've gone through addiction, I came out intact, I have a lot of knowledge and experience on the subject, and maybe I can really help and contribute to the crisis going on. I could either forget it ever happened and move on, or I can be part of the solution, maybe save some lives and help some families." I decided it would be very selfish of me not to at least try to help if at all possible. What has manifested from that decision is the book you now hold in your hands. And a second book I'm currently working tirelessly on titled "2nd Ripple," which is more geared and directed toward mothers and fathers, family members and friends who have a loved one dealing with substance abuse issues—to help them understand exactly what's actually going on with their loved one, and offer helpful suggestions on things I believe will help, and things I know will not help, so families have a more equipped arsenal when dealing with substance abuse! My father is going to contribute to the book also, giving his insight and perspective on what he went through as a parent with his children dealing with these same issues. Who knows what path the good Lord will take me down. But as long as I keep doing the right thing, I'm sure it'll be good.

There aren't very many things that I'm absolutely 100 percent certain about. But one thing I know for sure is that as long as I maintain a certain level of self-discipline and inner awareness, that will have a significant positive effect on my life and the experiences I happen to encounter during my lifetime. I now know what to do in certain situations and also what not to do. I've always been an extremely analytical individual. Now I keep it simple for the most part. That simplicity usually lays a path before me that won't invite too much chaos into my life.

I wrote this book with the intention of helping with this addiction epidemic we all face together. Addiction does not only affect the ones who use the drugs, take it from me. Substance abuse causes a giant ripple effect on society, economy, and family. I have examples galore. Some stories I can write of are quite unbelievable. But the fact of the matter is that we don't need stories. We need solutions, answers, and insight into the subject of substance abuse written in laymen's terms so it can be understood by all. That is what's going to help. Not stories. Stories don't help—they're for entertainment. And if you, reading this, believe you have a problem with drugs (or know somebody who does), you don't need stories. Chances are you have a few of your own.

I don't believe substance abuse disorders are as hopeless and helpless as they're sometimes portrayed to be. If an addict wants a better life bad enough, they could have it. And they could have it without substituting one thing for another. They could have it by simply looking inward.

I imagine some people reading this book and thinking, *This guy must be messed up in the head.* I led a rough life for twenty years. I poisoned my body and mind excessively for years. Miraculously, I'm fine. I don't need therapy, I sleep well at night, I don't take pills to cope. I don't want to undermine individuals who legitimately require a personal therapist, psychologist, or medication due to chronic depression or extreme anxiety, people suffering from an actual psychosis, serious mental depression, or personality disorders that are causing them serious pain in their lives. Bipolar disorders, manic-depressive disorders, etc. Yes, most people have heard those terms. But just because most of us generally know what bipolar and manic-depressive disorders mean, that doesn't mean we all understand what it is. I won't pretend to understand them either because I don't have them. However, I have read medical journals and psychology books that have explained them somewhat. From what I've seen, many individuals who claim to have these disorders in fact do not. It seems that many people *need* something to be wrong with them, almost as an identity, so they can refer to their "disorder" when they feel like shit. They went and told their doctors that they were depressed. I imagine some—not all—but many conversations between doctors and patients going like this:

"Doctor, I'm so depressed! I can't sleep or eat."

"Well, was there something that happened recently that could be causing this?"

"Well, I lost my job a month ago, and I was very upset. But I got a new one, so I was happy again. But then my boyfriend broke up with me and I've been devastated since."

"Let me ask you this, were you happy before you lost your job?"

"Yes, I was."

"Well, from what I've gathered in our ten-minute conversation is that you're having moments of relative happiness followed by depressive states. You were happy, then sad, then happy, then sad again. I'm going to diagnose you as a clinically depressed individual."

"Oh my God! I knew it, Doc. I knew something was wrong with me. I want to be happy all the time, and not get so sad when things happen in life that constitutes sadness. What can I do?"

"Well, we can try medication. I'm going to write you a prescription for Xanax, which is a highly addictive benzodiazepine which will literally change the chemistry of your brain, and I'll also give you some Valium in case your moods start to dip too low. Then I'll cross my fingers and hope you don't turn into a drug-dependent, neurotic, pill-popping junkie, seeing that you're only twenty-three years old and not a fully developed mature adult yet."

Then, because a doctor told them, they start believing that they are clinically depressed or have issues with anxiety and talk themselves into believing they actually need these pills and that it's all legit because it's "prescription." In my eyes, when someone is happy, and then they get sad for some reason, and then the sadness wears off, until some other shit happens, those are not legitimate bipolar or manic-depressive episodes, or even true anxiety. That's life. People nowadays tend to look to doctors or therapists to tell them they are normal and to be prescribed some miracle drug that makes life bearable.

Please don't get confused here and think that I'm saying there is no need for certain professional outlets or medications. I don't want to undermine people who really need these doctors or medications. What I'm trying to say is that many, many Americans are completely misdiagnosed. That's not my opinion. That's a fact. I can't tell you how many completely normal young men and women I've seen who have prescriptions for Xanax.

Everybody who is alive is going to get sad, pissed off, angry, lose their appetite, won't be able to sleep sometimes, have some anxiety or get depressed. It's called neurosis. It's normal, especially nowadays with our fast-paced, overstimulating world we live in, and in no way should drugs like Xanax, Klonopin, Valium, or any of these other drugs be prescribed for it unless it's an extreme case. Those drugs are for individuals who have crossed over to an actual psychosis, and doctors passing these drugs out like candy are causing a major problem. In my opinion, the risk of becoming addicted to benzodiazepines and the ultimate and inevitable outcome of that is a lot worse than sucking it up and learning to deal with life's ups and downs in a more natural and healthy way, other than popping pills.

What is happening—apparently and obviously—is that these doctors give these highly addictive pills to their patients, the patients get hooked on them, and when the doctors don't refill the prescriptions, or their tolerance levels go up and the doctors don't give them enough pills, these people are now addicted to benzodiazepines or opiates and are all of a sudden cut off. Then what happens is these addicts discover street drugs are more powerful, easier to get, and cheaper, and *boom*! The result is millions of drug addicts running around, crime going up, prisons becoming overcrowded, and families being torn apart. It's a real problem in our society, and it's getting out of control. It's now to the point where it's actually uncommon to meet somebody who doesn't know someone who's an addict, or who has experienced addiction themselves, or within their own family. Don't even get me started on fentanyl and the *southern border*.

If you get a little depressed, or sad sometimes about the "horrible" things happening in your life, instead of going and getting a prescription for Xanax, try this: Board a plane to a third-world country.

Let's say Somalia. Real places that are stricken with AIDS, malaria, Ebola, hunger and starvation, terrorism, and extreme poverty. Places with no running water, or grocery stores. Where open defecation still takes place. Kidnapping, rape, and murder are commonplace. Spend a week there. Then get back on your plane, back to America, realize the problems in your life aren't really that bad—comparatively—stop complaining that you hate your life, or can't stand your boss, or your girlfriend broke up with you, or you have to sit in traffic for ten minutes every day, etc. Chill out, eat some fresh food, drink some clean water, take a hot shower, and go to sleep in your nice warm safe bed and say to yourself "things could be a lot worse. At least I don't live in a third-world country," and move onward with your life. Shit happens! Eating pills and zoning out is not a healthy coping tool. Obviously, nobody is going to fly to a third-world country. But you get the point. We need to stop believing in the notion that there's a pill to fix everything, or that they make anything any better. Because most of the time they do not. In fact, most of the time, in the long run, they make things much, much worse.

Since the war on drugs began with President Nixon, the prison population in America has grown exponentially. The United States of America only makes up about 5 percent of the world population—yet we incarcerate 25 percent of all the world's inmates. There are over two million people incarcerated in the prison system of the USA—the majority of them petty drug offenders, and petty theft offenders for, you guessed it, stealing for drugs. All of which receive absolutely no professional treatment in prison, and the vast majority who will be released back into our communities in a very short time, and in most cases worse off than they were before they went to prison. This is not an opinion of mine. It's a fact. The whole point of prison is to protect society from people who commit crimes. However, these old judges who send our young men and women to prison for drug and drug-related offenses, where they know damn well these people aren't getting treatment and will be released in the near future, well, these judges aren't protecting society. They're actually making society a worse place in the future. Prison does not cure addiction.

I'm not one who blames others for my mistakes. I'm not one of these psychopaths who say "Free all prisoners." I understand the need for prisons and consequences, and the fact that some people belong in prison. But people with drug addictions do not belong in prison; they belong in treatment. It is well documented and well understood in the scientific and health community that drug addiction is a type of disorder that requires treatment. That sending people to prison is doing more harm than good. Yet in just about every courthouse in the country we have state's attorneys and judges, most of whom have never gone through substance abuse and don't truly understand it, sending our young men and women to prison on a daily basis. And this addiction crisis is getting worse, not better. We can only build so many prisons or spend so much money on locking people up. One of these days hopefully the super smart people who make these decisions and run our states will wake the fuck up. For all our sakes. Over one hundred thousand young men and women dead from opioid overdose annually! Seriously!? To put that in perspective, fifty-eight thousand Americans died in the entirety of the Vietnam War!

I'd like to be able to say that writing this book was a very enjoyable experience. And although I enjoyed writing some parts, for the most part, it wasn't. It was hard. It's hard writing a book. Not the fact that certain things were emotionally draining for me to get out and down on paper—but the process itself was hard. To compose a story that's coherent and makes sense. That flows so the reader stays interested. This book took me about three years to write collectively. I rewrote it five different times. It actually became an obsession of mine. For about twelve months straight, I worked on it for ten to twelve hours a day. But it had to be done. I wanted to give up on it many times. I'm glad I didn't.

I'm honored to be able to share my story of addiction and substance abuse. I hope that many will read this book and gain some understanding and hope. In regard to addiction, that's my story. But the story isn't as important as what I've learned from my experience. There are countless people who led or are leading a similar lifestyle I once led. I'm not unique. Well, maybe I am in some ways. But in regard to addiction, there's nothing overly unique about my story.

I also hope that I explained some things or answered some questions my family members or people who know me personally may have had. I'm sure many of them just thought I was a bad apple or a lost cause. God was teaching and molding me, that's all.

I've spoken to many people in my life who've been clean from drugs for long periods of time. When I was still using, I'd say to myself during these conversations, "They couldn't have been as screwed up as I am, because I can't quit. I'm way more messed up than they were." That wasn't the case, though. They were just as screwed up as I was. Some were a lot worse. And they got clean. And so did I. And so can anybody.

I also hope that I've shown some authenticity for anyone reading this who has a substance abuse disorder or knows somebody who does. I want my readers to understand that I've lived it. I truly understand what you're going through. And knowing that, you might take into consideration what I'm going to write in part two of this book.

If you're an addict, I hope that after reading the rest of this book, all your doubts and fears about kicking your habit vanish, and you realize that you have it in you to live the life you were put here to lead. If any book has one paragraph or one idea that changes a person's life, that is a good reason for reading it, and then passing it on. I hope this will be that type of book.

The greatest task—in my opinion—that we face as human beings is to understand why we go through what we go through, learn who we are and why we are here, and then use our wisdom, compassion, and personal experiences to help each other. Life is not just about consuming, buying nice things, and being happy twenty-four hours a day, seven days a week. Realistically, life often includes a lot of suffering (or Ripples). However, suffering is quite pointless unless we learn the lesson behind the reasons we suffer. We must first understand and embrace our suffering, then we can learn from it. It's all about how we deal with our own personal situations and what we choose to do—or not do—about it. And that's where our wisdom comes from.

The following quote I'm about to share may not have to do with addiction. My father has a big framed poster of this, and it was hung on the wall in our home throughout my childhood, and I've read it in passing many times. It was something that always stuck with me, and I believe it can pertain to many things in life, especially regarding the continuous battle we all face in life to become better versions of ourselves. I'll end my story with it.

### What It Takes to Be Number One
### By Vince Lombardi

Winning is not a sometime thing; it's an "all the time" thing. You don't win once in a while; you don't do things right once in a while; you do them right all of the time. Winning is a habit. Unfortunately, so is losing.

There is no room for second place. There is only one place in my game, and that's first place. I have finished second twice in my time at Green Bay, and I don't ever want to finish second again. There is a second-place bowl game, but it's a game for losers played by losers. It is and always has been an American zeal to be first in anything we do, and to win, and to win, and to win.

Every time a football player goes to ply his trade, he's got to play from the ground up—from the soles of his feet right up to his head. Every inch of him has to play. Some guys play with their heads. Thats okay. You've got to be smart to be number one in any business. But more importantly, you've got to play with your heart, with every fiber of your body. If you're lucky enough to find a guy with a lot of head and a lot of heart, he's never going to come off the field second.

Running a football team is no different than running any other kind of organization— an army, a political party or a business. The principles are the same. The object is to win—to beat the other guy. Maybe that sounds hard or cruel. I don't think it is.

It is a reality of life that men are competitive, and the most competitive games draw the most competitive men. That's why they are there—to compete. The object is to win fairly, squarely, by the rules—but to win.

And in truth, I've never known a man worth his salt who in the long run, deep down in his heart, didn't appreciate the grind, the discipline. There is something in good men that really yearns for discipline and the harsh reality of head-to-head combat.

I don't say these things because I believe in the brute nature of men or that men must be brutalized to be combative. I believe in God, and I believe in human decency. But I firmly believe that any man's finest hour—his greatest fulfillment to all he holds dear—is that moment when he has worked his heart out in a good cause and lies exhausted on the field of battle—victorious.

Coach Vincent T. Lombardi

Please read the following section of this book with an open heart and an open mind.

My baby sister Jessica, my sister Cara, my mother and myself

My sister Jess, my mom and myself, doing our duty in 2016

My sister Cara, my cousin Kelly, my sister Jessica and myself.
My three favorite girls.

Hard work

My Aunt Terry (my Godmother)

My cousin Jake and myself

My father, mother, sister Cara, and myself

My sister Cara and I on the porch of the home we grew up in on 92nd and St Louis and Evergreen Park Illinois

Me and my Superman pajamas the morning I
realized that Santa Claus didn't exist!

My sister and the infamous pink Barbie car that made
me realize these gifts came from my parents.

My dad and I

My sister Cara and I in trouble, sitting in the corner.

My step-brothers Patrick and Daniel and myself

All-Star game, I was probably 12 years old in this picture

Me and first base, my dad coaching first base. Like father, like son.

The two most influential men in my life. I am the man I am today specifically because of these two men – my grandpa McCann, and my father.

My grandma and grandpa McCann

My grandpa Seminetta and myself

My dad and my stepmom Dona

My mother, my two sisters, and myself

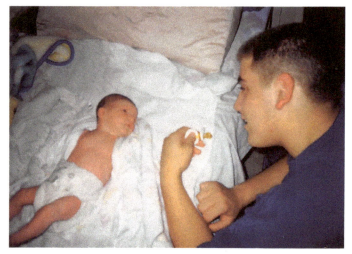

The day my baby sister was born, October 12th, 1999. I was 15 years old.

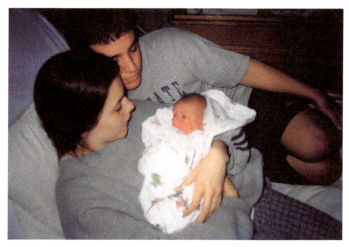

My two sisters and myself. Best buddies!

My sister sitting on Santa Clause's lap at a family party...which is me!

My sister Cara and myself. My best friend. I may have wrote
this book, but it's just as much Cara's story as it is mine.

My brother Daniel, his wife Carrie, and my grandma Senese

Grandma Senese and my stepmom

The old crew (from left to right), my sister Cara, my cousin Kelly, yours truly, and my cousin Jacob

My father and I, Chicago Cubs home opener in 2016. We broke the curse…You're Welcome!

This is what it looks like when you keep doing the right thing.

# PART 2

We are changing—we have got to change. We can no more help it than leaves can help turning yellow and coming loose in Autumn.
—D. H. Lawrence

You do not become good by trying to be good, but by finding the goodness that is already inside you and allowing that goodness to emerge. But it can only emerge if something fundamental charges in your state of consciousness.
—Eckhart Tolle

# CHAPTER 13

Allow me to begin part two of this book with a question: How does a man climb Mt. Everest? If you don't know the answer to that question, you'll have to read on for the answer.

This section of the book is for insight. Not only for addicts but also for the families and friends of addicts who have no idea what has become of their loved one, so they may understand a little more about why their loved one is the way they are. Utilizing the information and suggestions I propose, I hope, may give you all some clearer understanding of why us addicts do the things we do (or why they do the things they do), and in turn, help rectify the problem.

The content of this book is not a "cure," yet in my heart of hearts, I believe it will assist anybody who is suffering to find a better way. As I said, this book is for both addicts and for families and friends who know someone who is suffering from substance abuse and want to offer help, love, and support. So please know that I will be going back and forth addressing both parties.

This book is a recollection of my experience with drugs, and my experiences with many other addicts. Each and every addict reading this, and families and friends of addicts reading this, must develop their own battle plan and strategies. I obviously can't know the family dynamics of every person who reads this book. However, I do know the dynamics of addiction and all the bullshit that comes with it. My guess is that if you bought this book, everything I'm about to write will be relatable. I can only hope that by implementing some of my suggestions, some may be inspired to turn their lives around.

When an addict is in the process of getting clean, they must turn and look in the mirror. That's a hard thing to do, I know. When your conduct has consisted of lying, stealing, disappointing, and poisoning your body for a significant amount of time, it's hard to face that. My first suggestion is for addicts: We have to stop running from our problems and from ourselves. We are the problem! We must learn how to bring mindfulness and awareness to our problem. Only then can we learn how to be kind and caring to ourselves instead of beating ourselves up about it all the time. We have to learn how to accept ourselves as individuals who are struggling. To not use that fact as an excuse, but to simply accept it. From my experience, acceptance seems to happen only after we've given up our struggle to try to fix ourselves with drugs. In recovery programs, this is known as the "gift of desperation." When everything we've tried has failed and we come to the point where we understand fully that as long as we keep using drugs we will continue to be miserable, then we'll be the most receptive to accepting the fact that we've lost all control and that we need help. This usually happens around the time that our faith has vanished, our mind has exhausted every form of experimentation at attempting to clean ourselves up on our own volition without some form of help, and our lives remain in complete shambles. This is "rock bottom."

At this point, it is also our opportunity to move our focus towards waking up and at least begin to make attempts at doing what we know is right without thinking about it too much and allowing our brains to talk us out of it. My brain has failed me countless times in my life. My heart, on the other hand, has never failed me once. We need to learn how to listen to our hearts. Listen to that quiet, still voice within yourself that always speaks up first—right before our minds chime in. In doing so, we can usually free ourselves from a lot of unnecessary grief—believe me.

For the families and friends of addicts: It's very easy for anybody who has never personally experienced a serious chemical addiction to develop a false conception of substance abusers. I can attest that some of these misconceptions are mingled with disgust, anger, confusion, and perhaps a bit of pity. Little do most people really understand the continuous fight for normalcy, peace, and happiness that an addict desperately strives for on a daily basis—no matter how misguided they may be. The need for sobriety when chronic addiction is realized, yet still not being able to stop. The desire for a good friend, or a hug. It may seem that addicts just don't care. In the majority of cases—that couldn't be further from the truth.

If you, reading this, are not an addict, I'll ask you to please keep an open mind about those who are. I'm not by any means asking you to give them a free pass. And I'm not going to be making any excuses for addicts. I'm just simply asking that you have an open mind while reading.

I won't pretend that I believe that within every addict a wonderful, loving angel lies underneath all the ugliness. Believe me, I know that's not the case. Many addicts are downright vindictive, pessimistic individuals. They may be selfish, hurtful people who seem to just not give a damn. I've met these types. I do not know much about the cloth they were cut from or why they are the way they are. I've never been a hurtful person. Have I acted like a jerk before and done things I'm not proud of? Yes, I'm guilty of that. But I've never been a blatantly mean person. So, I'm only speaking on substance abuse alone. And what I do know for sure is that there is a lot of misunderstanding going around about men and women addicted to drugs. A lot of that misunderstanding can be found among the families and friends of addicts, but it can also be found in the media and throughout society as a whole.

Most doctors who concern themselves with the subject of addiction understand that it is a problem that goes well beyond being able to be controlled or corrected by willpower alone. Even the addicts themselves, toward the end of the chronic stage of addiction, realize that something is very wrong within themselves, even though they may not understand it and might not want to admit it right away.

For all the heartbroken and confused mothers and fathers whose drug-addicted children are walking all over, stealing from, and totally disappointing—let me tell you this: they're just as hurt and confused about it as you are. Maybe even more so. And although they don't show it all the time, if ever, their hearts are also broken. I beg you, please, don't give up on them. They need your love and support more than you can understand. The crazy thing is that often they don't even understand how much they need it themselves.

I'm not a doctor or a psychologist. I have no degrees. Every word I've written throughout this entire book came from my mind to my pen, and onto paper. I've naturally adopted certain ideas and writing styles from all the books I've read in the past—sometimes consciously, sometimes unconsciously—but this book is entirely authentic first-hand experience. I didn't spend hours upon hours researching addiction in libraries and in schools. Literally 80 percent of this book was written in a jail cell, and the only thing assisting me was my personal experiences and tons of freeze-dried Taster's Choice coffee.

Yet even though I may not have a degree, I am somewhat of an expert on the subject. Though my conceptual knowledge doesn't come from studying in a school. It comes from pure experience. I know that if it wasn't for the love and support of certain people in my life who've never given up or turned their back on me no matter what I did in my addiction—people like my father, my grandfather, my baby sister, or my cousins who know me the most, Johnny, Jacob, Kelly—I would've never broken the cycle and had the desire to get out of that lifestyle. In fact, I'd probably be one of the ones who ran out of time and died before I woke up. So again, try not to give up on them. And don't take anything they do or say personally. It's not personal.

I realize that sometimes your heartache that goes out to the one you love who is wrapped up in addiction can become too much of a burden for you to handle. It can often get to the point where it starts to affect your own health and well-being (physically, emotionally, financially). It's not your fault, and you're not a failure as a parent or friend if you just can't take their crap any longer. Fault implies intent. Nobody intended for any of this to happen, them turning into addicts, acting like jerks, and in turn you wanting to get the hell away from them.

So like I said, it's nobody's fault. If you're fed up, you're fed up. Completely understandable. An addict can be like a constant tornado in your life, and you have to let them go. Just don't stop telling them you love and miss them, talking to them, or praying for them. That's all I'm saying. Remember that their actions while in active addiction did not emerge from the essence of who they truly are. Reread that last sentence.

Now, to my readers who are the addicts and still using drugs, let me tell you this: people are only going to put up with your bullshit for so long. For your families and friends to keep letting you disrupt their lives and hurt and use them is unhealthy not only for them but it's also unhealthy for you. If you're an addict, chances are you're going to have to learn the hard way, and before you really start changing there's the possibility that you're going to get pretty beat up. I'm sorry to suggest that, but it's statistically true. There's no reason to keep hurting, lying to, and walking all over your own loved ones while you go through this. It's wrong. And it's disrespectful.

It would be wonderful if an addict could read this book and just magically stop. Most likely, that won't happen. However, you can use your experiences (and this book) to your advantage. See this situation as an opportunity rather than as a tragedy. An opportunity to really get to know yourself better. If you are going to get clean and be successful, you're going to have to get out of denial and face what isn't working in your life. You obviously need to change, right? The problems you are facing because of your addiction cannot be solved by the same level of thinking and acting that allowed them to be created in the first place.

That means you're going to have to completely change yourself. The way you think. The way you deal with stress, sadness, anger… happiness. You're going to have to change a lot. And change—even when it's in our best interest—is uncomfortable. I know. I went through it. Nobody wants to feel uncomfortable. That's why we use drugs in the first place. It was hard for me to stop using drugs because for a long time, I believed they were the only thing that gave me any type of comfort. Ironically, though, they were exactly what was causing all my problems.

I'm not going to sugarcoat anything. I'm not going to write a bunch of crap or try to sell you the idea that this situation you've got yourself into isn't going to be extremely hard to overcome, just so my book sounds good. Trust me, it's going to be hard. I'm only going to present to you, in the raw, how I see things. I've been through it myself, and I've seen, literally, hundreds of people go through this. Some of them are very close to me. Some of them are still in active addiction. Some of them are dead.

Do people get clean without completely destroying their lives? Yes, it has been known to happen. I hope you're one of them. But don't arrogantly think you'll just bounce back because you simply tell yourself you're not going to be like those "other addicts." Just prepare yourself for a long trip towards recovery. I know a little bit about this game you've managed to get yourself involved in. And if you're reading this book, chances are you're knee-deep in it. If you want to believe what I say, or not, that's completely your affair. But for those who truly want to turn their lives around, read on with your full attention. I must warn you, though, you may not want to hear (or like) what you read. But as my father would say, "Tough shit."

I wish you luck, though. And know this—when you do make it through this storm of addiction (or Ripple) you're going to realize that what you and your family have gone through has caused you all to evolve and come together more than ever. You'll understand love a lot clearer, and the words "Family" and "Friend" will have a stronger meaning for you all. And from then on, you'll be able to overcome anything life throws at you.

You'll learn that you only have control over three things in your life: The thoughts you think, the images you visualize for yourself, and the actions you take. The life you currently live is the direct result of all your past thoughts and actions. From now on, you're in charge of what you feed your body and mind. If you want something different, you're going to have to do something different.

In a lot of twelve-step programs, they describe insanity as "doing the same thing over and over and expecting different results each time." If you keep living your life as a drug addict, you're going to keep getting the results that drug addicts get. And that's a life of struggle and despair with hardly an ounce of happiness. My guess is that you want to stop being "insane," right? You cannot live a meaningful, happy life and be a junkie or a crackhead at the same time. I mean, come on! If you believe that you can be a drug addict and live a fulfilling, happy life at the same time, contrary to all the evidence and experience proving you can't—then drug addiction may not be your only problem. If you want true, genuine happiness, you're going to have to drop the act that you're fine and in control. You have to stop utilizing drugs as a solution for the way your life is. There's no other way around it, so you might as well stop trying.

## Chill Out…It Could Be Worse

The majority of people who tend to fail at everything they do in this world are people who have a bad habit of making excuses. I was one of them. And I failed often. And just as often, I made up an excuse for why I did. When I did get clean, I stopped blaming, whining, and thinking that my life was "so bad" because I learned a few things about life. I learned that my so-called problems were actually relatively meager compared to some people—people with real problems.

I knew people throughout the world suffered from horrible medical conditions and diseases. I knew people were abused or impoverished. But I was never really conscious of the extent of just how bad some people have it. When I got clean and actually started working on my screwed-up character, my selfishness started to diminish, and I became aware of how lucky I was that my major problem was just a heroin addiction. I developed a profound sense of awareness that there are people in this world who've had it a lot worse than I did.

I'm not suggesting that you undermine your addiction. Chemical dependency wrecks lives and can be very dangerous and potentially deadly. But I will attempt to get my readers to see that it is a situation that can be beaten. Little children who are bedridden, dying of cancer? They cannot control that. Whether their disease claims their lives or not is completely out of their control. There are people born blind. They can never see their mother's face, watch a sunset, or drive a car. And they are happy to be alive. People are born crippled or immobile. They spend their lives in wheelchairs and endure hardships I can't even imagine—and their spirits glow.

There are children who are beaten, raped, and abused by their own fathers or some other grown-up for years. They are defenseless.

They can't help themselves at such a young age. There are third-world countries filled with violence and war. Women and children are being killed. Females aren't allowed to read books or educate themselves. They spend their lives cooking, cleaning, and basically being raped whenever their "husband" wants sex. Period. Thats their life. Some of these girls are twelve to fourteen years old when they are forced to marry men twenty to thirty years older than them. There are families all over this planet who can't afford to feed themselves because they are so poor and impoverished. There are young girls all over the world who are kidnapped, hooked on drugs, and sold to underground prostitution rings for the personal profit of some sick pig. They spend their lives being physically and emotionally abused and forced to have sex with scumbag perverts. They are helpless. Literally thousands of children die each day from malnutrition and starvation. This shit is happening as you read this sentence. It's real. People are really suffering in this world.

All I'm trying to portray is that there are people who are a lot worse off. After realizing that the American young man or woman who has the world in the palm of his or her hand with every opportunity imaginable as long as he or she works hard for it but suffers and fails because he or she gets high all the time, well, that doesn't hold much merit. Yes, addiction is a serious problem. But it can be fixed. One can overcome it. That's a proven fact. Be grateful for that. Some people don't have a choice, like a child who is born with cancer. They can't help that they have cancer.

We cannot control what life throws at us. But we can control how we feel toward it and how we respond to it. A drug addict always has a choice. You have a choice. Even when our willpower seems to be gone and nothing seems to be going well in our lives, there's still that little part deep down inside us that knows what has to be done. And seeing how us addicts are extremely diligent and resourceful, if we put half the energy into straightening out our lives as we put into screwing ourselves up, most of us will excel in life.

One good thing is that by you reading this book, a seed will be planted in your mind. You may not be aware of it quite yet, but it's going to grow. The human mind is a natural goal-achieving machine.

If you give your subconscious mind a goal, it will eventually achieve it—as long as that goal is aimed at something good and worthwhile. Hopefully, that goal is getting clean and getting your life back on track. If it is, then this seed I just spoke of will grow if you nurture it and allow it to. But it will take time.

Word of advice: Relax. You didn't become a full-blown addict overnight. You're not going to get clean and figure it all out and put all the shattered pieces back together overnight either. Strap in and embrace the journey. And no matter how many times you stumble and relapse during your personal fight for sobriety, don't give up. You cannot fail as long as you keep trying. Just as long as those attempts are genuine and not half-assed.

The first step is trying to locate the problem before implementing a solution to see what works for you. And a quick hint—drugs are not your problem. Something within yourself is the problem. The drugs and all the bullshit that comes with using them is just a manifestation of that problem. One thing that really helped me in my recovery was actually understanding the clinical aspects of addiction and what I actually did to my brain from using drugs and why I was doing the things I was doing. Things I knew were wrong but couldn't stop doing. We'll start there.

# CHAPTER 14

One evening, an old Cherokee Indian told his grandson about a battle that goes on inside all people. He said, "My son, the battle inside us all is a battle between two wolves. One wolf is evil. It is anger, envy, sorrow, regret, greed, arrogance, self-pity, guilt, resentment, lies, false pride, and ego.

The other wolf is good. It is joy, peace, love, hope, serenity, humility, kindness, empathy, generosity, truth, compassion, and faith."

The grandson thought about this battle for a minute and then asked his grandfather, "Which wolf will win the battle?"

The old Cherokee replied, "The one you feed."

When I was a young boy, my mother used to buy those giant boxes of freeze pops for my sister Cara and me. Looking back, I see that I had a compulsive nature very early on. If my memory serves me correctly, there were two hundred individual freeze pops in each box. And after a day of playing ball or swimming in the pool, I'd sit on the couch and have a freeze pop. Only I couldn't eat just one. In fact, I couldn't eat just a few. I would sit there and eat fifty freeze pops. No exaggeration! I would actually feel full from eating freeze pops. Then I'd eat a few more.

I'm not implying that young ones who like to eat a lot of ice cream are going to grow up to be drug addicts. What kid doesn't love ice cream? There's that line, though, that can be crossed when indulging in things that are good or feel good. Eating sweets, video games, etc. This line is very hard to recognize, but if you notice fifty freeze pop wrappers in the trash can, keep an eye on the little one. He or she probably has a compulsive nature. Although that may not be a serious problem at such a young age, when we begin to travel through our teenage and young adult lives and begin to indulge in things other than ice cream, it can develop into a problem when our character includes a compulsive nature.

Individual personalities develop a lot during the first ten years of a child's life, and that same personality often carries over into young adulthood with the same compulsions, attitudes, and character traits developed in early life. I won't say all, but a large percentage of teenagers will at one point in their growing-up stages experiment with drugs and alcohol. Marijuana, drinking, nowadays there's a prescription drug abuse problem like never before (the four main pills being Vicodin and OxyContin—which are both opiates and lead right to heroin use, and the other two being Xanax and Klonopin—which are benzodiazepines, which completely change one's brain chemistry and leave them miserable in the long run), and overdoses and deaths are at an all-time high.

We all know that young people go through a rebellious stage. Most people do. They go wild for a few years, they drink, go clubbing, they may go to spring break, eat ecstasy, and take their tops off for beads, they get stoned. Then after a few years of cutting loose and enjoying their youth, they may meet that special someone, have a baby, grow up, start a career, cut back on the partying, go to work, and start raising their family. But for the ones who ate the entire box of freeze pops in an hour when they were young—the compulsive ones? They might have a little bit of a harder time giving up all the fun they're having when they're young and partying.

## Mental Attachment

The human memory is pretty fantastic. For instance, when we were all very young, at one point or another, we got thirsty. Maybe we were playing on a hot summer day, running around, playing sports, or riding our bikes, what have you. We overexerted ourselves and we became dehydrated and got very thirsty. So Mom gave us a juice box or made iced tea, or we stood at the water fountain in the park and chugged water from the fountain until the kids standing in line started saying "save some for the fish." The point is something happened in our brains. The body was dehydrated, we felt thirsty, we drank a bunch of water, and within a minute the problem of our thirst was solved. We became hydrated again. The imbalance was balanced. Why? Because we drank the water. The brain will always remember this. From then on, when we get dehydrated and feel thirsty, our brain's memory tells us that a nice long drink of water will fix it and make us feel better.

The solution to thirst is to drink something. The physical brain does not care if this is right or wrong. Indulging in things that may or may not be good for you is of no concern at all to our actual physical brains. Right and wrong is our minds' (or souls') concern. All the brain cares about is getting balanced. It only concerns itself with what it knows will work immediately. And whether or not drinking water is right or wrong—it works. It quenches our thirst, and nobody can talk your brain out of that knowledge. Now obviously drinking water is good for you. And I do have a point to all this.

There comes a time in all our lives when we sometimes feel like crap or just need to have a good time. Maybe we lose a job, bills are due, our parents are driving us nuts, relationship problems, financial problems, whatever. A potential addict doesn't have to be a chronic drug user at the time, but they do indulge in drugs or drink to excess sometimes. So a potential addict gets aggravated, and we go out with our friends and do Jägerbombs all night, maybe do a line of blow in the bathroom. We have a great time, and we become relaxed and feel happy again. Well, just like the cool drink of water when we were a kid, our brain remembers this. It remembers that when we get a little sad or stressed out, or we just want to be happy and have a good time, a few shots of Jägermeister or Captain Morgan and a couple of lines of coke will make us feel good and lubricate our brain. And it always works. It becomes a solution. It's a learned behavior and becomes part of our personality. We've all known these types or were that type ourselves—the "crazy" ones who like to party. We became mentally attached to using or drinking. And in the very beginning, there are no negative consequences from these actions, so most of us who were hard partiers were hesitant to stop doing it. It's fun, it feels great, and we're in control. Why stop?

## It's Better than Sex!

Most of us have heard that saying that drugs are better than sex. Well, I've done pretty much every drug out there, and now that I no longer do drugs, I've come to realize that no drug is better than sex. Real sex, that is. You know, with someone you love and care for, and your chemistry is in tune. Nothing compares to that. But when I was using drugs and living that fast life, I believed that drugs were better than sex. I believed that because it was true for me. It was true because I didn't understand the feelings you could experience when you make love to somebody who is close to you, you know each other's desires, and you're clearheaded. It's awesome! That good passionate sex where…well, you know. Sorry, I digress.

When I was screwed up on drugs, though, when I had sex, all I was doing was chasing a feeling. In this case, an orgasm. And at the time, getting high was a better feeling. Really. That's why that saying exists. Because getting high on a powerful drug feels better than a quick orgasm. Here's why:

Drugs—particularly heroin and cocaine—affect the brain's "reward circuit," causing a flood of the chemical dopamine. Normally, when dopamine is derived from some natural occurrence like having sex, the dopamine recycles back into the cell that released it, shutting off the signal between nerve cells. When drugs like heroin and cocaine are introduced into this brain function, they prevent dopamine from being recycled, causing large amounts to build up around the nerve cells. This flood of dopamine in the brain's reward circuit strongly reinforces the desire to take these drugs. A normal reward system motivates a person to repeat behaviors that cause joy, such as eating good food or having sex. Likewise, drugs like heroin and cocaine cause a surge of dopamine in the reward circuit and cause people to repeat the behavior again and again. And the more one uses these drugs, the brain begins to adapt to them. These adaptations lead to the person becoming less and less able to derive pleasure from things they once enjoyed, like going out to eat, sex, or doing fun activities. Those things produce dopamine, but not nearly as much as taking drugs does.

When a person does drugs like cocaine or heroin, the high they're feeling is caused by the mass production of dopamine and it literally flooding your receptors, ten times more so than having an orgasm. Literally. So the high from the drugs has the potential and often is ten times more enjoyable than sex. It's not just a saying. It's more of a physical fact.

## Transition from Social User to Addict

The problem is that this dopamine produced when a person takes drugs is produced artificially. It's not natural. They're inducing pleasure unnaturally with chemicals. One of the attributes that sets humans apart from other animals is that we have a thinking mind. A person can understand with their mind that the drug is producing this extremely good feeling or high and that it can (or has) become a problem. The physical brain, on the other hand, doesn't see it that way. The drug feels good. That's all the brain knows. It's like gasoline. A person knows that premium gas is better than low-grade gas, and that low-grade gas is not good for your V8 engine. Your actual engine doesn't care. It'll use what you put in it, even if it causes problems in the long run.

When a person takes drugs and induces pleasure with an actual foreign chemical like cocaine or heroin, it allows the brain a chance to take a break, so to speak, and it doesn't have to work as hard. Instead of actually having to recognize pleasure through the senses, produce dopamine, then send it on its mission through the brain to the pleasure receptors—the drugs bypass all of that. Not only do the drugs do all the work, but the feeling is more intense. The problem lies in the fact that the more one takes drugs, the lazier their brain becomes. The more they induce the drug that, in turn, produces an extreme amount of dopamine, the harder it gets for their brain to produce it naturally. And eventually, if they keep using drugs (which most people keep using them because there aren't any significant consequences in the beginning to make them want to stop), it gets to a point where their brain pretty much forgets how to produce dopamine or feel good without drugs. Then the serious problems begin.

Now before they realize it, they cannot feel happy or joyful or content without drugs. Their brain is now always seeking drugs. They have become dependent on that drug—hence the phrase "chemical dependency." The natural brain function that used to produce the raw stuff that allows them to feel good has been on vacation per se, and it's very rusty. The only thing that can lube it up is a shot or a snort or a hit. So the daily question becomes: Do I feel like shit all day and act crabby and feel depressed, or do I do a little dope so I can get out of bed and feel good as I go about my day? Hmm... "I'll use just today. I have things to do. I have to go to work. I can't lay here and be sick." And that decision to use becomes our solution. To everything. It's quick and easy, and it always works. If you're lying there feeling horrible, your brain knows that using will make you feel better. It knows that it will work, and that you can breeze through the day.

By the time we realize that we're using drugs almost every day, the damage to the brain is done. If one has an addictive nature, they just became a drug addict. The fact of the matter is that their brain has now developed a new solution to ease the stress of life. It has learned an easy way to deal with anger, pain, sadness, depression... and when they do feel a little bit of happiness, it's just not enough, and they say to themselves, "Why can't I just be happy? Why can't I feel comfortable in my own skin?" Well, their brain now knows how to enhance their mediocre happiness.

I believe this is what was going on with me when I was in eighth grade CCD and got caught smoking pot before going to a Chicago Bulls playoff game. I had to get high before I went. It's like, if I didn't get high beforehand, I wouldn't even want to go. I'm sure a lot of addicts can relate to that. There comes a point when we don't want to do anything without getting a buzz beforehand. Whether it be watching a movie, or going to a sporting event or a concert, or cutting the lawn. By this point, there is only one way for the brain to feel good, and it's not natural. It's to use our drug of choice.

Not all people who use drugs or get drunk when something bad happens, or when they go out for a good time, are going to become a drug addict or a raging alcoholic. I'm not saying that. What I'm saying is that the ones who party a little more than others and too often induce dopamine surges in their brain can develop an addiction. Using drugs is slowly becoming their solution when they feel like shit. And they start feeling like shit more and more often. Basically, they feel like shit every time they don't have drugs.

The transition in one's attitudes and how they deal with problems, stress, and their emotions with using drugs is a learned behavior, and the habit develops so slowly in most cases that they don't even notice it happening. Until they wake up one day and realize that they've used drugs every day for the last six months. It's like going bald; over the span of a year, your hair is getting thinner and thinner. You don't really pay too much attention to it. You notice it, maybe, but you still have hair so it's not that big of a concern and you don't worry about it too much. Then you wake up one day, catch the light just right in the mirror, and say, "Holy shit, I'm bald!"

That's kind of how addiction takes place. We wake up one day and say, "Holy shit, I can't stop!" Nobody wants to or expects to become a drug addict. Drug addiction is characterized by drug seeking and drug using that becomes compulsive and becomes very difficult to control despite the harmful consequences that inevitably begin to happen. Repeated drug use leads to brain changes that strongly challenge an addict's self-control and makes it nearly impossible to resist the brain's intense urges to use drugs again and again. Now the obvious solution would be to stop using drugs, right? Right. That is right. However, the way a drug user damages the way their brain feels good, at the same time, something else is also being damaged in the process. Enter the prefrontal cortex.

I'm not a neuroscientist or a doctor, but I'm pretty sure that the frontal lobe is the part of your brain that is responsible for making critical decisions. For example: Let's say you're coming home from work and as you pull up to your house, you notice that it's on fire. The whole house is ablaze. There's fire coming out of all the windows. A thought enters your mind suddenly that your season tickets for the Green Bay Packers are on the kitchen table... Actually, no big loss. Okay, bad example. Let's say they were season tickets for the Chicago Bears. Now that's a tough situation! – Just kidding.

Anyway, it's times like this that we would be grateful for our frontal lobe. The frontal lobe says, "Dude, forget about the tickets. The house is on fire! If you go in there and try to retrieve the tickets, you can get burned or worse. They're replaceable." The frontal lobe analyzes and evaluates risks. So you stand there in the street safely with your family and you choose not to risk your life running into the house while it's on fire for some tickets. And ultimately, your frontal lobe made the right decision.

When people—especially young people—are going through their rebellious stages and partying a lot, the ones who party and use drugs just a little bit more often and a little harder than the average person, they are damaging something in the process, their frontal lobe. The drugs have actually rewired the brain and changed the way their frontal lobe operates. We've all heard that saying before, "Rewired." However, most people downplay it as a cliché way of saying somebody makes dumb decisions. Most people don't really realize that an addict's brain being "rewired" is exactly what has happened. Literally. The brain starts making very rash decisions.

Now their brain might say, "Well, if I go through the kitchen window and stay low, I might be able to grab the tickets and bolt out the back door. I probably won't get burned. I can do this." The more an addict uses drugs, and the longer they use drugs, the more they change the way their frontal lobe works. And the more their brain changes, the harder it becomes to make the decision to stop using them. By the time noticeable problems start occurring in an addict's life, the damage has already set in, and their decision-making becomes a lot more compulsive. Now instead of, "The house is on fire, I can't go in there, my tickets are gone," it's more like, "Shit, my tickets! Hurry." And *boom*! Without a second thought, they jump through the kitchen window. Their brain no longer registers the potential hazard, danger, or stupidity in what they're about to do. All they think about is the tickets. That's the end of the thought. The idea of their actions being borderline suicidal never arises in their head. They now just act off their impulses.

This is exactly why people who first start using heroin snort it and say, "I'll never shoot it." Most heroin addicts have said this.

"I would never stick a needle in my arm. Not me. I hate needles." However, as the brain is continuously changing from using the drug for some time, the same brain that once said "I'll never shoot it" is not the same brain after six months of using the drug. Before they know it, they're sticking a needle in their arm, their arm full of track marks.

Once an individual with an addictive, compulsive nature reaches a certain point in their drug use, where it has become their solution to life, they get to the point when they no longer think about the consequences or dangers of using drugs. They don't think, "There's a bag of heroin or cocaine. It sure would feel good to get high... But I just got out of jail for a possession charge. I know I have a problem and I can't stop once I start. Although it would feel great, maybe I shouldn't. Drugs cause problems for me." Instead, their thought process becomes, "Oh, a bag of dope. It'll feel great to use it, so I will." And BOOM! They make the impulsive decision to use. Not because they don't care about the consequences, but because the consequences don't really enter their thoughts. And if they do momentarily, they are quickly pushed aside by the brain's extreme urge to use again. It actually gets to the point, as crazy as this sounds, where the consequences are not nearly as bad as how they feel if they don't use. That's something that's real, and most non-addicts don't truly understand. The thought that doing a hit, or a snort, or a shot will feel great and relieve whatever physical or mental pain they have pops into their head and that's the end of the thought process. The high, or good feeling they're desperate for, is sufficient enough to push all other thoughts aside and their brain makes the decision to say, "Fuck this. I'm going to get high. I'll worry about this shit tomorrow." The sad thing is that when tomorrow comes, they're even deeper into their addiction than they were the day before.

The high we get from using is very short-lived. But the effects it has on our brains are not. When we use drugs, we're changing the way our brain operates, as I've been saying. It happens over time, some longer than others. That's why it's not common for drug users to quickly realize we have a problem and make the logical decision to stop using before we cross that threshold. It's fun in the beginning and offers relief. Why stop doing what's fun or feels good? Once we realize that it's become the only way to have fun, or just to feel okay, it's usually too late to "just stop." Now we are no longer able to feel pleasure or contentment without drugs—plus our frontal lobe is now damaged, so we can't just make a simple logical decision to stop. This is when what's commonly referred to as the vicious cycle starts to occur. Vicious cycle is also one of those cliché statements we've all heard before, referring to somebody who keeps getting high and in turn causes all kinds of problems in their lives. Very few people realize the dynamics of this vicious cycle, and just how embedded it becomes in an addict's life.

## The Vicious Cycle

Once an addict is experiencing this cycle, they're using drugs on a daily basis. It's not just a weekend activity anymore. It's become a necessity in their life. They have developed an actual daily craving to use because their brain knows that when they use, they will feel normal, balanced, and relaxed. There is no fun or pleasure without drugs anymore. And this is how the "vicious cycle" goes:

An addict will wake up in the morning (or late afternoon) and not feel right. They may not be going through withdrawal yet, but often they are. And when I say that they don't feel right, what I mean is that there is an actual chemical imbalance in their brains. It's not just that they may be going through withdrawal and feeling physically sick. This imbalance is very real, and the brain knows something is wrong. Just like it knew they were dehydrated when they were a kid. And just like the knowledge that a cool, long drink of water will fix their thirst, their brain starts to think, "What will fix this imbalance? What will make me feel normal?" The answer: My drug of choice. Their brain knows this will fix it instantly. It doesn't care if it's right or wrong. It only cares about what works—what will fix the problem in the moment, and quickly.

So the thought or memory of using pops in their head and the cravings begin. And since the frontal lobe is not capable of making clear and rational decisions, the decision becomes simple. "Drugs.

Hurry! I feel like shit and I have a million things to do." Their frontal lobe no longer plays out the whole scenario. It makes its decision off impulse. The addict doesn't think about a ten-year drug habit. They don't think about jail, or losing their job, or car, or relationships. They don't think about disappointing their family—again. They only think about that moment. What will work right now. They say to themselves, "I'll use this last time. Just one more time."

So they use. Then after they do, they realize that they just did the same thing they promised themselves and their loved ones the day before that they'd stop doing. They used "one more time." After they use and their brain balances out and feels better, then comes the shame, guilt, and the realization that they have a serious problem that they seemingly can't control. So now they feel disappointed in themselves and maybe sad and weak, and on top of that, everything in their life is coming apart. Now that they feel horrible about using again, they want to get over it and dull the pain. What will make this horrible, depressing, shameful feeling go away? Well, since their brain forgot how to balance itself naturally, there is only one way. Ironically, it is to use more of their drug—the very thing that is causing all the problems.

They don't think about using every day for the next ten or twenty years. They just think about using that one time so they can say, "Ah, that's better. Now let me get through the day." So once again, they use. And once again, they feel ashamed of themselves, guilty, and weak. And again, they feel like shit, and their brain says, "How do I fix this fast? I can't take it." And again, they use.

This is the vicious cycle, and it gets worse every time it is repeated. And the longer it gets repeated, the harder it becomes to break the cycle. In fact, the issue will not even be questioned or really looked at until one realizes that this cycle is destroying their life. Recovery won't even be considered or attempted (in most cases) until they're absolutely sure that all the "relief" drugs give them is a complete illusion. There is no happiness in their lives anymore. There is no balance. Not even with the drugs. And in my opinion, a standard of happiness has to exist in our lives; otherwise, what's the point of life? An addict's mind (or soul) knows this is wrong, harmful behavior at this point—their physical brain just wants to feel normal and balanced and get through the day. Period.

## What Constitutes an Addict

When I see somebody drink an entire bottle of liquor or stay up for two or three days straight geeked out on blow and go through two 8 balls of cocaine and they say, "I'm not an addict or alcoholic, I can stop. I just don't want to. I enjoy it. I like the way it tastes, or the way it makes me feel"—first, I'll laugh because that's ridiculous. Then I'll say, "I enjoy an ice-cold Dr. Pepper now and then. I love the way it tastes. But I can't ever recall sitting down and drinking twenty-four cans of it in a night or spending $200 to $300 a day on it." Being an addict has nothing to do with liking it. It has to do with developing a strong urge to do unhealthy things over and over again and an inability to stop or admit we lost control and overdo it.

According to the Big Book of Alcoholics Anonymous (don't worry, I'm not going to be ramming AA propaganda down your throat), in the 'Doctor's Opinion' at the very beginning of the book, what constitutes an addict or an alcoholic is a physical craving and a mental obsession to use or drink. I will not try to explain it better than the Big Book of AA because the entire book explains it well. It's probably one of the best books in regard to describing an addict or alcoholic.

Basically, addiction is just that. An addiction. Addicts are sick, both mentally and physically. Honestly, I'm not big on twelve-step programs. My feelings about them are conducive to my personal situation, experiences, and feelings. Personally, they didn't help me much. But I'd never speak subversively about them. I respect them, but I'm not entirely in agreement with them.

For one, I do not believe in the concept that addiction is a disease. A disorder, yes. But not a disease. I understand addiction. I don't claim to know everything, but I know a hell of a lot about it— and I experienced it personally firsthand. Addicts have a tendency to make excuses and judge themselves harshly when things are screwed up. This is adding insult to injury, and many addicts use the disease concept as an excuse. In my opinion, it's not a disease. It's more like a loose screw that needs to be tightened or fixed in our subconscious. There's just so many screws in the brain that it takes a while to find and fix the problem. It takes persistence and inner awareness to fix it. And understand that I'm not making an implication that once it's fixed, we can use drugs again safely. I'm implying that once it's fixed, not only do we know we can't use drugs again but also we don't want to.

Diseases, in the normal sense of the word, are involuntary occurrences. Nobody plans on them, or knowingly participates in being infected with them willingly. Nobody says, "Let's go do some hepatitis," or "Let's go drink some influenza." Addiction, on the other hand? We drank or used drugs way too much and have ultimately created a serious physical and mental disorder. We screwed up. We twisted our brain up a little bit (or a lot-a-bit). Now we need to wake the hell up, detox, and start trying to fix it by understanding ourselves better. Or not. I just don't personally latch on to the idea that I have a disease.

I cannot speak for others. I can only speak for myself and about what I was feeling when I was living in active addiction. At first, I had a lot of fun. I knew it was wrong, generally, but it was fun. When I'd buy a keg of Coors Light on the weekend when I was a senior in high school, wheel it into the woods behind Shepard High School on a dolly, and proceed to throw a party in the woods at seventeen years old—yes, technically I knew it was wrong. My friend and I were all underage teenagers, trespassing in the forest preserves, and getting extremely intoxicated in public. Was it immoral? I don't think it was.

Drinking a lot, smoking pot, dropping LSD, snorting cocaine—I knew this was all wrong when I started doing these things, at least from a standpoint of them being illegal. But since I had not yet experienced the full consequences from doing these things, I was barely hesitant to do them. I didn't say to myself, "I'm going to become a full-blown junkie, drug-addicted loser and bounce in and out of jail for ten years." When it happened, though, and I began to realize deep down that I had a problem and realized I couldn't stop, I was very upset about it. The thing was, I couldn't stop. It wasn't that I didn't want to stop. I literally couldn't stop. And I couldn't explain it.

I didn't enjoy disappointing, hurting, and pissing my father off, but I continued to use. I didn't enjoy going to jail, but I continued to use. I hated that I couldn't engage in a healthy relationship with girls I dated (because either I was screwed up, or we both were), but I continued to use. I lost great jobs. I blew the opportunity to join the Sheet Metal Union at eighteen years old, then blew the opportunity to join the Plumbers Union a couple of years later, but I continued to use. I went to rehab and continued to use. I was pushing and turning my entire family and social network away from myself. It hurt, but I continued to use. So obviously, there was an apparent, deeper, more serious problem other than being a dumb kid who did drugs and got into trouble all the time, as if I enjoyed it.

Needless to say, I wasn't enjoying myself. My life was in complete disarray. The only solution I knew of that would balance me out and give me a sense of ease was to get high. Then the drugs stopped working too. I was broken by the time I was twenty-two years old.

The thing about addicts is that using drugs becomes our solution. They become our solution to everything. When we're sad, we use. When we're angry, we use. When we're depressed, down, feeling blue, we use. And when we do have a brief interval of usually fleeting happiness, it's not enough. Our girlfriend/boyfriend breaks up with us, we use. It's our birthday, or any celebration at all, we're using. It doesn't matter. If we're awake and riding the waves of life, most likely we have some chemical running through us. It sounds crazy, but the drugs literally become our fuel. At some point, using drugs became a very big part of our lives.

If you're an addict and your solution to life is to use drugs, you first have to evaluate how that's working out for you. If it's not going so well and you recognize that you have a problem, chances are you're not going to be able to just quit with the snap of your fingers. Try it. If you can, great. Try to stop using drugs completely for thirty days. Not a pill, or a snort, or a puff, or a shot – nothing. If you can, again that's great. But be honest with yourself. You don't have to announce that you're doing this to everybody you know. It's for you and you alone to learn about. Don't use any type of drug for thirty days.

Now, if you're saying, "Why? I'm fine. I don't have to quit. I could if I wanted to, but I don't want to." If that's what you're saying to yourself, let me ask you this: If you could take it or leave it, what's the big deal? If you could name one—just one—positive or healthy effect using drugs has on your life, then go ahead, use until your heart's content. If you're saying, "I'm just having fun. There's nothing wrong with that," let me ask you this: why do you *have to* use drugs to have fun? Can you not have fun without them?

If you can't stop, or you can't honestly have a good time without drugs, you may want to address that. If you think you may have a problem, it's worth learning about it early on. If you can't stay away from it, you're addicted to it.

I'm not saying that it's wrong to cut loose once in a while and have fun. Have a few drinks, shoot some pool, play the jukebox, then get a big fat burrito when the bar closes and go home with your significant other and take a roll in the sack. This is life; enjoy yourself. But trust your intuition. If you believe you might have a problem with drugs or alcohol, you have other things to worry about other than who your pool partner will be, or what you want on your burrito when the bar closes.

If you honestly try this test for yourself of remaining clean for one month and you find that you cannot do it, it's not because you are weak or that you're a bad person. It's because you have no other solution. Your main go-to solution for dealing with any emotion or your desire to have a good time is to use drugs. Like when you were a kid and learned that a cold drink of water cures your thirst. It's just what you do. It always works for you. If this is your situation, trust and believe me, it's going to stop working.

The only way to fix this problem is—well, it's not as complicated as people make it seem. It's not very mind-boggling when you become aware of it. This is how you fix it. Are you ready? Okay, here's the key to the mint: you have to find and learn another solution! It's not going to be easy—but it's as simple as that. Until you do, you'll continue to use the one you're using. And that's to get high.

And the only thing that will change is that your life will continuously get worse.

If you're an addict and have learned that you have a problem, or if you're someone who has a loved one or a friend with an addiction problem—there is a journey to endure. Reading about sobriety will not get somebody sober. All the knowledge in the world will not get somebody clean. Knowledge is what you get from reading. Wisdom is what's important. Wisdom is what we get from personal experience. Wisdom takes time to gain. But most importantly—addicts need to believe in themselves. Again, addicts need to believe in themselves. Belief in oneself is one of the most important things when somebody is trying to get clean. Finding a positive solution for ourselves takes time. But we can only discover what works for us by actual experience. Trial and error method.

I'd like to offer some suggestions to any addict reading this book, or to the family members and friends reading this book who refuse to give up on their loved one who is chemically dependent. These will only be suggestions. But hopefully, they will be suggestions that, if taken with an open mind, will ultimately lead you— or them—to a personal solution. The solution itself is for you—or them—to figure out. That's important to understand. The addict has to figure it out, and the solution has to make sense to them and invite happiness into their lives; otherwise, it won't mean much to them. Trust me, though, when it's found, a new healthy solution to life's problems, it'll be well worth the effort. It'll be priceless.

We cannot find our solution without searching for it. It took me about two to three years of battling my own false pride to admit I had a problem and realizing I had to find another solution to life. Then it took me about five good years of searching to actually find a better way that I understood and that felt right for me. Then it took me another couple of years of introspection and learning how to keep my ego under control while it made a few last attempts at keeping me sick, high, and unconscious.

During that time—from about twenty-two to thirty-two years old—I went to rehab twice and jail/prison several times. I put myself and my family through hell. I angered a lot of people. I lost jobs, cars, friends, girlfriends. I slept on couches, in cars, and lived in motel rooms. It got to the point where I literally didn't want to be alive anymore. I thought about suicide almost nightly, lying in bed thinking myself to sleep. The only thing that kept me from killing myself was the thought of hurting my family even more, mainly my sisters.

If you're an addict, you're going to have to go through some hardships on the road to recovery. Suck it up. What doesn't kill you will only make you stronger. We cannot question or change the way God has chosen to teach us the lessons He wants us to learn. Do not try. Don't resist it; it'll only cause you more problems and more grief. Learning how to spend time with my pain and confusion was essential to my recovery. Recognizing physical and mental pain is a very important tool. It's an indication that something is wrong. It made me think about and contemplate my life. We can only push our problems under the rug for so long. We have to stop postponing dealing with our problems. If we cannot be present and accept our most difficult times, we won't learn anything from them and we'll be doomed to keep repeating them. Resisting the problem creates more suffering. Accepting it will start alleviating our suffering.

Accept the fact that you're screwed up. Accept the fact that you have a lot of work to do. It's not about what life hands you, but how you respond to it that matters most. Just don't give up. Keep moving forward and making attempts at recovery, and you'll begin to learn things from your experiences that cannot be learned from listening to others or from reading books. Remember that nobody ever became who they wanted to become or beat something that was bringing them down without a fight and without falling down a bunch of times.

To gain a new skill—in this case, that skill would be finding another solution to life other than getting high, everybody—or to get better at anything in life, we have to be willing to keep moving forward in the face of fear and change. Do not give up. Be persistent. The longer you hang in there, the greater the chance that something good will happen. No matter how many times you relapse, or get into trouble, or stumble—always remember that you can do it. Believe in yourself. You have a choice, and you have a chance. Always remember that there are people out there—like myself—who won't judge you and who will help you if they can. There are people who have gone through this, beaten it, and who understand. There are people who will give you a hug—or a kick in the ass—if you need one. Use these people.

Do not underestimate yourself, or your human spirit. If there is a problem, the human spirit knows it. It really does. Learn to listen to it and give it a chance. Even if your drug-saturated brain says, "You're fine. You don't have a problem." Deep down, your spirit knows that's bullshit. Give yourself a chance. And if you screw that chance up, give yourself another chance. Just try not to run out of chances, or time. Don't take second chances for granted. They can run out. And running out of time or chances—that's truly "Rock Bottom."

If you reading this are a family member or a true friend who is trying to help an addict, please know that you cannot save them. The only way you can help them is through love and support. And when I say support, I ONLY mean emotionally. Don't support them in any other way (we'll talk about this in the next chapter). Praying for them and loving them is the only way you can help them. They're going to need a lot of love. Don't constantly remind them that they're screwed up, or that they did this or did that. Trust me, they know. They haven't forgotten about the horrible things they've done or that they're completely messed up. Constantly bringing these things up will only cause aggravation and fighting. Sometimes they just need a hug.

The transformation is a wild experience. Transcending addiction and growing into a normal, productive individual takes time and effort. Don't give up on them. You're going to cry, you're going to get pissed off, you're probably going to want to kick their ass sometimes. You may have to kick them out of the house. In fact, if that thought has already crossed your mind, you probably need to do it. It'll be a wake-up call for them and maybe exactly what they need. Don't be afraid to do it. Don't let them manipulate you into letting them stay at home—and they will. Don't put up with it (I'll explain why this is so important in the next chapter). All in all, if you really want to help your addicted loved one, it's time to realize how serious this is, learn and understand the nature of addiction, and get tough.

If you reading this are an addict, it's time to start waking up. Life is passing you by. In order to change, you have to grow and start trying to get clean. Start by accepting who you are today, no matter how incomplete and screwed up you may be. Instead of beginning sobriety with the notion that something about you is "diseased" or "incurable," look at it in this light: "I'm broken and something needs to be fixed. I'm confused and scared, but I'll figure it out. And I won't give up on myself and my family. I can do this."

Now before I make a few suggestions and tell you what I did to get clean and get my mind and life back, I'd like to address the families and friends reading this book who have a loved one in active addiction. Chances are, if they're out running the streets getting high every day, they're not reading this, you are. So this next chapter is for you all.

# CHAPTER 15

"When people seem the least lovable, that's when they need the most love." I came across this quote listening to a great Hindu Sage teaching while I was on a six-month spiritual retreat in the Himalayan Mountains in Northern India... Just kidding. I actually heard it on an episode of *Full House*. That doesn't make it any less true, though. So again, "when people seem the least lovable, that's when they need the most love."

I write this chapter as a former addict myself—somebody who has been through that lifestyle and has inside knowledge of how addicts think and feel. But I also write this chapter as somebody who has been on both sides of the fence. My mother is a recovering addict. I've witnessed her crash and burn many times. I'm not going to name any others, but there are people in my life whom I love dearly that have gone through substance abuse. So I know how it feels to try and help or change someone who is destroying themselves—someone you love and care about—and not being able to. I truly understand that feeling of helplessness, confusion, and anger. I know how it feels to be lied to, let down, manipulated, taken for granted, and stolen from. I've put all my faith and hope that they will pull through, get their lives back on track, and regain the glow in their face, and it never happens. Or if it does happen, a short time later they start using again. I mention this because I don't want my readers to think to themselves, "Yeah, this guy knows all about getting high, being an addict, and acting like an asshole, but he doesn't know how it is to watch somebody you love slowly killing themselves." I do know. I know exactly how you feel.

So with that being said, I'd like to offer some insight that I believe will be beneficial to my readers. Again, I don't know everything; I still have a lot to learn about all this. I'm only thirty-five years old as I write this sentence. I still have a long life ahead of me. I just want to offer some assistance—my only aim is to help. That's what this book is about—helping addicts to wake up, and at the same time helping their families who have no idea what's happening to their child or loved one.

During my using days, I walked all over a lot of people. Not because I was an inherently selfish person or because I didn't care about others' feelings—it was because it eventually got to the point where getting my next fix took precedence over everything in my life, including my morals. I was like a tornado in my family's lives. So, the only thing I could think of now to give back and contribute to this sociological problem is to try and alleviate the suffering addicts are causing to themselves and to their families.

## The Three Stages

There are many types of addictions: gambling addictions, sex addictions, eating disorders, etc. All addictions are very similar in nature regarding their effect on our reward circuit. It doesn't matter what one is addicted to. What matters is that it has become their solution to feeling good, and it's screwing up their life. But I'm only going to write in relation to chemical dependency. Even though all addictions are unhealthy, drug addiction is a little more severe because addicts are actually ingesting chemicals into their bodies, not just playing poker or watching porn. In my eyes, there are only three stages of drug addiction.

The first stage is pretty common. The individual is in high school or maybe junior high, and they start hanging out at the neighborhood parks, going to little house parties, social gatherings, etc. Their social network is widening. They're at the age where Mom and Dad aren't "cool" anymore. They start noticing the opposite sex (and realizing that cooties aren't real). They start going to parties at the houses of vacationing parents. Along the way, they're drinking alcohol and smoking pot on the weekends. They start indulging in the "gateway drugs." They're just being teenagers and having fun.

Which is fine. They should be having fun. I'm not advocating drug and alcohol use or saying that they should be getting high and drunk when they go out with their friends, but often that's what they do. Not all teenagers do this, but a lot of them do. And they'll party a little bit, go wild for a few years after high school, and eventually snap out of it and take care of their responsibilities in a sober manner. But we're talking about the potential addict here.

At this stage, you can't really recognize that there may be a serious problem slowly evolving. To the parents, and to them, they're just going through a stage, and nobody believes that they really are developing a drug problem. Unfortunately, for those with an addictive compulsive nature, this stage is going to be harder for them to emerge from unscathed. They're not going through "a stage." They're going through "the first stage." This is a stage with a very fine line. They're either going to grow out of it, or their indulgence in drugs is going to progress.

The second stage is when they choose to indulge in substances even more. Maybe they've changed a lot over the last year. Their attitude, their conduct, the people they hang out with. The subject that they're drinking a lot or smoking a lot of pot, or maybe you've found pills or empty baggies in their rooms, their grades are slipping, or they just aren't the same anymore may have come up as a topic of discussion between yourself and them. Of course, everybody changes, but the changes you notice are different. You intuitively know—even if you don't want to believe it—that your loved one is messing up, doing drugs or drinking to excess, and living unhealthily or heading in a bad direction. Their drug use is starting to surface. They're still not honest with you about it, but you know they're getting high on something. Something other than smoking a little pot. They're sleeping late all the time. They're losing interest in school, or sports, things like that. Maybe they're never home anymore. And when they are, they stay in their bedroom or in the basement, secluding themselves from everyone. Red flag!

At this point, they're most likely using drugs other than pot. And more than likely, they've developed the type of mindset where they want to be high or buzzed for any activity they involve themselves in. Stage two can last a while. Some may stay in this stage for a few years. Some can move onto stage three a lot faster depending on their character and what drugs they're doing. If cocaine is involved, especially crack cocaine, it'll progress fast. If it's heroin, it'll progress extremely fast. Unfortunately, if they have reached this stage, there's a high probability that they're going to hit stage three at some point in the near future. They've become addicted, and most addicts at this stage lack the willpower to just quit without some type of intervention.

The final stage—stage 3—is the most progressive stage that ends in chronic addiction. This stage usually takes a while to reach, perhaps a year or so. Drug addiction is a progressive disorder. Nobody starts shooting heroin or smoking crack right away. As I said before, some may stay in stage 2 for a couple of years. Everybody is different. Once they reach stage three, however, you'll know it.

First of all, the fact that they're using hard drugs is out in the open. The family knows it, and they know that you all know it. They also don't deny it anymore. They still lie about their using but only because they're embarrassed about it, they don't want to talk about it, and they'll lash out and try their best to deflect the conversation every time you bring it up. They are well aware that they have a problem, though. Chances are they've tried to quit and found they cannot. They always use "one more time." They still lie about it because they refuse to accept the fact that they've lost control and their willpower is not functioning.

You can compare this mindset to a baseball player. Even if they're down by ten runs, it's the bottom of the ninth inning, and they only have three more outs to get eleven runs for the win. But the bottom of their lineup is up—their seven, eight, and nine hitters. They're pretty sure they're going to lose. Plus, the other team just put their closer on the mound, and he's throwing a ninety-eight-mile-an-hour fastball. But your team doesn't just say, "Okay, we're beat. No point in finishing the game." No matter what the score is, a ballgame will always go to the end. Admitting defeat is a major blow to the human ego. Nobody wants to lose—or admit that they've been beaten. That only happens when the game is over. It's the same with addiction. An addict will keep trying to control their drug use until they're totally beaten. It's human nature. Stubborn, stubborn, human ego.

My father used to ask me, "How are you?" He'd say, "You're still using. I can tell you're high right now. Stop lying to me! I'm not stupid." I wouldn't say to him, "I'm screwed up, Pop. I'm weak and pitiful, and I can't stop. I hate myself." No, no, no! Instead, I'd say, "I'm fine, okay? I'm not high, I'm tired. Stop staring at my eyes! God, you're always on my case." Then I'd proceed to get into an argument with him—on purpose. This way, I could feel justified when I stormed out of the house, which I wanted to do, anyway.

As their drug use progresses, you'll start noticing more significant changes. Weight loss, appetite loss, acne, mood swings, irritability. They're never smiling anymore. Your beautiful daughter used to spend an hour getting ready to leave the house, even if she was just running to the store. Makeup, hair, the whole nine yards. But lately, she just throws her hair up in a ponytail, splashes some water on her face, and within fifteen minutes of waking up, she's running out the door. This is how drug addicts act. They're gone all day, and when they come home, the gas tank is completely empty, and there's 150 miles added to the mileage on the family car. You ask them where they've been all day, or why they haven't returned your calls, and they roll their eyes or come up with some chaotic story. You know they're lying about where they've been, and you wonder why. They're lying because they don't want you to know what they were actually out doing. People who have nothing to hide don't lie. Period.

Eventually, they may start experiencing some legal problems. Maybe DUI, drug paraphernalia, or drug-possession charges, or petty theft. If they manage to hold onto a job, their paycheck is gone in a day or two after getting it. When you show concern or question this, they get upset. Maybe you've noticed money missing out of your wallet or purse. Or the change jar in your bedroom is getting lower and lower even though you throw your change in it every day. When you bring up their drug use and try to discuss it with them, they get upset, argue, rationalize, and leave—or they just shut down, stay silent, or try to brush it off and change the subject.

It will get to the point where they just don't care who knows that they use hard drugs every day. They cease putting effort and energy into hiding it. They do this because there is no energy left to hide it. All their energy and efforts are focused on and centered around one thing: balance. And by now, they only have one way to get balanced and feel okay. And that is to use "one more time." It's become their only solution. Their lives are spinning out of control, and no matter what you say or do, they just don't stop using. They continue to get high, and it gets worse and worse and worse.

The sad thing is, and I'm sure the hardest thing to accept as a parent, is that it's up to them and only them how long they stay in stage 3. There is no other stage. They're either going to continue to use drugs and things will continue to get worse, or they're going to get clean. You have no control over what they choose to do, or when they decide to do it. They alone can change their course. Not their family, their parents, their better half or significant other, not their pastor or church, not the court system, not jail or rehab. They and they alone have the power to change and fight for their sobriety.

Commonly, they will try every way imaginable to live a normal life without giving up their drug or drugs of choice. Giving up their drug is frightening. It's all they have to feel good and normal. And without it, they feel not only physically weak and sick but also emotionally and mentally exhausted. Giving it up is stepping into the unknown. They will avoid and resist that change completely. Eventually, they will try everything to keep living their lives without taking the drugs out of the equation, and everything they try will be exhausted to failure. This will be the turning point—hopefully—because they will realize that getting clean is the only option left. This is the "gift of desperation" I spoke of. And by this time, believe me, they want to be clean more than you can possibly imagine.

Patience is key on your part. It could take them a while before they really start to realize how bad their situation is, realize that it's only getting worse, and start making attempts to get their lives and minds back. They may get high for years before they make a whole-hearted decision to try and change. They may go to rehab two or three times, jail or prison a couple of times. I believe, statistically, it takes an addict five to seven times, either going through some type of rehab program or doing a jail term, usually a combination of both, before they quit for good. Maybe they'll end up in a hospital once or twice for some reason related to their drug use. You'll have to remain patient and hopeful. Learn to be extremely patient. Hopefully none of what I just mentioned will happen, although prepare yourself for it. Even after making the decision to get clean, the road to recovery begins, and that can be just as bumpy.

They may continue to use drugs. They may go to rehab or jail, get out, and a week after getting out they get high—breaking the promises they made to you that they wouldn't use again. Understand that they're not breaking their promises because they want to hurt you or because they didn't mean all the good promises they made while they were clean. They're sick. They literally do not know how to not use. Recovery is a growing process, and it takes time. They have to learn what works for them, while breaking the habit of what they've been doing for years, and they have to do this while usually feeling depressed, aggravated, and tired all the time. And until they find what works for them (that new solution) and learn how to be happy again, they're going to slip up. The important thing is that they're trying. They're on the long and bumpy road to recovery.

Yes, it is true that you can't change them or force them to get clean. But taking a passive approach won't help. I'm not saying to just sit back and watch them destroy themselves. There is action you can take that will help. First, you must truly and completely understand that they're not doing drugs and using them so recklessly because they're stupid or that they don't care or that they can just simply stop if they wanted to. They're doing drugs because they're addicted to them, and they keep doing them despite all the problems they're well aware of that are happening because they just can't stop.

The most important positive thing you can do is to take a communicative approach with them. Learn to open up healthy dialogue about it with them so they feel they can talk about it with you without being judged too harshly. When you yell at them about it, or tell them how upset you are with them, they're simply not going to be comfortable talking to you about it. And they won't.

What will help them get motivated to seek help is that you continuously remind them that you love them and that they're important and that they're part of the family. You don't have to always talk about their drug use and messed-up lifestyle. I'm sure there are other things you can talk about. Talk about happier times when they were clean. Once in a while, just walk up to them, wrap your arms around them and squeeze. Don't say anything other than "I just want you to know that I love you." Period.

Maybe you can go to your local bookstore and purchase a book on chemical dependency and substance abuse. Give it to them without commentary. Just say, "Here, I came across this and thought you might like to read it." They will eventually read it or flip through it. It may accumulate some dust first, but they'll come across it at the right time. And they'll appreciate the gesture more than you know. These are the things that helped me. It showed me that my family missed me, loved me, and that life was going on without me. It made me realize that I was really missing out on life, and it provoked positive thoughts for me.

Sometimes my father and I would go get some pizza together at Rosie's. He knew I was all screwed up; I knew he knew. But he wouldn't hound me about getting clean because he knew yelling at me about it wasn't going to make me stop, and that if he did, I'd get defensive and probably get up and leave. Talking about shooting heroin is not a normal conversation to have between a father and son. My dad knew that my life and mental state was enough stress for me to take without having to talk about it too every time we had a conversation. Sometimes I just needed a slice of normalcy. To know that there was a normal life waiting for me if I decided to fight to get clean. So we'd sit there and share a pizza and enjoy each other's company and talk about sports or work.

Or my cousin Johnny—whom I love with all my heart—would call me up or come by the house and say, "What's up, homie? Just thought I'd see if you wanted to go to an AA meeting with me, then maybe grab some coffee and bullshit for a bit." These were the times when I'd say to myself, "Man, I have to stop this shit and get my life back on track. I have to stop disappointing all these good people."

Instead of people telling me I had to get clean, it forced me to mentally acknowledge to myself that I had to get clean. And it meant so much more to me when that acknowledgment came from within myself.

Constantly remind your loved one that they are part of the family and that the family isn't complete without them. Chances are they're not going to be able to quit using immediately. But when they fall, or when they're really down and having a hard time, they will be more comfortable asking for help because they know their family is not going to have an "I told you so" attitude or shun them. They'll be a lot more susceptible to going to treatment. There's nothing worse than being lost and needing help and being too uncomfortable to ask or talk to your family about it.

These little gestures of love and compassion you show them are what's going to help them realize the status of what their lives have become, and what they're missing out on. It's going to help them fight to get clean. Think of it like this: if an addict's entire family has turned their back on them (even though it's probably because of their own actions), they have no friends, no life, no happiness, no love, or nothing to fight for—what's the point of getting clean? Why? For what? Now as a clearheaded, logical-thinking man, I realize that what I just wrote is complete nonsense—but that's how addicts think. They're not clearheaded, logical-thinking people. Their brains simply say, "Screw it. I'm getting high." And that's why it's important to keep reminding them that they're loved and needed and part of the family. And no, I'm not saying to let them do whatever they want and to never bring up the fact that they're screwed up. I'm not saying to allow them to lie to you, use you, or walk all over you. All I'm saying is to let them know in subtle ways that you love and miss them—in between the inevitable fights and arguments.

If they're stealing from your wallet or purse, or electronics start coming up missing, or there are young ones in the home, you may have to kick them out of the house. This is a touchy subject that comes up a lot with addicts and their families. Almost every addict I've ever known, including myself, has been kicked out of the house. So let's talk about this.

I can imagine that this could be a very hard thing to do. I've never had to kick a family member out of my house. But I have been kicked out, and I understand how that feels. It felt horrible. However, in retrospect, that's exactly what I needed to feel to open my eyes up a little bit more. To tell your own flesh and blood that they can no longer live at home must suck. But sometimes it comes down to that when dealing with an addict, and is necessary. When the health, safety, and well-being of the rest of the family is at stake, you shouldn't hesitate to tell them they have to leave.

They may cry, fight, tell you they hate you. Whatever. Don't take it personally. They don't hate you. They don't mean the hurtful things they say. They're sick. And in the end, they'll get over it and they'll understand why you did it. Tell them you love them, but as long as they continue to use drugs, they can't live at home. It'll be a major wake-up call for them. At first reaction, they'll say something like, "Screw you, I hate you, you'll never see me again," and storm out. When they're gone, sitting somewhere by themselves, that's when they'll think to themselves, "What the hell is wrong with me? I have to get myself together."

Believe me, my father did it to me. And I can't tell you how many drug addicts I've sat with who had just been kicked out of their house. Not one of them ever sat there bashing their family. It was more like, "I'm messed up, Mikey, what am I going to do? I should just go to rehab." When it happened to me, it made me realize how bad things were getting. As long as I was living in my father's house—I had a roof over my head, food to eat, a bed to sleep in, a TV to watch, no bills, no responsibilities—it enabled me to focus on getting high and nothing else.

When he kicked me out, I finally had something to think about other than my next fix. I've heard many people say, "I'm afraid that if I kick them out of the house, something bad will happen to them, or I'll never see them again." Let me say this, and I can't be more real with you; if they continue to live in the house and are allowed to focus on nothing other than getting high, that day may come a lot faster when you'll never be able to see them again. Many drug overdoses happen to young men and women who live at home. They're found dead, locked in their bedroom. They had nothing to do or worry about other than spending all their time, energy, and money on getting and using drugs. They didn't have to worry about shelter or food. They had no bills to pay. No responsibilities. And all their motivation revolved around getting more dope.

When drug addicts have everything taken care of for them, they tend to have worse habits. If you have the notion that letting them stay at home because you're scared something bad will happen to them is helping them—it's not. I'm not trying to sound like a jerk. I understand your motives. I'm just being real. They can harm themselves a lot easier in the comfort of their own homes. Not only do they have more time and money on their hands, but they also have no significant reason to change, living at home. And if you kick them out and something bad does happen, that something just might be the thing that opens their eyes.

Mothers, fathers, and family members can get so wrapped up in dealing with a loved one with a substance abuse problem that they often sacrifice their own well-being. Remember that it's unhealthy for you to allow someone to use you as a doormat. Unfortunately, addicts treat people like this. They walk over everybody in their lives. They're unconscious, and deep down they don't mean to be so cruel. It's the nature of addiction to be destructive. Getting one more fix has become their ultimate everyday priority, and nobody is going to stand in their way of achieving that. It's sad, but it's true.

Do not let them manipulate you. Don't let them think they're getting over on you. If an addict's mouth is moving, most likely they're lying. If you know they're lying, tell them, "I know you're lying." Don't let them bullshit you. And if they're disrupting the entire household so badly where you have to kick them out, don't worry about all the stuff they say when you do. "I hate you! You'll never see me again! I'm going to be sleeping in the streets! Blah, blah, blah."

Listen, they don't hate you. You'll see them again. And if they have to sleep on a park bench, that's their fault—not yours. Maybe they need to feel that pain. They need to understand that this is what happens when they use drugs, that they'll end up on a park bench.

Believe me, they're only saying all those horrible things because they don't want to deal with their problem. What they want (I should say what their drug-saturated brain wants) is for you to take care of everything so they can lay in the basement with no responsibilities and get high all day. If you allow that to happen, you're hurting them more than you're helping them. In fact, all that's doing is hurting them. It's not helping them at all. Not one bit. And someday when they get their head out of their ass, they'll apologize for all those mean things they said.

Do not give them money—ever! If they are using drugs and ask you for money for such and such a reason (I know, the stories us addicts spin can get pretty elaborate and insanely amusing sometimes), there's a 99.89 percent chance that the money you give them will be spent on drugs within thirty minutes of giving it to them. The stories are sometimes so elaborate, in fact, that they're actually believable. You think to yourself, "Wow! There's no way they're making that up" They are. They probably made it up four minutes before they told you. If you're willing to take that chance and hope they're telling you the truth about needing $50 because "Cindy is sick and needs to get her prescription from the pharmacy, but her family is out of town, and she lost her wallet, so she can't get money from the bank or ATM because her ID and ATM card was in her wallet. She really needs her medicine, and she promises she'll pay you back when she gets her paycheck in two days,"—well, if you're willing to play the odds that they're being truthful, you should probably stay away from Las Vegas. No matter how believable their story sounds or how bad you want to believe them, chances are they're lying. Do not let them lie to you, and do not give them money.

There will be times when you pity them and feel so bad, or you just don't want to deal with them, and you break down and give them $20 to $40. Understandable. But don't let them drain your checking account, though. They may squeeze a few bucks out of you every once in a while. But if you don't draw the line sometime, they're only going to ask more often, and it'll get harder on you emotionally to say no. Stand your ground.

Because there is so much emotion—love, care, disappointment, anger, sadness, confusion—involved in dealing with somebody who is addicted to drugs, it can get very stressful and can mentally drain you completely. There is no perfect way to deal with this. This book I wrote is not "the way," but I believe it will help you understand the situation more, and maybe help you deal with it better and prepare you for things you may have not fully understood—that's why I wrote it. But dealing with your child, loved one, or friend can only be perfected by you. You know them better than anybody. What I think is right might not seem right to you. My suggestions may not appeal to your nature. Maybe you've been through as much as you can take to even want to try anymore. If that's the case, may God give you the peace you need.

But if you refuse to give up on them, like my father refused to give up on his son and daughter, I salute and applaud you. If this is the case, I have a suggestion to offer you: as soon as you put this book down, go find them. No matter where they are—the basement, their room, a friend's house, a motel, etc.—and no matter what time it is, go to them, walk right up to them, put your hands on their shoulders, look them straight in the eyes and say, "I love you. I love you, and I miss you, and I'll never give up on you." Then give them a big hug. A big long bear hug. Forget about all the bullshit they've put you through. Forget about the money they stole, or the embarrassment they caused you, or the mean things they've said. Just for a moment, put all of that aside and give them a hug and some love. Don't put it off until tomorrow. Even if it's 2:00 a.m., go do it right now. If they're in jail or rehab, write a letter or plan a visit. But express your love to them as soon as you possibly can. If you've already done this, do it again, and again. And do it every day if you have to. It won't change them immediately, but it's a powerful start and it may open up a good conversation. It will have a positive effect on them—trust me.

So go ahead. Put this book down and go to them right now. Give them a big hug and tell them how much you love them. After that, tell them to read this book. I have some things I'd like to say to them in the following chapters.

# CHAPTER 16

To my readers who are addicts and still actively using drugs, I'd like to ask you a few quick questions. Now, obviously, we've never met. I'm just a guy who wrote a book that you're reading. I'm not some snobby famous rich person whom you couldn't relate to, who has some magical ability that allowed me to write this book. I'm just a regular, down-to-earth, normal everyday dude. I live in a regular little house on the South Side of Chicago. I drive a regular car, and I start speeding when a good song comes on the radio. I order from the dollar menu at McDonald's, and I get my coffee from Dunkin' Donuts. I have horrible spending habits, and I still watch *Family Guy*. I'm not special, and there's nothing extraordinary about me. I'm probably not much different than you are.

So here are my questions to you: after reading my story, do you believe that I've been through all this shit, have a lot of insight about it, and understand exactly what you're feeling and going through? Do you believe that I would never tell you to do anything that would hurt you or make your situation worse? Do you believe that your best interest was in my heart when I wrote this book? If you've answered yes to those questions, please believe what I'm about to tell you. Don't think about it. Don't allow your screwed-up brain to muffle your intuition and your heart. Just trust me, please, you have to go to detox and treatment. You have to.

I know, I know…you have work and can't lose your job. You have to pay your car payment. You can't lose your apartment. Your boyfriend/girlfriend needs you. You can quit on your own. You don't need treatment or help. Blah, blah blah, blah blah, blah blah! Come on, stop it. You know damn well with all your heart and soul that that's bullshit, and that your life is more important than your job, your car, or your apartment, or any other rationalization you make for not going to rehab. You also know damn well that if you get your shit together and start becoming the person you really are and living up to your potential, you'll get a better job, a nicer car, and a better place to live, and you won't be giving all your money to drug dealers. You'll be better, healthier, and more happy. You know I'm right! I'm not some person in your life who is going to buy that shit that you can't go get your life back on track and, in turn, stop using drugs because of some job, or boyfriend or girlfriend. I can poke a thousand holes into that logic that anything is more important than you getting clean.

Come on now. You've read my story and know me intimately. It's me—Mikey Seminetta. Let's be honest here. You know that you can't keep living like this. You know that you have to go to detox and treatment. And I know, and fully understand, why you don't want to go. And we both know that it has nothing to do with a job, or a car, or a fucking apartment. If you truly believe that all those replaceable things in your life are more important than yourself—you're wrong.

Usually, when a person goes to a rehabilitation center, they're required to go through a three to six-day detox before they can even start the rehab program. If you're serious about getting clean, this is a must. You have to first stop getting high and detoxify your brain. Until you do, you're not going to be able to think rationally or make any other healthy decisions. This is the tricky part for addicts. Their brain being saturated with drugs is exactly why they keep using them and procrastinating getting clean. Believe me, I know how it feels to know that your only solution to life—the only thing that gives you some "relief"—is not going to be available anymore. It's almost equivalent to being told you can't breathe anymore. There's a reason it's called drug dependency. It's because we're completely dependent on drugs. That's why going to rehab is such a hard decision to make. It's not so much that we don't want to go, or because of some bullshit responsibility we tell ourselves we just can't neglect, it's that we don't want to not be able to use our drug. We know if we go, we can't use. And that's terrifying.

People have just stopped on their own due to some very rare circumstances, but it's very, very unlikely. You're going to need some help. So be brave. For once in your life, take a chance—for yourself. You can't tell me that after all the hard times and suffering I'm sure you've gone through over the years, you can't handle detox. Suck it up. Yes, there are mental and physical reasons we keep using drugs, clinically speaking. But in layman's terms—the reason us addicts resist detox so much is because we act like a bunch of freaking babies when we're on drugs. I was that way. "Oh, I can't do it. I'll be sick. I'm helpless. Waaah." Think about a child lying in a hospital bed dying of stage four cancer. What do you think they would say if an addict said to them, "I can't go to treatment. I'll be sick. I'm just going to keep destroying my life. I'm helpless." They'd call us ridiculous, probably tell us to get the hell out of their room.

Pick up a phone, call a rehab center, and make an appointment. Don't be afraid to step into the unknown. Go to rehab, you silly goose...or don't. Keep getting high. Keep lying to everybody you love and who love you. Keep telling them you're clean when you're not. Believe me, you're only lying to yourself. And you'll continue to be miserable. Like I said, this is all up to you. Life isn't going to pause itself for another year, or ten years, until you decide to get clean. For real. Life is going to keep on keeping on—with you or without you. It'll be nicer for yourself and your family if you're around.

When you're out there in active addiction, getting high every day, you're not only wasting your life, but you're also robbing the rest of humanity of your potential. Who knows, if you get clean and get your head out of your ass and start doing what you were put on this earth for, you may be somebody who changes the world for the better. Maybe you'll invent something important, or come up with a cure for something, or write a book—maybe save some lives. Your purpose is not to get high and make drug dealers rich. You have a real important purpose. We all do. It's time you figure it out and start living your life. Again, don't think about it. Just do it. Just say, "You know what? I'm going to trust this Mikey Seminetta. I'm going to rehab." Then pick up a phone. Put a smile on your family's face for a change.

Have you ever seen a puddle or a small body of water where you can clearly see the reflection of the sun as if you were looking in a mirror? Say you take your foot and disturb the puddle or throw a stone and cause ripples. What happens to the sun? Does it disappear? Or is it just clouded by the mud being stirred up, or from the ripples? Just because you can't clearly see the sun anymore doesn't mean it's not there. It's the same thing with substances. Your inner light and desire for happiness are there—it's just fogged by the drugs. No matter how strong the urge to see the light clearly is, it'll never be possible as long as it's clouded and fogged up.

So let's say you go to a twenty-eight-day or ninety-day rehab program, or got locked up for a few months and did a treatment program in jail. That's great—but don't get complacent. You're not "cured." After you've been cleaned out for a month or so, either from jail or rehab, as soon as you get back out into the real world again, it's all about those first few days. Most addicts develop an attitude or mindset where we need immediate gratification. If an addict doesn't feel happy or "normal" in the first few days, our minds tend to go into what's called the "fuck-it" stage. After a few days of boredom with no feelings of purpose or happiness, or feeling overwhelmed, we quickly start looking for it in familiar ways. And we find it in using drugs. Addicts do this because they need to feel something good so bad, and this is still the fastest way to feel something. They do not yet know how to just be happy and comfortable in their own skin. That's why so many people relapse hundreds of times while trying to get clean.

If you did make it through a rehab program and paid attention while you were there, you know a little bit about how to begin and what to do. Honestly, I didn't learn much when I went to rehab. I went once and stayed for five days of detox and twenty-eight days of rehab, and my only focus was hooking up with these two girls, Nicky and Tammy. I didn't pay attention because I didn't go for myself. At the time, I thought I could still control it myself. I went to appease my father. But I did learn some things about programming and what it basically entails. Unfortunately for me, my path didn't include a bunch of rehab retreats. My path included a bunch of jail/prison stints. To each his/her own, I guess.

The important thing is that you've become aware of what recovery is and of all the programs that will be there with open arms when you become willing and honest enough with yourself and decide to use these tools. AA, CA, NA, fellowship clubs, volunteer work, church, praying, meditating, family, clean and sober friends. These are all things to get involved in and back in touch with. The major thing is that you avoid toxic people and activities. One thing I believe in wholeheartedly is that individuals become like the people they hang out with. We're only as good as the company we keep. I wish I would've learned this a long time ago before I continued to reach out to or to let certain people back into my life.

Until you reach the point in your self-development where you no longer allow other people to influence your behavior or affect you with their negativity, and manipulate you into thinking they care for you, you need to stay away from them. I can't stress this enough or be more real than this for those trying to stay clean: Fuck being nice and friendly. You're trying to get your life back before you burn every last bridge, end up in prison, or dead. Don't get distracted because your so-called "friends" want to see you, or because she looks cute, or because you're lonely. Don't associate with the same people you associated with while you were using. And if they keep trying to slip back into your life, tell them to fuck off.

I understand that some of these people you've used drugs with are not all bad people. Maybe it's an ex-boyfriend/girlfriend or a couple of your really good friends who happen to be drug addicts also. Just because they are still using doesn't make them bad people, and I'm not implying that we who happen to be clean should ever judge them or think we're better than them. If anything, we should stay clean and become better versions of ourselves and lead by example— show them a better way if we truly care about them. But we can never do that if we keep backpedaling. All I'm saying is that in the beginning, you're better off spending time alone than spending time with people who are going to hold you back, influence your action, and bring you down with their toxic mentality and screwed-up standards, even if they don't mean to. You need to make a conscious effort to surround yourself with positive, uplifting people. People who believe in you, encourage you, and who bring out the best in you. That is what true friends do.

I wasted years caring about, trying to be nice to, and loving a certain girl who could care less about me. All because I was lonely, and because I was never looking out for myself and putting the effort into my own life that I should've been. I spent a lot of time and money trying to make others happy when I was myself miserable. And none of these "friends" could give a shit. All they cared about is what they could get. And when the well was dry, or I was down and out, or locked up—they were nowhere to be found. The ones I took for granted—my family—they were the only ones there for me. So, if you ever find yourself in a situation where a certain person in your life just takes and takes and never gives, stop wasting your time.

I just do not hang out with people that bring out the bad in me. Period. If they mirror selfishness in any way or are not on the same path I'm on, I stay away from them. I only hang out with people who are happy, growing, and want to learn and succeed in life. And that makes a giant impact on my life. Birds of a feather, right?

Please don't allow my personal feelings to influence your view, unless they seem right to you. But because I'm being completely honest throughout this book, I must say that I'm not a big fan of twelve-step programs. I was involved in AA on and off for a decade. It didn't keep me clean. And yes, I tried. I'm not one of those people who went a handful of times and said, "I tried, it doesn't work." If I were to say this to a die-hard AA member, they'd probably say, "Well, you didn't try hard enough." I can recite about 75 percent of the Big Book from memory. I read it literally over twenty times through and through. I've worked the steps. In fact, that's how this book came to be. It started off as my fourth step—"We made a searching and honest moral inventory of ourselves." I've gone to tons of meetings. I've emptied ashtrays, made coffee. I didn't become a serious member because, well, because I just didn't. It never really helped me. But it seems to help others, and that's great. What works for you is what's important.

I respect AA and twelve-step programs. But personally, I needed something else. From my experience, the majority of members who were in fact clean were older men and women who had spent twenty to thirty years drinking and drugging. Personally, I think their sobriety is more so a result of personal experiences and life lessons learned from using drugs and alcohol for half their lives—not specifically because of a twelve-step program.

Again, I'm only speaking on my own feelings, and I do not want to offend anybody. There are things about twelve-step programs that I don't agree with. For instance, I do not believe in the second step. Now, the second step is, "We came to believe that a power greater than ourselves could restore us to sanity." Let me be clear; I'm not saying that I don't believe in God, or that I don't believe that God could restore us in any way. I just don't believe that that fact has anything to do with me getting clean.

I think a lot of, or I'd say most of the AA members that I've known have identified themselves by some denomination of Christianity: Catholic, Baptist, Protestant, etc. But this is only based on my geography. Obviously, there are members of all religions, but for me, this has been my experience. The thing I find interesting is that if you really dig for the true meanings of what Jesus taught, he taught that all his power and insight and salvation lies within us all equally. I'm not a devout believer in the dogmatic rules and teachings of any religion, but I do believe in the basic lessons and righteousness taught by all religions. In the Bible, it says that God created man in his image. So for those who are devout believers, I believe that means that we are a reflection of God. *God* is consciousness. I believe in the human spirit—in *God*—which in essence is everyone, including you. God is within us all. We're one and the same.

In my personal view, when people pray *to* God, I believe they are separating themselves from the essence of God. Saying that you are praying *to* God implies that you are here and God is over there or in heaven, and you're praying to him. I believe that God is not outside ourselves. When people say, "God is inside us all," that doesn't mean he's sitting on our hearts just chilling out. I believe that means that God is within us in a sense that, once we fully wake up and become enlightened (as the Buddha put it) or enter into salvation (as Jesus put it), we'll realize that we're one and the same, essentially. There is no separation. There is no us and God. There is only God. People like the Buddha and Jesus realized this. Most of us have not—yet—fully realized this, myself included. I still struggle with attachments and my own ego. I'm still in this world and of this world.

I hated sitting in meetings and hearing people say, "My higher power, whom I choose to call Jesus, keeps me sober." In my opinion, that's just not how it goes. If you believe in biblical text, God let his only son be crucified on the cross to fulfill prophecy. The night before in the Garden of Gethsemane after the Last Supper, Jesus went off alone to pray. He knew what he was about to go through, and he asked God to "let this cup pass from me." God did not stop it. That was Jesus's path. His destiny to salvation. So God is not going to get us off drugs. God wants us to get sober and clean and be happy and help others, but God's not going to do that for us. God wants us to evolve and grow and learn the lessons of life on our own. That's how we discover the true meanings of our struggles.

Think about this: if God is all-powerful, then he obviously allowed us to become addicted to drugs in the first place from our own free will. So because we chose that path, that's how we're going to learn our lessons—hopefully. If we're on that path of self-destruction and God wants to teach us valuable lessons in life, why would he just take all the pain away because we prayed for him to? To me, that doesn't make sense. God wouldn't have allowed us to become screwed up in the first place. This is all happening to us for a reason.

All I'm trying to say is this—if you've been clean for some time, you got your relationships back in order and amended, you established a nice home again, and you've learned how to be happy without using or drinking, you made that happen! Not *God*. God may have been cheering you on the entire time, but you did it. I hated sitting in those meetings watching everybody undermine their own inner strength and power (given to them by God) with this talk of a higher power being responsible for their success, calling themselves "powerless." "I'm powerless over my addiction," they'd say. I'd think to myself, *Okay, then why the hell are you here? If you're clean and sober, obviously you're not powerless.* Nobody is powerless. Jesus, one of the greatest spiritual masters of all time, taught that himself. It's just that oftentimes "we have eyes but do not see."

Instead of acknowledging to themselves that they had the power within themselves to beat their addiction themselves, they'd give the credit to their higher power. I understand we have to be rid of selfishness and all of that. But it's not selfish to admit to yourself that you have the power to overcome anything you put your heart and mind to. So if you want to give the glory to your higher power, great. But give yourself the credit. I believe that when a twelve-step member is giving all the credit to their higher power, thinking that they—in and of themselves—cannot stay clean, at the same time God, Jesus, Buddha, or whomever are sitting in heaven, or in the astral planes saying, "Great job! I knew you could do it," I believe that when we overcome our trials and tribulations and learn the lessons along the way ourselves, that's what makes God happy.

Personally, I think that experience is what gets people clean, not sitting in meetings reading and talking. Just please understand that these are my own feelings. I'm in no way trying to influence anybody's beliefs or say that I'm right and they're wrong. Not at all. I'm simply telling my readers how I feel. Twelve-step programs are a great beginning or introduction to sober living. I believe they are a powerful force. I just don't believe in many of their root concepts. It works, though. I've seen it work for others. If you're an addict and want to find a better way of life, please try out a twelve-step program, whatever it may be, and stick with it if you feel you should. It will start to work eventually because it is an introduction into living a spiritual life. And once that lifestyle takes hold, the road ahead naturally gets better. That's why twelve-step programs are great.

It teaches you how to get in touch with yourself and the human race again. It'll point you in the direction of enlightenment, or salvation, or nonsuffering if you work hard at correcting your attitude and flaws. You'll learn how to interact with sober people, accept help for yourself, be humble, and help others. You'll learn how a simple hug could brighten up someone's day—or yours.

One of the things I learned in AA was that if something isn't working, then you have to move on to the next thing. The next thing for me had nothing to do with "programming" or twelve steps or going to meetings. I still enjoy going to a meeting every once in a while. I listen and I learn—and keep my mouth shut as much as possible! These AA guys are pretty hard-core. They'd kick my ass if I said any of this in a meeting! Just kidding. AA, honestly, for the ones who are serious about getting and staying clean, they're a great bunch of men and women. They really are. Awesome people.

When I do go now and then, it's usually with my cousin Johnny, and we'll go have some coffee afterward or just drive around and chew the fat. I don't go much, but when I do, I enjoy it. I respect the program. But for me, personally, if I depended on meetings and prayer and a higher power to keep me clean, I'd be loaded right now. I've learned through my experience that nothing, absolutely nothing outside myself would keep me clean. I had to turn inward.

## Jumping on the Wagon

Stopping using drugs is hard. However, staying stopped is the real challenge. For me, I needed a very strong spiritual foundation to begin my recovery and growth because I felt disconnected from everybody and everything. I'm not talking about religion. I'm talking about spirituality. Now I don't want to sound like a flake, like some holy roller preacher, but it is important in recovery. Spirituality is personal and can only be understood in our own individual authentic way. It's a matter of self-discovery rather than becoming something else or adopting the ways and beliefs of some religion. Spirituality is about learning who we truly are and not taking ourselves so seriously all the time. It's about going beyond our old ways of routine thinking.

I think it's about getting in contact with ourselves and our source of power—our "inner God." But what I think doesn't matter in your recovery. What you think and believe in matters. What mattered for me was that I started to believe in myself again. That's what I needed—to believe in myself. Nothing or nobody was going to get me clean. It was something I had to do for myself. And if you truly want to commune with God, you have to put in the work. We can never do that if we don't believe in ourselves.

I got clean by not giving up on myself. For years, I kept falling down, drying out, relapsing, going to jail, relapsing, going to rehab, relapsing, going to prison, relapsing. For about ten years, my life was like a freakin' roller coaster. Up. Down. Up. Down. Up. Down. There are two reasons why I'm not a junkie anymore. First, I never gave up on myself. And second, I kept searching for alternate solutions to life and happiness. And I only found it through experience. The ups and downs.

I would get out of jail, and my father would say to me, "What's different this time? Why should I believe you're going to stay clean this time?" Well, what was different each time was that I was a little more knowledgeable about my condition, a little bit more aware of my situation, a little more focused, a little more wise, a little more serious, a little less confused, and a little more dedicated to getting and staying clean. What I did the last time didn't work, so I tried to figure out another solution. And eventually, those "little mores" ended up being enough. I learned how to stay clean over time. Like when you go to an AA meeting, and a lot of the young newer members are obviously still a little screwed up and a lot of them are still using—the older members who are completely clean? They're clean because they all spent twenty to thirty years drinking and getting high, and they finally figured it out.

Everybody who has learned to ride a bike had to learn by falling down a bunch of times. Eventually, we stopped falling. And down the line, we eventually felt comfortable enough to take the helmet off. We started to believe in ourselves that we weren't going to fall anymore.

## Recovery—Recovering? Recovered?

There are two stages of recovery: recovering and recovered. Recovering addicts still need the steel and concrete beams in their lives. A recovering addict still does not act rationally or logically regarding drugs. They're not yet "cured." They can still fall off the wagon or tightrope. They don't have to be perfect right away, but as long as they're trying and genuinely striving to stay clean and live a more virtuous life, they are recovering.

A recovered addict, in my eyes, is not an addict. They're "cured." They act sanely toward drugs. That doesn't mean they can use drugs once in a while and control it. What I mean when I say they're cured is that they know with every fiber of their being that they cannot. Not only do they know what will happen if they do use "one more time," they don't want to use. If I find myself in a situation where somebody offers me drugs and I say, "Oh, I can't, I'm an addict," to me, I'm probably not recovered yet. If the sole reason I'm saying no is because I'm an "addict," that probably means that I'd like to get high, but I figured I shouldn't, which is a good decision. However, when a former addict is fully recovered, it's not "Oh, I can't, I'm an addict," it's just "No thanks, I'm all good." When one is fully recovered, they say no because they literally do not want to get high. An addict is someone who is addicted to something. If you're not addicted to something, you're not an addict. Of course, if a former addict relapses, they will become addicts once again. And I understand that all former addicts will probably always have a stronger susceptibility to become addicts again, but that doesn't mean that they will always be addicts—unless they spend the rest of their lives being addicted to something, actively or inactively.

Someone who has fully recovered has transcended their former selves. They've evolved. They bypassed that immature mentality. "Let's party" is no longer a part of their thinking process. Yet they don't rest on their laurels and get complacent. They are sane, normal people once again and they feel no need to use drugs for fulfillment. They found another way which is much, much better. They are happy people, and they understand that the only reason they're happy is because they don't use drugs anymore.

## Things That Proved Helpful to Me

Again, for myself, acquiring a strong spiritual foundation was very important in my recovery. I needed to find meaning in my life, or I didn't want to live it anymore, literally. I read a lot. Now reading an inspirational book isn't going to transpire an immediate and total awakening and recovery. Learning who we are takes time. I'm not talking about the egotistical us. I'm speaking about the essence of who we are—our true selves. The "I Am" that Jesus spoke of. The word *Buddha* means "awakened one." When the Buddha was asked if he was God, he simply responded, "I am awake," something Jesus said five hundred years later. When the Sanhedrin asked him if he was God, he simply said, "I Am."

As Americans, we've been conditioned to think and to look outside ourselves for pleasure, happiness, and answers. We want some *higher power* to fix our problems. That's what many religions teach. Spirituality will show us how to look, not outside ourselves, through people or things or money, but inside ourselves for answers and peace and happiness. Spirituality teaches us that yes, there is a higher power—you. Your true, pure, uninfluenced self. I'd like to suggest a few books right now for you to read if you wish. These books helped me more than I can explain:

1. *The Power of Now* by Eckhart Tolle
2. *The Alcohol and Addiction Cure* by Chris Prentiss
3. *Awakening the Buddha Within* by Lama Surya Das
4. *Peace Is Every Step: The Path of Mindfulness in Everyday Life* by Thich Nhat Hanh

These are not religious books. If you're a Catholic, chill out. You can still be a Catholic. If you're Baptist, great. Muslim, Hindu, Rastafarian, Atheist—awesome. Whatever you believe in and identify with is your business. These books will not try to change your religious preference. They'll teach you about yourself. Probably more than you've been taught by any other book or institution. They will teach you to be mindful. And mindfulness is what we, as recovering or former addicts, all need. If we're mindful, over time, we'll acquire meaningful insight about life. We'll understand people a lot more and more importantly, we'll begin to understand ourselves a lot more.

We don't have to believe in a specific religion to make sobriety work. All we have to believe in is ourselves. The best approach, to me, is to be open-minded, honest, and flexible. And if you're a total drug addict like I was and you want to get clean, you better damn well learn how to open yourself up to new concepts and ideas. Obviously, what you're doing—or not doing—isn't working out all that well. I'm not suggesting that those few books I mentioned are going to magically cure you. But if you read them with an open mind, they will teach you how to set up your personal foundation. But it's your job to build your castle.

I was raised Catholic. But I'm not completely identified with it. I like to go to church for the sole reason of seeing my grandparents, putting a smile on their face, and enjoying breakfast with them after mass on Sunday. That and the stained-glass windows and statues. I believe in the factual Jesus of Nazareth. Not the fictional "God" Jesus portrayed by many religions—particularly the ones who tell me that if I don't believe in everything they tell me, I'll be cast into a burning "lake of fire." I don't believe in dogma. I don't believe in a God who would cast two-thirds of the human race into a "lake of fire" simply because they're not Christians. That's a bunch of bullshit. And if it were true, I personally don't want any part of it.

I don't believe in this "lake of fire." In fact, I don't believe that hell and heaven are actual physical places. I believe they are states of mind and states of existence and consciousness that we create for ourselves and for each other in the here and now through our actions, thoughts, and deeds. I think the entire Bible could be wrapped up in one parable: the Sermon on the Mount. That really gets down to the heart of the matter. Jesus is the truth! He was a man—*the Man*—and an enlightened spiritual master.

I always wondered to myself how somebody could act like that and live their life like that. Basically, how can one be like Jesus. And I've found that the best tool to attain that type of personality and to achieve that level of perfectness would be the practice of Buddhism. Think about this: despite what religion you're part of, if there was a tool that you could utilize to better understand what spiritual teachers like Jesus taught more clearly, and in turn bring you closer to your truth if you choose to use that tool and take action, wouldn't you want to know what that tool was? It's sad to me that some people are so identified through their religious institution that most of the time they're completely missing the point of the lesson, and their minds snap close at even the mention of a different religion other than their own. I'm not saying that this is the mentality of every religious person. There are many religious people and religious leaders who have evolved spiritually enough where they no longer have a divisive attitude toward religion but a unifying one. There is a great book called *The Good Heart* by the Dalai Lama. He collaborated with the Catholic Church and gave a Buddhist perspective on Christian teachings. It was such a good book. Anyway, there are those people who truly do not understand. "I'm right, they're wrong," "I'm going to heaven, they're going to hell," "Thank God I was born into a family who believed in the *right* religion," and so on. What nonsense! I think that Jesus, Buddha, Gandhi, Emerson, Mother Teresa… Jerry Garcia—they're all sitting together in spirit right now shaking their heads indignantly at people with this "I'm right, they're wrong" attitude. Jerry Garcia is saying, "What the hell is wrong with these people?" And Jesus is saying, "Well, they have eyes but they do not see." And Buddha is laughing. And Mother Teresa is telling Buddha, "Stop laughing, it's not funny." People who have that "my religion is the right religion" attitude who judge and criticize others for not believing in what they believe in and believe that the nonbelievers are going to hell—even if those nonbelievers are good moral people—they're not spiritual people. They're egotistical people. I was that way for a long time. I'm not judging them. Hey, people are who they are. But the fact is, spiritually evolved people don't have that mindset.

These spiritual types of books I was speaking of helped me out tremendously. They helped me understand life, other people, and myself so much more clearly than I ever had. I learned how everything in this world is impermanent, including ourselves. Everything and everybody changes, and unhealthy attachments only cause me suffering in the long run. I learned many concepts that made me realize how much I love being clearheaded and drug-free and that I don't need any of that stuff to make me happy.

Another thing I realized over the years is that throughout my addiction, I developed a very reclusive attitude. I became so detached from life, society, family, friends, and so on I was always alone. Being lonely gave me an excuse to get high. Being by myself meant that nobody had to know what I was up to, and I'd give myself an excuse to get high based on that. It wasn't the only excuse, but it was one of them. Sometimes (well, most of the time) us addicts hurt and piss off a lot of people when we're using drugs. Try to patch up these relationships, no matter how hard it seems. Learning how to say sorry and enjoy a good hug afterward helps more than words can explain.

## Remember Your Imagination?

Get out of the house! Go miniature golfing. Bowling. The batting cages. Or join a bowling league or start golfing. Join a baseball or softball team. Go camping. Great America. Fishing. Read a book. Learn how to cook. Make love. Join a yoga class. Go to a museum, an art gallery, or the zoo. If you live in Chicago, go to the Shedd Aquarium or The Planetarium. Roll up your pants, take your shoes off, and walk along the beach. Play volleyball or just sit back and watch the girls play. If it's wintertime, go drive around and look at the Christmas lights. Go sledding, ice-skating, skiing. Build a snowman. Have a snowball fight with the neighborhood kids. Make hot cocoa with marshmallows. Build a fire. Go Christmas caroling.

Remember your imagination? Start using it again! In case one of the thirty suggestions I just mentioned aren't appealing to you, here are some more…

Get a job. Go to school. No GED or high school diploma? Go get one, either at a campus or school or online. Go to the mall. See a movie. Pray. Meditate. Take up drawing or writing. Write a book! Go to an AA or an NA meeting. Make some sober friends who will be a good influence in your life and who will call you out on your bullshit because they actually care about you. Buy a bike. Start bike riding. Buy a pair of Rollerblades. Buy a dog, or a cat, or some fish. Plant a garden. Join a fitness club and start working out. Lift weights and jog—transform your body into a Superman or Superwoman.

Sit in the sauna. Swim some laps. Meet some pretty, healthy girl or a good-looking, nice, healthy guy. Ask them to dinner. Go on a date. Learn how to play chess. Go buy some board games. Remember Sorry or Trouble?

Do whatever it takes to enjoy yourself and have some fun. Just don't use drugs. We have to practice doing healthy activities. For God's sake, just go outside and walk. Enjoy the sunshine. Enjoy the singing birds. Live! We only get one shot at this life. Whatever you want to do with it, start doing it. Stop wasting yourself and your life. Live healthy and be good. You'll feel better.

You're unlikely to really feel good about yourself after a day of lying, cheating, stealing, and getting high. When you break that cycle and lifestyle, you'll feel much better about yourself. Start focusing on the good within you. It'll have a major impact on your self-esteem. If you don't think there is any good in you, then start creating some. And sex? Oh man! When you're clean and healthy and clear-minded and you make love to your girlfriend/boyfriend or husband/wife—it's amazing. Sorry, I don't want to sound inappropriate, but many addicts' sex drives are practically nonexistent when they're strung out on drugs.

When I finally got clean and stopped using heroin, it didn't matter if I was in prison or in paradise. I was basically a happy person again. I realized how beautiful life is without that stuff. All I had to do was open my eyes and my mind. And after years and years of trying and struggling, my eyes opened up. I haven't had a "horrible" day since.

Using drugs is no fun. I mean, come on! If you're a junkie or a crackhead or a drunk, come on. Honestly, aren't you sick of that? Don't you want more out of life? I ask that rhetorically. I know that you do. There is so much fun and happiness out there waiting for you—go grab it!

But first, you have to make a decision. Right now. Not later on or tomorrow or after you get "one more." Right now, make a decision. Do you want to live? Not just be alive. Do you really want to live? If your answer is yes, then I want you to do something right now: go stand in front of a mirror in silence and look into your own eyes. I know this sounds a little lame, but try it. The eyes are said to be the window to your soul. Look yourself in the eyes and declare yourself a powerful and beautiful individual who will overcome this addiction. Declare your dedication to your sobriety. Believe that it will come, and it eventually will. Then be brave and pick up the phone. Call a detox/rehab center and talk to them. You have to detoxify your brain. Trust me, you can handle it.

Then start searching for alternative solutions to life. Try new ones out. If they appeal to you and make you happy, adopt them. If they don't, move on. Just don't run out of time or chances.

# CHAPTER 17

There is no one way to battle an addiction. There is no instant cure for it. If that's what you're looking for, stop. It doesn't exist. If you do not believe that, ask any recovering addict, former addict, addiction counselor, doctor, psychologist, etc. I'm sure they will all agree with me when I say that getting clean is an extremely hard, uphill battle. This battle is between an addict and themselves, and it takes place on an extremely narrow road. In the beginning, it's like walking a tightrope. One false move, one twisted thought, one minute of going out of focus, and we fall. And when I say "fall," I mean get high. It's likely to happen a lot in the very beginning. It's okay to get angry at ourselves for using "one more time." We should get angry, or disappointed, or sad and discouraged. That means we're serious about getting clean. It'll help us get off our asses and try again.

See every fall or relapse as an opportunity for improvement. I'm not saying it's okay to relapse on purpose. Yes, relapse is a part of recovery. However, that doesn't mean we can use that as an excuse to just consciously relapse whenever we want to (like I used to do). If or when you do, though, just take a deep breath and realize that it's all part of the process on this journey. Everything in the past happened for a reason.

Think about it, ask yourself why you relapsed, cry if you want to, but then drop it, suck it up, and move on. Don't get discouraged and don't let other people discourage you. The people in your life may get mad or upset when they find out you relapsed. Rightfully so, but don't let them discourage you when they put their two cents in. It may not be what you want or need to hear. If they call you a failure or say, "I knew I shouldn't have believed you. You'll never change," etc., just realize that they truly do not understand. And if they are not addicts or have never experienced addiction themselves, then they shouldn't understand. Don't get upset with them. Remember that what other people think about you is none of your business, especially if what they think or say is totally negative.

We cannot learn how to stay clean until we start trying to figure it out. Then when we've found something we think may help us, we practice. As I write this sentence, my baby sister, Jessica Lynn, is twenty-two years old. Ever since she's been able to walk and talk, I've been giving her a piece of advice (something my father always told me when I was younger) that is the most basic, priceless advice, and it applies to everything we do in life. Whenever she'd be trying something new that she's never done before, still to this day, she had a tendency to get aggravated easily when she can't do it correctly right away, no matter what it may be. She'll cross her arms and say, "Hmmm, this is stupid! I'll never be able to do this." Then I'd say to her, "Hey! What do I always tell you? Jess, answer me." "Practice makes perfect, Mikey, but—" And I'll cut her off and say, "But nothing. Keep trying, you'll get it." And before she knows it, she's a little pro.

## Practice Makes Perfect

I'm not going to sit here and tell you to do this or to do that. You're going to have to figure out what works for you personally. You have to seek and search for it yourself. The specific things I did are only conducive to my own personality and mindset. I'm in no position to tell anybody what they should do. But I think you'll find that every experience you have and every different solution you try will yield more insight that you can apply in your own way. Trust your intuition. All I can do is tell you how I came to the point where I just knew that I'd never stick a syringe in my arm again.

Reading this book will not get you sober. I hope it helps you, but it's not going to get you clean. Your parents, siblings, family, or friends—they cannot get you sober. AA, NA, CA, and every other recovery program under the stars will not make you get clean. The Bible, the Quran, the Jewish Torah, the Hindu Vedas, the Buddhist

Pali Canon, the Church (whatever church you prefer), a priest, an exorcist, rabbi—none of these will get you clean. And this is a personal belief of mine, but God *himself* is not going to move the cosmos to get you clean. So if you're waiting for God to intervene and snap his fingers and make you stop using drugs just because you prayed long and hard for it (without putting forth a genuine effort yourself), you're going to be waiting a long time. Honestly, if the Supreme Being of the universe just went around fixing all our problems for us just because we asked him to, I think human beings would be very shallow individuals. We'd never learn anything meaningful about life. God wants us to be clean, but he's not going to do it for us.

What I'm getting at is that whatever God or concepts you believe in, they will not give you sobriety. There is but one person who will get you clean and sober. And that person is you.

Please don't misunderstand me here—AA, NA, going to church, praying, meditating, family, and friends—you're going to need all these things to assist you. We all need help at one time or another. But ultimately, you are the one who has to make the decision to get clean if you decide that's what you want. Your personal feelings and drive and experiences are what's going to get you clean. Those inner thoughts and dreams you think about and visualize when you're all alone and daydreaming? Those aspirations are going to play a major role in who you become. They did for me.

Visualize being drug-free. Don't allow getting high to be a part of your thoughts. If they pop into your head, don't entertain them. Think of what you really want out of life. Hopefully, the eradication of drugs from your everyday life is one of the things you want. Visualization is important. It will activate the power of your mind to accomplish all your dreams.

An affirmation is a statement you make either in your head or out loud that describes what you want and how it will be in its completed state. Think like and act as if you are already where you want to be in life. Maybe you want to be a strong independent woman, go back to school, start a career, meet a nice man, have some babies, start a business, whatever. Or maybe you're a man who wants to work your butt off and save your money so you can start your own business, build a house, start a family, whatever. Whatever it may be, start visualizing it now. Don't get bogged down in planning, analyzing, and hoping. Take some action! Visualize it, think about it, then take action. All action is conceived in thought. I'll repeat that: All action is conceived in thought.

I understand how it is at first when you're first trying to get clean. Addicts' lives are usually pretty screwed up by the time we realize that we really have to change. Your family is pissed off at you, and more so hurt. All your friends (your good friends who aren't drug addicts) stay far away from you. You have legal problems, you're on probation or parole, you have financial problems, etc. It's hard because everything sucks, you're constantly depressed and lonely. And you have that voice in your head that keeps saying, "Just go get high, you need to feel better, then you can figure this all out. Just one more time."

You have to dig down deep, to that feeling deep within your heart that knows you have to stop this lifestyle and get clean. You have to recognize that those thoughts telling you to get high again are not who you are. Find that inner desire for serenity and happiness and hold onto it. Turn all that self-loathing and self-pity into an aggressive force and aim it at change. Then take action. Again, all action is conceived in thought.

When I first realized just how sick and screwed up I was and how chaotic my life had become, I wanted one thing. It wasn't sobriety at first. It was happiness. Period. I wanted some happiness in my life. I needed it more than I needed to eat or breathe. Just some true genuine happiness. Then, after jumping through hoops like a neurotic madman for a few years, trying to find happiness and still use drugs at the same time, I realized that for people like me, there is no happiness without being clean.

When my cousin Johnny used to drag me to AA meetings at twenty to twenty-two years old, at first, I'd sit in those meetings and say to myself, "This better give me some sobriety and happiness," as if going to a meeting would get me clean just from sitting there. And even though that, in the long run, twelve-step meetings weren't a good fit for me personally, they did help me a lot as far as recognizing I really had a problem. I've learned that twelve-step meetings are a catalyst for getting clean. They're not a cure like I believed in the beginning. You have to put in the effort.

From the ages of eighteen to twenty-four, I went to a lot of meetings. You know why? Because I was trying to manipulate everybody. My father wanted me to go. He'd say, "Michael, if you don't go to meetings, you're not living in my house." So I'd go. I'd sit there and chain-smoke, drink coffee, and space out. A couple of times, I hooked up with girls after the meetings. Girls going for the same reason I was going because their family was forcing them into it. We'd meet in a meeting, and afterward go get high and screw around. I was more interested in that than getting clean and taking my life seriously like a grown responsible man. The point being, I was completely detached from these meetings—at first. I still thought I could control my addiction without any help. I was a stubborn little jerkoff, if I'm being honest with myself.

My cousin Johnny knew I should be going. He'd always call me up and somehow talk me into going in subtle ways. It would be easier to just go than to keep making up bullshit excuses of why I couldn't. Johnny was always able to see through me. I felt too pathetic trying to lie to him and manipulate an excuse to not go. Quick story:

My cousin Johnny called me one morning when I was about twenty-two years old. This wasn't uncommon for him to do. It was about 10:00 a.m., and he asked me if I wanted to go to a meeting with him later that evening. All chipper, he said, "It starts at seven o'clock. There's going to be a good speaker. It'll be great." I sighed and said, "Yeah, John, I'll go." He told me he'd pick me up at about 6:30 p.m. I hung up the phone and said to myself, "What a pain in the ass this freaking guy is."

About two minutes later, my dad comes downstairs and tells me that he and my stepmother were going to a wedding at 4:00 p.m. Four o'clock rolled around, and I had the house to myself. I took a quick ride to meet my drug dealer. I got back home about 5:00 p.m., shot a bag of coke, topped it off with a big shot of heroin, and headed for the liquor cabinet. I grabbed this fifth of vodka in this pretty little gift canister. It wasn't regular vodka. It was like this exotic expensive vodka (about a month later, when my dad discovered it was gone, he told me that it was a gift to him and he didn't plan on drinking it, which made no sense to me at the time. Vodka that you don't drink? That's ludicrous!).

Anyway, that day, I took the big bottle of vodka, grabbed a small glass, and went downstairs to the basement. I popped in a Grateful Dead CD and proceeded to have my own little party. I was shooting pool, and in between games of 9 ball, I'd gulp down a big mouthful of vodka. Before I knew it, it was 6:45 p.m., the bottle was almost entirely gone, and my doorbell was ringing. "Who the hell is ringing the doorbell," I thought. I hid all my stuff, ran upstairs, and peeked out the curtains in the front room, totally expecting to see a SWAT team ready to raid the house, and there was my cousin Johnny standing on the porch. I completely forgot he was coming to pick me up. "Let's go, bro, we're gonna be late," he said. "Shit!" Instead of being honest and telling him I was in no shape to be going to an AA meeting, I said, "Okay, I'll be right out."

I was drunk too! Not like high school keg party drunk or "I had a couple too many" drunk. I was completely impaired. Stone drunk. No exaggeration, I had just drunk about twenty to twenty-five shots of vodka in the last hour and a half. On top of that, I was jacked on cocaine and had just shot about six bags of heroin. I got into Johnny's car, and still to this day, I cannot believe he didn't know right away how messed up I was. And if he did, I cannot believe he took me to an AA meeting like that. But he did.

The meeting was held in a church basement in Oak Lawn. I walked into the room, sat in this little fold-out metal chair, and lit a cigarette. The meeting began almost as soon as I sat down. I didn't even make it through the initial readings from the chairperson. As this guy was reading "How It Works," I was sitting there, and I could smell the alcohol that was profusely seeping through my pores and engulfing me like a storm cloud. I had this feeling that people— sober people, mind you—were looking at me, and they knew I was hammered. I just couldn't sit there any longer. So, about five minutes into the meeting, I leaned over to my cousin and said, "Listen, I'll be waiting outside for you," and I got up and left the room.

Because the meeting was being held in the basement of a church, I had to walk up this huge flight of marble steps to get out to the parking lot. About halfway up the stairs, I just had to lie down immediately. So I did. I fell asleep on the steps of a church basement at an AA meeting.

Somehow, I woke up about a half hour later. Nobody had seen me (at least that I knew of), and I got up and went and sat on the front steps of the church to wait for my cousin. My cousin came out about ten minutes later, and we got in his car. I can't really recall that ride home, but I vaguely remember arguing with Johnny, telling him to drop me off at this girl's house. But by this point, he knew how messed up I was and insisted I go home. I don't remember walking into my house, but I do recall talking on the phone and my dad coming home, walking downstairs, and yelling at me because the basement smelled like alcohol. That's how drunk I was. I had finished drinking hours prior, yet the basement still smelled like straight alcohol, all from my breath and pores. I remember my dad yelling at me and nothing else. I don't recall stripping down to my boxers and crawling under the pool table to pass out, using a backpack for a pillow—but that's what I must have done because that's where I woke up about ten hours later.

I spent the next morning throwing up blood and dry heaving for about three hours while my stepmom argued with my dad, telling him that I should go to the hospital. Later that day, when I was finally able to hold down some water, I went to get my paraphernalia "kit" to do some dope, and there was the bottle on the floor in my closet. When I picked it up, the entire bottle was gone, just about.

At this point in my life, I had been to rehab, jail a few times, prison once, and I'd been going to AA meetings on and off for a few years already—and I was still doing stuff like that. My point being, getting clean is a process. I hope that my readers do not take as long as I did to wake up, but it does take time. Create a dream for yourself, figure out how to reach it, and keep practicing until you're perfect. Until you're truly happy.

If you fall or slip up or relapse—whatever you want to call it— don't beat yourself up too badly. Beat yourself up a little bit, but then get up and try again. And again, and again. That's how I got clean. If happiness is what you want, you can find it in clean living. You may not realize this right away, so just keep at it. If you do go to meetings, ask people to share their success strategies with you. Then try them yourself if they're appealing to you. Experiment with them. If that way of behaving works and feels right, adopt it. If not, drop it and keep looking and experimenting with different solutions.

You have to make a continuous and persistent effort in attempting not to use drugs. Not just at a meeting for an hour, or for an hour or two after the meeting when you're still feeling renewed hope from the meeting but continuously. I used to go to a meeting, and it would make me feel like, "Yes! I can do this. I'm going to be sober! I'll never use heroin ever again. Yeah." Then within a couple of hours of leaving that meeting, my mindset would change, I'd hear a Rolling Stones song on the radio, and out of nowhere, I'd be sitting in a Taco Bell parking lot waiting on a drug dealer. And I'd be right back to feeling helpless and hopeless. So, be persistent. You must continuously strive to be clean.

Often, addicts set such high standards and expectations for themselves that are practically impossible (and unrealistic) for them to reach and achieve right away. Then, when we can't do it right away, we get upset with ourselves. Then the "vicious cycle" kicks in again. Take your time. Start small. That's where the saying "one day at a time" comes from. Don't try to conquer this in a week. It won't happen.

My first goal was to stop biting my nails! It had nothing to do with drugs but with behavior. We can't just relate getting clean with drug and alcohol consumption. Getting clean means completely changing our behavior. Drugs and alcohol don't just jump down our throats or fly up our noses. Like I said previously, drugs are not the problem. Our behavior is the problem, causing us to utilize drugs as a coping mechanism. We have to train and condition our brains and behaviors just like any other muscle in our bodies. No pain, no gain, right?

It's important, however, that you never utter the words "I can't." Saying "I can't" disempowers you. Don't say that. Don't even think it. You can do anything you put your mind to and work for. Believe me, we can push ourselves harder than we often give ourselves credit for. Human beings are a tough, intelligent, goal-oriented species naturally. Look at Navy SEALs! If an individual can go through that caliber of training, training that goes on almost continuously for years, training that normal people like us can't even fathom and come out on the other end successful with their trident on their chest—then surely kicking a drug habit is well within the realm of overcoming. What did Yoda say in *Star Wars*? "Do or do not. There is no try."

You may be asking yourself, "How long before I get back to normal?" Let me tell you this: although it may take six months to a year of being clean for your physical body and brain to get back to normal functioning capacity, and it may take a year or two to actually stay clean completely and learn how to be happy and content without drugs every day by finding your personal solution, and it may take a couple of years to build a life for yourself where you have a nice place to live, a car, a bank account, your family trusts and likes you again, etc.—if you acknowledge right now that you have a problem and that you're going to start right now trying to correct it, you are back to normal. People who are not normal do not make healthy decisions. And acknowledging you have a problem and need help, and starting to make attempts at getting clean is a healthy decision, as long as it's genuine. Sobriety is built on attitudes and logical healthy decisions, not conditions. Remember that sobriety is built on attitudes and logical healthy decisions, not conditions.

Just because you relapse doesn't mean that you got off the road to recovery. Unfortunately, the road to recovery often entails relapse. You're not a failure because you slip up and get loaded. You're a failure if you give up fighting to stay clean. Don't underestimate yourself. You can do this. It's going to be a tough challenge, but it can be done. How is up to you. How you do it isn't really important. What's important is that you get clean, get your life back on track, gain some happiness, and give your family some peace. That's the point of getting clean, right?

When I first began trying to stop getting high, I was scared. I was scared that I wouldn't be able to live, function, and feel good and have energy without dope. It's okay to be scared. But be brave. Being brave doesn't mean that you're not scared. People who aren't scared in the first place have no need for bravery. Being brave means that you are scared, but despite your fear, you do what you have to do anyway. That's being brave. Picking up that phone sitting right by you and calling a detox/rehab center is being brave. Do what you have to do, what you know you have to do. Find something that works for you and practice it until you're perfect. Good luck and God bless.

# EPILOGUE

Give us rain when we expect sun.
Give us music when we expect trouble.
Give us tears when we expect breakfast.
Give us dreams when we expect a storm.
Give us a stray dog when we expect congratulations.
Dear God, play with us. Turn
us sideways, and around.
(Anonymous Prayer)

Whenever I have a momentary lapse of tranquility, I think of that prayer. Pretty cool prayer, huh? Anyway, where did it all go wrong? That's a question that used to frequent my thoughts quite often in the past. I now realize that nothing went wrong. Everything that has happened to me happened the way it was supposed to happen—precisely. And everything was right on cue for all the right reasons at all the right times. Everything eventually balances out. When I came to this realization, I stopped trying to fight myself, and my own expectations of how I want life to be, so much. I learned how to mellow out and just go with the flow of life, instead of trying to change everything and everyone to my liking. It's human nature to deny and run from anything that the mind cannot immediately understand and comprehend. I think that's what took me so long to wake up, stop being obstinate, and stop using drugs. *Testadura!*—that's Italian for *hardheaded*.

Fortunately—and I say this with no egotistical attitude—I'm getting better at life, and I'm learning a lot about myself. I don't focus on the ugliness and negativity as much now. Too often in the past, the little things that matter in life went completely neglected, ignored, or unnoticed because I had "better things to do." Those things usually consisted of bullshit and drama. I was actually drawn to it. "Oh, look, some bullshit and drama! Let me go jump in the middle of it." It seemed I always had something better to do or to focus on other than life itself.

I've realized so many things about life in the last decade. Most importantly, though, I've realized how horribly I've neglected and took for granted all the great and beautiful things and people in my life that really matter. And I've made a vow to myself to try my best not to let that ever happen again. As cliché as it may sound, you never really realize how much you need, miss, or love someone or something until it's gone or becomes totally unavailable to you.

When I was much younger, I recall the question, "If you had three wishes, what would they be?" being asked of me many times throughout my childhood. My answers usually were along the lines of what I've now come to view as total nonsense. "Ten million dollars, a Lamborghini, and a supermodel girlfriend." Honestly, all good wishes, but I realize now that if these silly things were my ultimate wishes, I would have dealt myself a very short hand. I wouldn't have led my life as I have the last twenty years or so, and that would have been a shame. I'd have missed out on countless deep and meaningful situations and experiences I've been through. Some very interesting people I would never have met. And many lessons would have never been learned, or at least thought about. I'd now be as unaware, unconscious, and arrogant as many people I know who grew up in a nice neighborhood, in a good family, and has never really had anything significantly life-changing happen to them. My life would have been completely different.

When I'm on my deathbed, I don't want the last thing I ask myself to be, "What have I gained in my life?" I think the more important question should be, "What have I contributed to life and to the human race? Did I make any kind of a positive difference, or did I just merely exist to consume and buy stuff?" I think everybody knows regret. I believe regrets are something we should be concerned about in the here and now, not when we're on our deathbeds. By then, it's too late. We're all going to pass on one day, and in those last few weeks or days or hours and minutes, I doubt any of us are going to be thinking about what kind of cars we had over the years or what kind of clothes we wore or how big our house was. What's that saying? You never see a U-Haul truck behind a hearse.

One of the more priceless lessons I've learned over the years is what it means to have compassion for others. Love is an abundance of feelings and emotions like patience, understanding, respect, and dedication. We embrace what's true and good about others, and we accept what is not. John Lennon said, "All you need is love." Wise man, that John Lennon.

I mention compassion and love because it was so important in my recovery. Real love has no strings attached. When we truly love somebody, we do it unconditionally. We don't need anything in return. Nothing. Family love is strong. There were (and still are) people in my life who loved me, had a lot of patience with me, and didn't turn their backs on me, and if it weren't for these individuals, I'd be gone right now.

I learned the word "altruism." Altruism means selfless concern for others. And in order to get clean, we need altruism from others, but we also need to be altruistic ourselves. We have to give of ourselves. That's what this book was all about. Love for, and concern and compassion for everybody who is dealing with a substance abuse problem and the families and friends who are being affected by it. This is my contribution. Good luck to you all. I, for one, will be in your corner, cheering you on always.

And I'll also be right along with you. I'm only thirty-eight years old at the time. It's going on four years since the last time I've stuck a needle in my arm (other than a minor six-month relapse). I don't want what I'm about to say to come as a disappointment, but I have to be honest. I still drink alcohol once in a while. I have a glass of red wine with pasta now and then. If I go to a ballgame or a barbecue, I'll have a cold Heineken. I don't get drunk. I haven't been drunk in as long as I can remember. It's been at least seven or eight years since I've had more than two to three drinks at a time. Any AA member would probably call me an idiot and bet anything that in a short time I'll be a full-blown junkie again. I don't believe that. I know I'll never use that stuff again. My former self would, but I'm not my former self.

If you're trying to get clean, the best route to take is one of total abstinence. I'm not suggesting it's okay to drink. I'm just being honest here, that's all. I never said I'm a perfect pillar of cleanliness. I still have a lot of learning and growing to do. I still make rash decisions. I still sit in front of the TV once in a while, watch *Family Guy*, and eat an entire half gallon of ice cream. I still goof off and do stupid stuff every blue moon. I still have a lot of life to live. The difference is that I'm now able to find logical, meaningful solutions to problematic situations I encounter in life. And most of the time, they make sense to me. I understand myself, I'm comfortable with who I am, and I feel I have a lot to offer. And that helps to keep me clean and clearheaded.

All in all, I suppose this book was about my perspective on addiction and life. But also, it was a story about making the continuous choice to keep moving forward and the constant yearning for peace and happiness. Not only that, but the decision to keep moving forward in the face of not only a particular bad time but understanding that a million other bad times are going to occur to me in life and, despite that knowledge, choosing to keep moving forward. It's the nature of life. Ups and downs. Sometimes you're up, other times you lose everything. I believe those are the tests that God puts in place for us. How do we handle them? For a long time, I didn't handle them. I ignored them, put them out of mind, procrastinated, and slammed heroin.

I still struggle with some of these tests. But I find that when I face them like the man I was raised to be, even if I don't have the answers or I'm completely confused, as long as I listen to that inner voice and try to do the right thing and respond rationally and logically instead of ignorantly and compulsively, the outcome is usually something I can handle. And I know that as long as I'm not all screwed up on drugs, then there is a gang of individuals who will help me out. And that's big for me because for the longest time I knew everything, and I didn't need any help. My dumbass was still believing that after my third prison sentence.

Our true selves want help; it's our egos that resist it. If the only help you're giving yourself in life is to get high and forget and mask all the bullshit with using drugs and acting like your life is just hunky-dory—you're going to have a pretty toxic and shitty life. That's the hard truth. That's not just my personal opinion. Look at every drug addict in history, especially the heroin addicts. Their lives were chaotic, unhealthy, and shitty—until they stopped using. Only then did they get better. It's a fact—you can't be a drug addict and be a winner at the same time.

People ask me why I named this book *Ripple* instead of *Ripples*, or sometimes I'm asked where I came up with the idea of naming it that. There are a few reasons. First, I like the word *ripple*. It's as simple as that. It's a calm, inviting, and visual word to me. I think people will see it and say, "Huh, *Ripple*. What's this book all about?"

Secondly, the book is centered around addiction and substance abuse. Yes, drugs will cause a lot of different ripples coursing through your life, especially if you allow yourself to become completely drug dependent. They will disrupt your life in more ways than you can imagine. Family problems, social problems, legal problems, friendship problems, financial problems, health problems (both physically and mentally), to name some. As human beings, we're going to have to deal with these problems and situations in life that sometimes happen to us regardless of whether we use drugs or not. But they are enhanced tenfold if these problems are stemming from drug use.

Picture a drop of water landing in a calm pond, and a bunch of ripples start to disrupt the water—it's that initial ripple that caused all the rest. The ripple of using drugs has caused a whole bunch of other ripples in my life, all completely avoidable if I just hadn't set them in motion by the initial *Ripple* I made when I stuck that syringe into my arm.

And the final reason I named it *Ripple*? It correlates to a beautiful song by the Grateful Dead called "Ripple." If you hear the words to the song, you'll understand why I chose it. The only difference is that they used music—I used literature. Their song, and my book are both "hand me downs."

My life hasn't dramatically changed since I've stopped using hard narcotics. I'm still just Mikey Seminetta from the south side of Chicago. However, the quality of my life has changed exponentially since I've stopped using. I now know how to enjoy myself without drugs. I like shooting pool still, but I don't have to be wasted to do it, and I actually have a more accurate shot—who would've thunk it! I love working out and running. I love going downtown still, laying a blanket in the sand on Ohio Street beach, and talking and laughing with friends while we sip on our Italian ice from Taylor Street. I still like going camping, or to see live music. The difference is that now I'm my own man. I don't need anybody or anything to make me feel comfortable. I'm totally aware of my worth, and I'm worth more than living the life of a drug addict.

My life is still not perfect. I still have shitty days, and I make mistakes, though now I actually learn from them right away. My thirty-eight years I've lived on this earth so far has been a wild ride. There were a lot of things I had to go through and endure to get to where I am today mentally. It wasn't easy.

The life I have lived in the past could have easily killed me. When I reflect on my past, I realize that I had to go through all of that in order to reach the life and the attitude toward life that I have today. If I didn't live that life, no way in hell would this book be complete. I never would've been able to write it. But I did, only because I was willing and able to, because I didn't give up, because I was clean. These pages are a complete manifestation of my past, and I can only hope that someone has learned from it and is now on the road to recovery.

I don't see things in a negative light anymore. I see every situation in a positive light—as a test and a challenge—whatever it may be. And the only thing that matters to me is the truth I find within my personal experiences. I recognize nonsense and bullshit immediately, and I stay away from it, unless it's unavoidable. And I no longer preach to people unless they want to talk to me about it. I don't run away if I happen to encounter an active drug addict. I don't have to leave an event or a party because people are drinking too much. If I leave, it's because I don't want to be around a bunch of annoying drunk people, not because I'm concerned about myself. I'm not afraid to be around that. If I was, how could I help any drug addict recover? I really have an excellent happy life now, and I don't want any of that crap. I don't judge others, and I don't try to change them. But I try to surround myself with positive, uplifting people as much as I can. I think I've used enough drugs for one lifetime.

I can't wait to meet a good, healthy, clear-minded, passionate, and beautiful woman, fall in love with her, and ask her to be my wife. My father always tells me, "If you're smart, you'll marry an Italian girl." Maybe I'll do just that. But it doesn't matter to me. She could be Irish too! As long as we love each other. I know what love is now, so I'm really looking forward to meeting her. I want to spend my life making hers beautiful.

And I'd like to have children. I want to be a baseball coach or a girls' softball coach. Or both. I look forward to changing diapers (well, I don't really look forward to it, but I'll do it), messy meals, teaching them how to ride bikes, going to school plays, teaching my son to be chivalrous and how to treat a lady, or aggressively introducing myself to my daughter's boyfriends. I'm good at it too! I had some practice already with my baby sister's little boyfriends the last few years. Family vacations. Holidays. Anniversaries. Waking up next to my girl on Sunday morning and tickling her to tears to wake her up. I look forward to all those little things that make life so great. And I know that as long as I stay focused, strong, and drug-free, there's a wonderful fulfilling life awaiting me.

I like to believe that I'm now as normal as I can get. By "normal" I mean that I no longer do things consciously that cause unnecessary hardships—or ripples—in my life. I have no desire or craving to get high. I don't want to party. I'm completely content and happy without all that nonsense. I enjoy peacefulness. I enjoy being involved in family parties. Birthdays. Holidays. I love decorating my mom's house like Clark Griswold when Christmas comes around. I enjoy getting up and going to work in the morning fueled by nothing other than a cup of coffee, and there's hardly ever any overwhelming stress involved. After living the lifestyle I did, it takes a lot to stress me out and throw me off my square. It's almost freakish how much bullshit I can take and still be able to smile during it. I no longer feel the need to *have to* jump up and go somewhere or do something. And that feels great.

Today I'm clean and drug-free. Again, as I write this sentence, I'm only thirty-eight years old, and it's been a long time since I've been high on any drug but marijuana. And as time goes by, that life-style I once lived is more and more of a distant memory. But I know what will happen if I use "just once." I'll crash and burn. Worse than before. It always gets worse. Always. So, you know what I do? I don't freakin' do it. Not even "once" because I know that saying "one's too many, a thousand's never enough" applies to me fully. I keep the fact that I have a compulsive addictive nature at the forefront of my attention if I find myself in a dangerous situation. It can easily get out of control if I forget that. I'm confident that I won't. And as time goes by, that confidence grows. It doesn't get complacent.

Many recovering addicts say, "I still think about getting high a lot." I can understand that. But personally, I don't think about getting high. I can't explain why I don't, but I just don't. Of course, I think about my past now and then, especially while I wrote this book, but it's usually thoughts of how bad drugs have affected my life. I don't think about the "getting high" part—ever. It makes me sick, even the thought of it. And I don't consider myself an addict anymore. I'm Mike, and I'm not a drug addict. I'm a son, a brother, a cousin. I can be a good friend. I can be a crazy S.O.B. sometimes, but I'm not a drug addict. I refuse to give those two words any power over me—and I always will, until I die.

Karma means that we don't get away with anything. We all reap what we sow. Karma actually translates as action and reaction. In the Buddhist perspective, there are no accidents. Every cause has an effect, and every effect has a cause. I believe in karma. I'm the type of person who needs to really practice before I get something right. I can't perfect myself in one lifetime. I'll probably need a couple more tries. It's okay to not be perfect right away. It's a growing and learning process—this life we all live.

You may have noticed all the quotes throughout this book. I hope you have enjoyed them and pondered them and learned from them like I did. I sometimes had a hard time formulating words that coincided with my thoughts and feelings while writing this book. So instead of deluding the thought by rambling for the sake of trying to sound like I have it all figured out, I decided to use the quotes. Greater minds and more enlightened individuals have explained certain things better than I ever could. A lot of these quotes can explain how I feel better than I can myself. So I shall leave you with one final quote, my personal favorite.

> To laugh often and much;
> To win the respect of intelligent people and the affection of children;
> To earn the appreciation of honest critics and endure the betrayal of false friends;
> To appreciate beauty, to find the best in others;
> To leave the world a bit better, whether by a healthy child, a garden, or a redeemed social condition;
> To know even one life has breathed easier because you have lived.
> This is to have succeeded." (Ralph Waldo Emerson)

*****

Okay then, what else, what else, what else? I guess I'm spent—for now. Thank you for reading and allowing me to share my story. Good luck and God bless. Oh! I almost forgot. As for my question at the beginning of part 2 of this book, "How does a man climb Mt. Everest?" well, the answer is simple: one step at a time!

Love,
Michael J. Seminetta III

Printed in the USA
CPSIA information can be obtained
at www.ICGtesting.com
LVHW070742131024
793680LV00005B/17